This Invisible Riot of the Mind

This Invisible Riot of the Mind: Samuel Johnson's Psychological Theory

GLORIA SYBIL GROSS

University of Pennsylvania Press

Philadelphia

Library of Congress Cataloging-in-Publication Data

Gross, Gloria Sybil.
   This invisible riot of the mind : Samuel Johnson's psychological theory / Gloria Sybil Gross.
      p.   cm.
   Includes bibliographical references and index.
   ISBN 0-8122-3146-5
   1. Johnson, Samuel, 1709–1784—Knowledge—Psychology.   2. Johnson, Samuel, 1709–
1784—Biography—Psychology.   3. Authors, English—18th century—Psychology.
4. English literature—Psychological aspects.   5. Psychology in literature.   I. Title.
PR3537.P8G7   1992
828'.609—dc20   91-39482
                                                                                                            CIP

Jacket illustration: Portrait of Samuel Johnson by Sir Joshua Reynolds. From the collection of
Loren and Frances Rothschild.

To my parents

Contents

Acknowledgments

THIS BOOK GREW OUT OF THE PLEASURE of studying eighteenth-century literature and Samuel Johnson with my teacher, Donald Greene. I am also glad to acknowledge the immense help and encouragement I have received from Paul Korshin and O M Brack, Jr. in Johnsonian studies; from Roy Porter in the history of medicine; and from George Rousseau, who guided me through the intricacies of interdisciplinary work. They will know why I single them out with affection and special thanks for their unfailing assistance and kindness. I am grateful for a Clark Library Summer Postdoctoral Fellowship at UCLA and for several grants from the Foundation at California State University, Northridge. I am indebted to fellow board members of the Samuel Johnson Society of Southern California, and our chairman, Loren Rothschild. I thank the readers and staff at the University of Pennsylvania Press for their close attention and contributions to this project. To my colleagues at Northridge—Lawrence Stewart, Gale Larson, Robert Noreen, Gwen Brewer, Lesley Johnstone, Elaine Plasberg, William Walsh, to Dean of Humanities Jorge Garcia, and to former Dean Jerome Richfield— I owe much for their welcome interest and excellent support.

Earlier versions of portions of what follows appeared in several papers presented at meetings of the American Society for Eighteenth-Century Studies and its regional affiliates, and in published form in:

"'A Child is Being Beaten': Suggestions Toward a Psychoanalytic Reading of Johnson," in *The Age of Johnson*, vol. 2, ed. Paul J. Korshin (New York: AMS Press, 1989), pp. 181–217. Copyright © 1989 by AMS Press, Inc.

"Johnson and the Uses of Enchantment," in *Fresh Reflections on Samuel Johnson: Essays in Criticism,* ed. Prem Nath (New York: Whitston, 1987), pp. 299–311. Copyright © 1987 by Whitston Press.

"Dr. Johnson's Practice: The Medical Context for *Rasselas*," in *Studies in Eighteenth-Century Culture*, vol. 14, ed. O M Brack, Jr. (Madison: University of Wisconsin Press, 1985), pp. 275–88. Copyright © 1985 by the American Society for Eighteenth-Century Studies.

"Johnson on Psychopathology," in *Greene Centennial Studies: Essays Presented to Donald Greene,* ed. Paul J. Korshin and Robert R. Allen (Charlottesville: University Press of Virginia, 1984), pp. 271–87. Copyright © 1984 by the University Press of Virginia.

Permission to reprint these materials is acknowledged.

Permission is also acknowledged to reprint portions of John Wain's English translation of "Know Thyself," in John Wain, *Johnson on Johnson: A Selection of the Personal and Autobiographical Writings of Samuel Johnson (1709–1784)* (London: J.M. Dent, 1976), pp. 182–84. Copyright © 1976 by J.M. Dent Co.

But this invisible riot of the mind, this secret prodigality of being, is secure from detection, and fearless of reproach.

—Johnson, *Rambler* 89

Introduction

> The dissipation of thought, of which you complain, is nothing more than the
> vacillation of a mind suspended between different motives, and changing its
> direction as any motive gains or loses strength.[1]

SO JOHNSON WROTE TO BOSWELL in December, 1763 about the fundamental ambivalence which lies at the heart of mental life and breeds its devastating disorders. No stranger to emotional crisis, Johnson, at the time, was
struggling with the black, uncontrollable depression that haunted him
from at least the age of twenty. Now rapidly descending into a maelstrom of
disorientation and what he believed to be threatened collapse into madness,
he characteristically recorded his experience. In a journal entry which
survives of April 21, 1764, 3:00 A.M., he tells of plunging into an abyss of
lethargy: "My indolence . . . has sunk into grosser sluggishness, and my
dissipation spread into wilder negligence. . . . A kind of strange oblivion
has overspread me, so that I know not what has become of the last year, and
perceive that incidents and intelligence pass over me without leaving any
impression." The numbness alternating with "vain terrours" reported in a
few sparse succeeding entries, he is much the same one year later, Easter
Day, 1765, "about 3 in the morning": "Since last Easter . . . my time . . .
seems as a dream that has left nothing behind. My memory grows confused,
and I know not how the days pass over me."[2]

No doubt Johnson kept many such records of his mental state, private
papers and journals he destroyed shortly before his death, including the
famous two quarto volumes with the detailed narrative of his life, to which
Boswell and Hawkins allude.[3] The fragment of Proustian autobiography,
saved from the flames by Frances Barber, was begun during the mid-1760s,
as we estimate, and it is the purest record extant of his efforts to recreate an
emotional history.[4] As he lingers in scenes from earliest childhood, by a
kind of stream-of-consciousness narration, we note the rudiments of what
was likely an ongoing self-analysis. These writings must have been an
important medium for sifting through and managing a tumultuous inner

life. What is more, Johnson's labors of introspection, consisting in so elemental a census of his thoughts and impressions, surely provide the matrix from which his theories of the mind originate. "Every man . . . may, by examining his own mind, guess what passes in the minds of others," Imlac proclaims in *Rasselas*, that most psychiatric of eighteenth-century texts. Clearly, Johnson owed an extraordinary understanding of mental phenomena to intense and painful self-analysis. His works contain some of the most astonishing portrayals before Freud of problems rooted in hitherto unperceived mental acts and agencies. Drawing upon diverse traditions—in medicine, philosophy, theology—but chiefly on his own experience, Johnson helps to pioneer a newly emerging science of the mind. With scrupulous honesty, he speculates on causes of mental affliction and relates symptoms in remarkable detail. And, often in defiance of long-standing canons, he writes courageously and judiciously to open the way for what were to become the central lines of development in modern psychological and sociological theory.

The intent of this book is to explore Johnson's psychological theories, as they develop and are represented in his writings. My principal inspiration has been the research of scholars such as James Clifford, Donald Greene, and W. J. Bate, among whom there is striking consensus about Johnson's penetrating insights into human emotions and behavior. An habitué of the early modern world, Johnson ranged the landscapes of the mind, delving to inner recesses, however dark or painful or incongruous, to construct a dynamic picture of mental functioning. His writings map the course of basic human wants, needs, and expressions and show how, when deprived and frustrated, they erupt into dangerous morbid symptoms. Preeminently informed of new currents in medicine and epistemology, he used fresh paradigms of psychological laws and demonstrated their heuristic value. With aggressive conviction, he made sense of the seething inner revolt that depleted health and ruined happiness. Needless to say, this study also owes much gratitude to historians of medicine, as well as of literature and psychology in the eighteenth century, by virtue of their many dedicated efforts to trace original sources and present a cogent analysis of psychiatric issues in Johnson's day. Such reconstructions help to provide the cultural idiom through which Johnson interpreted his theories.[5] At the same time, this study employs a classical psychoanalytic approach, which seeks to establish a coherent relation between Johnson's life, his fantasies, and his creative production.[6] In a variety of ways, an analytic mode well suits the unorthodox style of Johnson's own ideas and methods. "Johnson's own

sense of the working of the human imagination," writes W. J. Bate, "probably provides us with the closest anticipation of Freud to be found in
psychology or moral writing before the twentieth century."[7] Evidently,
Johnson's methodical, far-ranging forays into the foundations of the psyche
have an unmistakable affinity with Freud's. The principle of psychological
determinism, the view of the mind as dictated by forces in conflict, the
concept of the dynamic unconscious and the submerged power of desire in
all human activity, pervade the very texture of his writings.

Surprisingly, even through a twentieth-century lens, psychological
meanings in Johnson's works have been eclipsed by issues of morality and
religion, to be sure, the conventional modes of reference for his day. But
following that agenda too exclusively, we risk imposing all too narrow and
timebound a viewpoint. Much as the old set piece of the Great Cham used
to deflect any interest in his writings, so exhaustive debates about eighteenth-century Anglicanism and Christian ethics tend to lose sight of Johnson's remarkable unconventionality. Too often is he appropriated to van-
ished causes, the dull disciple of one or another system of belief. Too readily
are the tendentious and pious professions of his age made to furnish the
main battery of his ideas. And not only current scholarship but original
accounts have contributed to this stilted image. The early reviews and
biographies are saturated by anthems to his Christian piety, unhappily to
cast an uncongenial shadow over his works for the most robust and avant-
garde of eighteenth- and nineteenth-century thinkers.[8] Certainly a great
many valuable studies in recent decades have gone far to determine in their
own right a full and accurate picture of Johnson's religion and morality. But
to rest entirely upon one or the other of these specialized historical topics is
to miss the distinctive challenge and power Johnson drew from the inexhaustible variety of human experience. From the viewpoint of psychological analysis, many meanings remain to be captured by contemporary students, many resonances to be sounded on the deepest levels of our common
understanding. It is a testament to his astonishing modernity that while we
may be on easier parlance with, we are hardly more free from the mental
demons Johnson so fervently pursued.

Since this book is centrally about Johnson and psychology, it might be
helpful to indicate here the larger backdrop of intellectual aims and interests. Wrestling Johnson from the chokehold of many eighteenth-century
orthodoxies is a necessary task of any claim to read him psychologically.
The history of psychological thought from the Renaissance forward is
plagued by repressive views of mental experience, commonly proffered in

the name of a rigorous sanctimony. Whether patronized by consumers of religion or science, the great god of Reason served a zealous penchant for complacency and maintenance of the status quo. Ruled by Reason, man's nobler spirit was certifiably hallowed, and he was authorized to act with relative impunity. For Augustan intellectuals, much fêted analogies between the hierarchal government of the mind and subordinating offices of the state extolled the sovereign power of cool Rationality: the passions, just as the rude, tempestuous rabble, were no more than snarling derivatives of the subhuman, to be duly muzzled and confined. And despite far less parochial attitudes of the Georgians, now amply impressed by the iconoclasm of Locke, Hume, and the philosophes, the enclaves of irrationality were still jealously guarded by doctrinaire policies in modern dress as well as hidebound reductionism.

Johnson's original contribution to the advancement of psychological thought was his trafficking with alien worlds of meaning, sprung of his unshakable belief in the absolute reality of inward life. Undaunted by institutional evasions, he urged men and women to probe more deeply into themselves and into others. Spurred by his own ambivalent relation to obedience and authority, he found that Reason was not master in its own house. Thus he challenged many talismans of certitude, many bastions of revered conformism, which sealed the doom of those who stumbled in the shadows of sickness, disability, and suffering. Moreover, by the very nature of his liberal, energetic investigations, he made incursions into the holy ground of psyche, in clear prospect of the basic premises underlying Freudian psychoanalysis. That he has been so often misrepresented is only more telling of the ominous resistance to the inner, private and potent, realm of mind. If the unsavory tale of madness in the eighteenth century foreshadows the varied forms of massive denial weighing heavily on contemporary life—the disavowing of human wishes, values, and will; the lashing evangelical patriotism; the patrols of thought police consecrated by "political correctness"—then this book celebrates Johnson's essential humanity and intelligence.

The chapters to follow are organized chronologically, in order to investigate a developmental span. I wish to suggest that themes of Johnson's intrapsychic life directed the course of his evolving psychological theories, from the fiery outrage and injustice-collection of his early career to the worldly insight and judgment of his mature works. Chapters One and Two offer formulations of Johnson's inner history, as well as how he understood his troubling mental symptoms in the style and resources of the eighteenth century. Chapters Three through Seven trace recurrent ideas and images, rooted deep in the psyche, which Johnson reexamined and reworked as the cornerstone of his indefatigable research. The final chapter considers Johnson as a pioneer in a new scientific theory of the mind, forged independently more than a century before Freud and his followers. Opposing many biased, fashionable attitudes toward mental disturbance—the savage derision of the Tory satirists, the inquisitorial "judgment for sin" of the provincial middle class, the fatalism and mechanism of the associationists, to name a few—Johnson's views are distinctively enlightened and progressive. Despite his legendary reputation as the "great moralist," he helped free human beings from moral-punitive obsession and glib rationalization, as he probed the vital springs of emotion and experience. By exploring hazardous, often forbidden terrain, he unearthed layer after layer of the structures of the mind. It is precisely this unprejudiced quality that made him a unique geologist in the realm of mental experience. There is a mournful yet defiant image in Johnson's last English poem, written two years before his death, an elegy on his old friend Dr. Robert Levet:

> Condemn'd to hope's delusive mine,
>   As on we toil from day to day,
> By sudden blasts, or slow decline,
>   Our social comforts drop away. (*Works*, 6: 314, ll. 1–4)

The situation of relentless digging into mysterious, myth-laden caverns is a masterful metaphor for Johnson's life's work. This study is an effort to measure that rare and enduring expedition.

Notes

1. *The Letters of Samuel Johnson*, ed. R.W. Chapman (Oxford: Clarendon Press, 1952), 1:165 (no. 163). Hereafter cited as *Letters*.

2. *The Yale Edition of the Works of Samuel Johnson*, ed. Allen T. Hazen and John H. Middendorf, et al. (New Haven, Conn.: Yale University Press, 1958–), 1:77–78; 92. Hereafter cited as *Works*.

3. Of these diaries, Boswell writes: "Two very valuable articles, I am sure, we have lost, which were two quarto volumes, containing a full fair, and most particular account of his own life, from his earliest recollection. I owned to him, that having accidentally seen them, I had read a great deal in them; . . . I said that I had, for once in my life, felt half an inclination to commit theft. It had come into my mind to carry off those two volumes, and never see him more. Upon my inquiring

how this would have affected him, 'Sir, (said he,) I believe I should have gone mad' "
(*Life of Samuel Johnson*, ed. George Birkbeck Hill and L.F. Powell [Oxford: Clarendon Press, 1934–50], 4: 405–06—hereafter cited as *Life*). Hawkins in fact does take
two parchment-covered notebooks from Johnson's bedchamber during his last
sickness: "Johnson took me aside, and told me that I had a book of his in my pocket;
I answered that I had two, and that to prevent their falling into the hands of a person
who had attempted to force his way into the house, I had done as I conceived a
friendly act. . . . At the mention of this circumstance Johnson paused; but recovering
himself, said, 'You should not have laid hands on the book; for had I missed it, and
not known you had it, I should have roared for my book, as Othello did for his
handkerchief, and probably have run mad' " (*The Life of Samuel Johnson*, ed. Bertram
H. Davis [London: Jonathan Cape, 1962], pp. 271–72). For an illuminating view of
the controversies generated over these papers, see Paul J. Korshin, "Johnson's Last
Days: Some Facts and Problems," *Johnson After Two Hundred Years*, ed. Paul J.
Korshin (Philadelphia: University of Pennsylvania Press, 1986), pp. 55–76. See also
Frederick A. Pottle, "The Dark Hints of Sir John Hawkins and Boswell," in *New
Light on Dr. Johnson*, ed. Frederick W. Hilles (New Haven, Conn.: Yale University
Press, 1959), pp. 153–62.

4. For sources and dating of the manuscript, see *Works* 1: xiii–xv.

5. Prominent research in the history of psychiatry in the eighteenth century,
from that appearing most recently, includes Roy Porter, *Mind-Forg'd Manacles:
A History of Madness in England* (Cambridge, Mass.: Harvard University Press,
1987); Klaus Doerner, *Madness and the Bourgeoisie*, trans. J. Neugroschel and J.
Steinberg (Oxford: Basil Blackwell, 1981); George Rousseau, "Psychology," in *The
Ferment of Knowledge: Studies in the Historiography of Eighteenth-Century Science*
(Cambridge: Cambridge University Press, 1980); George Rosen, "Irrationality and
Madness in Seventeenth and Eighteenth Century Europe," in *Madness in Society:
Chapters in the Historical Sociology of Mental Illness* (Chicago: University of Chicago
Press, 1968), pp. 151–71; Richard Hunter and Ida Macalpine, *Three Hundred Years of
Psychiatry 1535–1860* (New York: Oxford University Press, 1963); "The Enlighten-
ment," in Franz G. Alexander and Sheldon T. Selesnick, *The History of Psychiatry*
(New York: Harper & Row, 1966), pp. 106–32; Michel Foucault, *Madness and
Civilization: A History of Insanity in the Age of Reason*, trans. Richard Howard (New
York: Random House, 1965); "The Age of Reconstruction," in Gregory Zilboorg,
A History of Medical Psychology (New York: W. W. Norton, 1941), pp. 245–341. For
studies specifically geared toward literary issues, see *Psychology and Literature in the
Eighteenth Century*, ed. Christopher Fox (New York: AMS Press, 1987); William B.
Ober, *Bottoms Up: A Pathologist's Essays on Medicine and the Humanities* (Carbondale: Southern Illinois University Press, 1987); Frederick M. Keener, *The Chain of
Becoming: The Philosophical Tale, the Novel, and a Neglected Realism of the Enlightenment: Swift, Montesquieu, Voltaire, Johnson, and Austen* (New York: Columbia University Press, 1983); Lillian Feder, "The Spleen, The Vapors, and the God Within,"
in *Madness in Literature* (Princeton, N.J.: Princeton University Press, 1980), pp.
147–202; Michael V. DePorte, *Nightmares and Hobbyhorses: Swift, Sterne, and Augustan Ideas of Madness* (San Marino: Huntington Library, 1974); Max Byrd, *Visits to
Bedlam: Madness and Literature in the Eighteenth Century* (Columbia: University of

South Carolina Press, 1974). See also David G. Schappert, "Selected Bibliography of Primary Materials," in Fox, ed., *Psychology and Literature in the Eighteenth Century*, pp. 303–45.

6. Doctrines of psychoanalysis are the product of modern intellectual history, with many of its ideas having become an accepted part of educated discourse. Terms such as *conflict*, the *unconscious, inhibition, compulsion, guilt, ambivalence*, and the like are common parlance and readily acknowledged, with the simplest definitions setting them clearly in focus. By "classical psychoanalytic approach," I mean the traditional humanistically oriented style of inquiry, as first developed by Freud and his followers and continuing to evolve in current research and clinical practice. This, in contrast to other psychological styles of inquiry, dominated by contemporary literary theory and often linked in spirit to French structuralism and deconstruction, i.e., "the dynamic relation between reader and text." For a critique and justification of classic psychoanalysis as applied to historical and literary texts, see Peter Gay's indispensable *Freud for Historians* (New York: Oxford University Press, 1985).

7. W. J. Bate, *The Achievement of Samuel Johnson* (New York: Oxford University Press, 1955), p. 93. Bate puts it even more emphatically in *Samuel Johnson* (New York: Harcourt Brace Jovanovich, 1975), p. 300: "As in no other classical moralist, we have a profound anticipation of what was to be the wide-scale nineteenth- and twentieth-century discovery about the mind that went on from the major Romantics down through the clinical exploration of the unconscious that followed Freud. That is, the discovery that the mind—far from being either a serene, objective, rational instrument, or, as the radical materialist thought, a sort of recording machine that works in mechanically happy union with whatever outside experiences press the button—is something unpredictably alive in its own right. And when something outside stimulates or pokes it into activity, it can start moving in any number of unforseen ways that are by no means in harmony with things outside it." Many are the allusions to Johnson's and Freud's common view of the mental apparatus. Some recent examples include James Engell: "Johnson probes the unconscious mind . . . with a brilliant, stubborn persistence unrivaled before Freud. He is aware that the door is always open between imagination and every impulse, instinct, and emotion, at every level from the rudimentary to the sophisticated. This leads to a less compartmentalized, more dynamic conception of the mind than is common among contemporaries writing in the 1750s" (*The Creative Imagination: Enlightenment to Romanticism* [Cambridge, Mass.: Harvard University Press, 1981], p. 61); Jean Hagstrum: "Johnson was of course aware that psychological links were automatically forged in the dark—that one vice, for example, could be magnetically attracted to another, sometimes a virtue to a vice, sometimes an excess to a defect—all this because of the very structure of the psyche, without volition, without choice" ("Towards a Profile of the Word *Conscious* in Eighteenth-Century Literature," in Fox, ed., *Psychology and Literature in the Eighteenth Century*, p. 42); Paul Alkon: "In recognizing the existence of unconscious motivation as well as in pointing out the importance of our disposition to forget whatever makes us uncomfortable, Johnson anticipates two major concerns of Freudian psychology" (*Samuel Johnson and Moral Discipline* [Chicago: Northwestern University Press, 1967], p. 138).

8. *Johnson: The Critical Heritage*, ed. James T. Boulton, pp. 1–41; James L. Clifford and Donald J. Greene, *Samuel Johnson: A Survey and Bibliography of Critical Studies* (Minneapolis: University of Minnesota Press, 1970), pp. 3–33; and O M Brack, Jr. and Robert E. Kelley in, both ed., *The Early Biographies of Samuel Johnson* (Iowa City: University of Iowa Press, 1974) and the *Samuel Johnson's Early Biographers* (Iowa City: University of Iowa Press, 1971), pp. 75–114 all note the sanctimonious bent of early reviews that make Johnson into a flawless moral hero. A couple of examples include, in his own lifetime: "May it be long before he seeks the place which only can supply a reward adequate to his private merits!"; and in 1842: "Though few or none can hope to emulate his *greatness*, all may, trusting in the same almighty Help, walk in the same *good* path with Dr. Samuel Johnson" (as quoted in Clifford and Greene, pp. 4–5). A typical rebuff by the avant-garde is Jeremy Bentham's characterization of Johnson as "that Pompous preacher of melancholy moralities" (as quoted in Boulton, p. 8). Alvin Kernan well sums up the basis for Johnson's stodgy reputation: "For Macaulay and most of the nineteenth and early twentieth centuries, he became the great Tory, the rational defender of the old order, the last voice, quirky and eccentric, but authoritative, of neoclassical values in a time of radical skepticism and social change" (*Printing Technologies, Letters & Samuel Johnson* [Princeton, N.J.: Princeton University Press, 1987], p. 116).

1. "Make Your Boy Tell You His Dreams": The Intrapsychic Life

RIDING IN A CARRIAGE by a Devonshire village churchyard with Samuel Johnson in 1762, Frances Reynolds recalls their sighting "a very stricking [sic] object of maternal affection, a little verdent [sic] flowery monument, raised by the Widow'd Mother over the grave of her only child." As she began to relate the sad tale of original love and loss, she was startled to find Johnson suddenly stricken by racking emotion: "She heard him make heavy sighs, indeed sobs, and turning round she saw his Dear Face bathed in tears." Some years later, Miss Reynolds reports how the scene must have haunted his imagination, for when reminded of it, he wrote, "I know not when I have been so much affected."[1] The way we interpret this remarkable incident surely turns a key to Johnson's intrapsychic life. In analytic terms, we mark the identification with a mythic lost child, the adoring mother's only son, the vanquished father's guilty heir, who, Oedipus-like, suffers the consequences. It is an opening to rich and mysterious depths of being, much as Johnson advised Mrs. Thrale to listen to the voices of the unconscious: "Make your boy tell you his dreams: the first corruption that entered into my heart was communicated in a dream."[2]

Psychoanalyzing Johnson is a fascinating project, in view of the abundant data available on his emotional history. Johnson's intense introspection, his scrupulous inquiries into the filigree structures of the psyche, combined with the detailed observations of those who knew him, have yielded some admirable studies in psychobiography. Under the Freudian auspices, twentieth-century views of Johnson explain a variety of lifelong symptoms, such as recurring melancholic episodes and fears of insanity, to be motivated by complex intrapsychic events. In condensed form, the clinical vignette would go something like this: Johnson's violent mood swings and attacks of severe depression can be traced to impaired relations with his parents, themselves the victims of what would appear to be chronic characterological depression.[3] Though he did not suffer from a lack of love, he was oppressed by a clumsily directed love, the victim of his father's irregular attentions, now doting, now aloof, and his mother's overprotective, fretful anxiety. Thus the small child Sam imagined and experienced their disapproval and rejection, affects which determined the adult regression to panic and despair. Johnson reified punitive images of his parents, which he repressed, and in this way, repetitive feelings of worthlessness, compulsive needs for reassurance, and paroxysmal terrors of abandonment made up the pattern of his neurosis. The two major depressions of his life—in his twenties after leaving Oxford and in his fifties after receiving his pension—are enactments of this process which depleted his energies and left him infant-like, helpless, and out of control. In his relationship with the Thrales, particularly Mrs. Thrale, he found parent-substitutes, under whose indulgent care he was able to repeat and thereby undo the traumatic experiences of childhood.

Wrestling with the issues of Johnson's intrapsychic life takes us over a wide circuit of research and scholarship from the past several decades. With frequent appreciation (though occasional astonishment), we may review selected psychobiographies, as they attempt to reconstruct the contours of a private, largely unconscious, world of meaning. Clearly, the best examples collect all the available evidence and provide a sound conceptual framework, bringing into the open otherwise inaccessible structures of personality.

Under the special heading, "Biography—Medical and Psychological Works," listed in Clifford and Greene's *Samuel Johnson: A Survey and Bibliography of Critical Studies* (1970), at least eleven entries out of sixty-three in all are exclusively psychological, while the rest frequently engage psychological topics. And these considerable numbers do not include more general assessments of Johnson's character, such as those in Krutch, Bronson, Watkins, Liebert, Balderston, and Clifford, which are listed separately. More recent studies which apply psychological theory to Johnson's life begin with George Irwin's admirable psychobiography, *Samuel Johnson: A Personality in Conflict* (1971), and I have counted some half-dozen others, many cited in Greene and Vance's *A Bibliography of Johnsonian Studies 1970–1985*, which fit the original "psychological" category, in addition to the well-known psychoanalytically-oriented biographies by Wain and Bate.[4] Indeed, Irwin's study becomes a watershed of sorts, marking the change from the early erratic, often wildly theoretical "case histories" to the later more factually informed, more integrated research into Johnson's emotional history. Like the pioneering accounts by Krutch and Clifford, which rely more on empirical analysis than abstract speculation—a method the subject himself would have thoroughly endorsed—Irwin's study shifts the emphasis from Johnson as diagnostic showpiece to Johnson the humanly compelling habitué of the modern world.

Many early psychological interpretations of Johnson, while notable for specifying his demonstrably neurotic behavior patterns, suffer equally from two main weaknesses: their overdetermination and limited scope. Despite Freud's famous warning about "wild psychoanalysis,"[5] these studies tend to cast Johnson into stiff diagnostic molds, reducing his problems to narrow sexual factors and using Boswell's *Life* as almost sole documentation. A typical example is R. Macdonald Ladell's "The Neurosis of Dr. Samuel Johnson" (1929), which states that Johnson developed an "anxiety hysteria," by which he "discovered himself to be sexually impotent. Denied all outward sex attraction he had concentrated his interests so exclusively on intellectual achievement as to divert the main stream of his libido from its natural goal."[6] Similarly, Charles Maclaurin (1925) finds that "probably all Johnson's psychasthenic involuntary movements which made him so strange a figure to his contemporaries, took their origin in unconscious memory of some affront to his childish masculinity, such as would be caused by taking him to Queen Anne to be 'touched.'"[7] And Edward Hitschmann (1945) believes "if Johnson had not repressed his archaic, very barbarian instincts, he would have bitten off the nipples of the breasts of his wet nurse, would have castrated and killed his father, blinded his brother and let him die of hunger, would have committed incest with his mother, slayed some of his enemies, and would have died from overeating."[8]

Needless to say, these are preposterous claims, even given the analyst's metaphysical license: the incomplete data and the lack of any comprehensive view or feeling for a living person lead one to suspect that here is the grotesque picture taken from Boswell (and very likely Macaulay's popular edition of the *Life*), but done up psychoanalytically. It is the sacrifice of the subject for a dubious theoretical rigor, applying what were then novel discoveries of Freud, Adler, Jung, and so on, in ways never intended.[9] More reasonable early uses of psychological interpretation are to be found in contributions by the eminent neurologist W. Russell Brain (1934, 1949), who pieces together a more sophisticated, if unfinished, portrait of Johnson from a larger variety of sources. Lord Brain traces Johnson's mental suffering to a "bondage to the past," and he pointedly diagnoses his subject's compulsive gestures as psychosomatic in origin, concurring with Sir Joshua Reynold's remarkable observation that "these actions always appeared to me as if they were meant to reprobate some part of his past conduct."[10] In a like vein, Lawrence C. McHenry, Jr. (1967) relates Johnson's abnormal movements to his "constitutional melancholy" and pervasive feelings of "everlasting condemnation," for which he also finds evidence in several sources.[11] These latter approaches represent more helpful discussions of Johnson's psychopathology, by virtue of their breadth of reference and disencumbrance from abstract theoretical dogma. But at the same time, their fixed intent—ostensibly, the clinical description of the "great man"— hence their limited results, give only a partial measure of the depth of Johnson's vastly complex personality.

A fuller and more rewarding account of Johnson's character and temperament begins with literary scholars, who combine psychological implications with solid historical knowledge of the man, as well as of eighteenth-century manners. While not strictly the stuff of psychobiography, which reconstructs a picture of intrapsychic life, these studies nonetheless contain reliable, well-documented treatments of Johnson's personal and social habits, and they analyze major events and relationships. Interwoven through the narratives is a predominant psychological theme, which attempts to explain the outbursts of turbulent emotion and intervening bouts of severe depression. Here is the principal concept of Johnson's mental life, to be developed more completely by Irwin and subsequent psychobiographers: the staving off of intense feelings of defeat and worthlessness, the chronic struggle against intolerable anxiety and guilt. Krutch (1944) names it, when speaking of the depth of Johnson's grief over the loss of his wife: "Since college days at least he had known that the abyss was just beside whatever path he trod, whether it was something he had inherited from a melancholy father or, possibly, something generated by some forgotten experience never examined in the light of day. At its bottom lay nameless apprehensions and fears, an obscure sense of guilt. . . . [His wife's death was] a rational incident to which floating and otherwise inexplicable distresses attached themselves."[12] Bronson (1944) infers much the same, as he interprets the rage and fury of the young Johnson's hard contention for literary reputation: "Mad, violent, and bitter; miserably poor, and conscious of intellectual abilities of a high order, yet unrecognized: the mixture spells, as always, Radical, Iconoclast, Enemy of the Established Order."[13] And Watkins (1939), likewise: "It was the turbulence and power of his imagination which put him so much on guard against it. . . . Rude, savage, outrageous . . . he spared himself even less than others, as his torturing sense of his own personal insufficiency shows."[14]

Drawing a similar conclusion, Clifford (1955) notices a deep resemblance between Johnson and his friend the renegade poet, Richard Savage, of whom "it would be hard to find anyone more emotionally dependent upon pain and disappointment, often self-inflicted."[15] And Liebert (1948), in perhaps the most penetrating psychological analysis of all, describes Johnson's poignant identification with failure and distress. Listing the denizens of Johnson's humble household, he notes: "In the frailties of Levett, the blindness of Mrs. Williams, the miseries of the sick and sorrowful for whom he was a sure retreat, there was anodyne for the pain of his own unceasing struggle, and with them he could be one in the fellowship of the afflicted."[16] Finally, Balderston (1949) suggests certain masochistic trends in Johnson's relationship with Mrs. Thrale, reconstructing, in part, his "compulsive fantasy . . in which the impulse to self-abasement and pain predominated. . . . [Mrs. Thrale] was . . . the unrecognized erotic object from whose ministrations his maladjusted libido sought relief."[17] Striking a rather sensitive note in Johnson biography and extrapolating perhaps a bit more precisely than the data warrant, the suggestion was enough to open the door once more to an analytic conceptual framework: the efforts to reconstruct Johnson's intrapsychic life, in this case, supported by responsible literary scholarship, prepared the way for Irwin's outstanding achievement.

Samuel Johnson: A Personality in Conflict (1971) is a daring and ambitious study, for its careful mapping of the course of Johnson's mental life, ranging from childhood and early education to middle age. Irwin's thesis is that Johnson, with the help of his unique relationship to Mrs. Thrale, recognized and treated his own mental disease: he made, as stated in the Preface, a "pre-Freudian recovery from neurosis, an event of unusual psychotherapeutic interest." According to Irwin, Johnson's neurosis entailed an all-pervading sense of fear, stemming from unconscious "mother-hate": "To hate the person whom one has from the first moments of reason been taught to honour, the person one is obliged to love; to hate that person to whom above all others one wants to be acceptable in order that one may be acceptable to oneself, is so repellent that mother-hate is usually repressed before it impinges upon the conscious mind. But, though Johnson could hide this hate from himself, he could not escape the resultant guilt and the self-punishing responses which subconscious guilt induces."[18] A major advantage of Irwin's approach is its generous sampling of quotes from Johnson's contemporaries, Robert Burton's *The Anatomy of Melancholy* (1621), and Johnson himself on the nature of mental suffering, thereby to establish an eighteenth-century psychiatric idiom. With a nice balance of history, critical imagination, and psychological insight, Irwin pioneers the difficult way to understanding how Johnson experienced and managed his emotional distress. At the same time, this is an introductory study, for while bringing together substantial literary and psychological data, Irwin by no means runs the full course of analytic interpretation. Instead, he presents more like a preliminary draft of an intrapsychic picture, which invites further research: if Johnson suffered from "unconscious guilt," it remains to explore a clinical vignette which encompasses the roles of his entire family—mother, father, and brother—as well as a wider range of affects—love, envy, rage, and the like. With the plentiful volume of materials at hand, it remains to construct a metapsychology which includes the fierce archaic images, the full gamut of internalizations and projections, determining the more thorough extent of Johnson's inner travail.

John Wain's full-length life and critique of Johnson (1975) is told through the medium of a novelist-poet, who creates the man and his world with stirring, generous compassion. While clearly not intended as psychobiography, Wain's book ever suggests the pattern of an inner life, in the best tradition of literary biography, so that we feel the presence of a living person. Speaking of Johnson's identification with the intractable Richard Savage, for example, Wain refers back to Johnson's relationship with his mother: "The resentment of Sarah for her failure to give him love and emotional security was buttoned down tightly out of sight and watched over by an unsleeping censor. All the more eagerly did he listen to Savage's tirades against the mother who had similarly, and far more spectacularly, failed him. Chords which his own fingers were forbidden to touch became vibrant at the eloquent recital of Savage's wrongs."[19] If Wain's life of Johnson is interlaced with a subtle analytic meaning, W. J. Bate's *Samuel Johnson* (1976) has a texture conspicuously Freudian, its principal concern being the mind and motivation of its subject. Combining technical concepts with a comprehensive knowledge of Johnson, Bate attempts the ultimate synthesis of life and works through classical psychoanalysis. Take this excerpt from an early chapter entitled, "Breakdown and Despair: Psychology of the Young Johnson," which interprets the cause, symptoms, and creative expression of Johnson's lifelong mental problems:

> This [feeling] was the fierce and exacting sense of self-demand—with its remorseless capacity, in some natures, to punish the self through a crippling sense of guilt and through the resulting anxieties, paralysis, and psychosomatic illness that guilt, grown habitual and strongly enough felt, begins to sprout. . . .

The part of himself from which he needed to escape was this remorseless pressure of "superego" demand, of constant self-criticism, and all the unconscious ruses of insistent self-punishment. . . . And in Johnson's own moral writing, which often anticipates psychoanalysis, he was to show—in a way close to modern psychiatry—how much of the misery of mankind comes from the inability of individuals to think well of themselves, and how much envy and other evils spring from this.[20]

Brilliant and wonderfully bold in scope and interdisciplinary design, Bate comes closest to formal psychobiography, though, like Irwin, he essentially stops short of the full intrapsychic picture. Yet to be charted is a more complete exploration of Johnson's intrapsychic life, of internal objects having developed from early experience, real as well as imagined, and of the projectively apprehended world, so indigenous to the psychoneurotic personality.

With the way to responsible literary and psychological judgment already prepared by Irwin and Bate, the three most recent psychobiographies of Johnson I shall now turn to are among the best. From the medical historian's point of view, Porter (1985) provides a detailed framework for Johnson's melancholy, as he "suffered his affliction—one almost says, enacted his passion—in the idiom of his day, above all perceiving derangement through the Lockean lens that located madness in the mind, the deluge of delusion invading the realm of reason."[21] To be sure, Porter's interest in Johnson is largely paradigmatic, for the sake of exploring a fuller record of mental disturbance in the eighteenth century, but in doing so, he solidly identifies Johnson's compulsions and phobias and extrapolates as to their cause and effect. More to the subject of Johnson's individual psychopathology is Newton's provocative analysis (1984) of Johnson's severe depression in middle life, tracing more completely than his predecessors a picture of his subject's intrapsychic life. Newton finds the cause of Johnson's acute attacks of anxiety and depression hidden deep within the psyche: "By 50, Johnson's characteristic melancholy was turning into madness, because he had lost all reason for living and because, in a world emptied of purpose, there was only the internal world of guilt and remorse, longing and loss, anxiety and conflict, the world of internal bad objects—the repressed hateful and hated, neglected and now dead wife and mother, the hateful and hated, long dead brother and father."[22] Finally, Meyer's exemplary, if brief, series of papers (1979, 1981, 1983, 1984) help to open many secret passageways to Johnson's intricately structured personality. With a rare combination of psychoanalytic and literary expertise, Meyer organizes the account of childhood and early development to form a striking psycho-dynamic picture. He demonstrates the congruity between Johnson's life and work and his unconscious wishes, all influenced to varying degrees by intense guilt and masochistic striving: "A careful scrutiny of Johnson's history as well as his fictional writing discloses that issues of captivity, incarceration, and escape played a prominent role in his own mental life."[23]

Certainly more work along the lines of the studies by Irwin, Bate, Newton, and Meyer needs to be done to create the full picture of Johnson's psyche, yet what we have so far suffices to tell a remarkably convincing story. We note consistent findings of a severe superego, in respect to which every pleasure must be paid for with painful guilt, self-punitive ordeals, and destructive acts, so common to psychoneurotic personality disorders. More than would be conveyed by the abstract term, "masochism," Johnson's entrenched suffering colored his entire mode of living, and nowhere does he strike so profoundly the note of his own experience as in his literary production. As he transforms private issues into public utterance, we trace a developmental pattern, from the projection of intense persecutory fantasies to the working through and modifying of that internal world of bad objects. The repetitive convictions of failure and chronic unhappiness give way to more conciliatory aims. The gnashing fury and unsettled traumas provide the impulse for his excavation of mental life.

Notes

1. *Johnsonian Miscellanies*, ed. George Birkbeck Hill (Oxford: Clarendon Press, 1897), 2: 279. Hereafter cited in text and notes as *Johnsonian Miscellanies*.
2. *Johnsonian Miscellanies*, 1: 159.
3. Surely we can afford to de-stigmatize Johnson's parents, particularly his mother, who has suffered some nasty aspersions over the past several decades. The stress on her middle age at marriage and childbirth, as well as her alleged ignorance and perpetual scolding, runs dangerously close to the popular mid-twentieth-century concept of "momism" (from Philip Wylie's expression, coined in 1942), the idea of a mother's excessive domination over her children and their ensuing difficulties in life. Needless to say, such an attitude is tactless, if not crudely reductionistic. Irwin's otherwise evenhanded appraisal of Johnson's mental problems, which stem, as he puts it, from unconscious "mother-hate," relies at times too heavily on this unfortunate dictum.
4. Clifford and Greene, *Samuel Johnson: A Survey and Bibliography of Critical Studies*, pp. 70–74; Donald Greene and Johnson A. Vance, *A Bibliography of Johnsonian Studies, 1970–1985*, ESL Monograph Series, No. 39 (Victoria, B.C.,: University of Victoria, 1987), pp. 13–14.

5. *The Standard Edition of the Complete Psychological Works of Sigmund Freud,* trans. and gen. ed. James Strachey (London: Hogarth Press, 1953–74), 11: 221–27.

6. Ladell, "The Neurosis of Dr. Samuel Johnson," *British Journal of Medical Psychology* 9 (1929): 321.

7. Maclaurin, *Mere Mortals: Medico-Historical Essays* (New York: George H. Doran 1925), pp. 38–39.

8. Hitschmann, "Samuel Johnson's Character: A Psychoanalytic Interpretation," *Psychoanalytic Review* 32 (1945): 215–16.

9. Even as late as 1971, Dutch psychiatrist E. Verbeek offers the unwieldy and frankly baffling thesis of Johnson's "degenerative personality" disorder, drawn in even more baffling detail by alleging his "epileptic depressions" (*The Measure and the Choice* [Ghent: E. Story Scientia, 1971]). If there is a saving grace in Verbeek's essay, it is his acquaintance with more than just Boswell.

10. Brain, "Authors and Psychopaths," *British Medical Journal* 2 (24 Dec. 1949): 1429–30. See also "A Post-Mortem on Dr. Johnson," *London Hospital Gazette* 37 (May, June 1934): 225–30; 288–89.

11. McHenry, "The Neurosis of Dr. Samuel Johnson," *British Journal of Medical Psychology,* 9 (1929): 166–67.

12. Krutch, *Samuel Johnson* (New York: Henry Holt and Company, 1944), p. 108.

13. Bronson, "Johnson Agonistes," in *Johnson Agonistes & Other Essays* (1944; rpt. Berkeley: University of California Press, 1965), p. 2.

14. Watkins, *Perilous Balance: The Tragic Genius of Swift, Johnson, & Sterne* (Princeton, N.J.: Princeton University Press, 1939), pp. 89–90.

15. Clifford, *Young Sam Johnson* (New York: McGraw-Hill, 1955), p. 209.

16. Liebert, "Reflections on Samuel Johnson: Two Recent Books and Where They Lead," *Journal of English and Germanic Philology* 47.1 (1948): 85.

17. Balderston, "Johnson's Vile Melancholy," in *The Age of Johnson: Essays Presented to Chauncey B. Tinker,* ed. F. W. Hilles (New Haven, Conn.: Yale University Press, 1949), pp. 11–13.

18. Irwin, *Samuel Johnson: A Personality in Conflict* (Auckland: Auckland University Press, 1971), p. 50.

19. Wain, *Samuel Johnson* (New York: Viking Press, 1975), p. 105.

20. Bate, *Samuel Johnson* (New York: Harcourt Brace Jovanovich, 1975), pp. 121–22.

21. Porter, "'The Hunger of Imagination': Approaching Samuel Johnson's Melancholy," in *The Anatomy of Madness: Essays in the History of Psychiatry,* ed. W. F. Bynum, Roy Porter, and Michael Shepherd (London: Tavistock Publications, 1985), 1: 80.

22. Newton, "Samuel Johnson's Breakdown and Recovery in Middle-Age: A Life Span Developmental Approach to Mental Illness and Its Cure," *International Review of Psychoanalysis* 11 (1984): 113.

23. Meyer, "On the Application of Psychoanalysis in W. Jackson Bate's Life of Samuel Johnson," *Journal of the Philadelphia Association for Psychoanalysis* 6 (1979):

158. See also "Dr. Johnson's Secret Padlock," a paper read at the New York Psycho-analytic Society, New York, 26 Feb. 1980, abstract in *Psychoanalytic Quarterly* 50 (1981): 469–70; "Notes on Flying and Dying," *Psychoanalytic Quarterly* 52 (1983): 327–52; "Some Observations on the Rescue of Fallen Women," *Psychoanalytic Quarterly* 53 (1984): 153–61.

2. Medical Psychology in the Eighteenth Century

IF WE ARE NOW EQUIPPED with a view of Johnson's tempestuous inner life, we need also to establish his relation to eighteenth-century medical psychology. How, for example, did he understand his affliction in the era deemed by the late Michel Foucault and his followers, the "great confinement," or by another noted medical historian, "a disaster for the insane"?[1] In what way did the cluster of beliefs about the mind and madness influence Johnson in advancing his own theories? If his fears of insanity were part of a larger cultural stigma that sequestered disturbed individuals for being evil and dangerous, to what extent did he help to remove that mark of disgrace and reproach? And in its place did he substitute merely another repressive regime of Rationality, à la Foucault, or would it be better to stress an empiricist view, alert to his formulation of the dynamic unconscious? These are questions to be explored in the chapters following, but it is useful to begin the matter here.

Themes of medicine and disease run deep in Johnson's writings, and it is clear that he kept apprised of current developments, especially the key ideas from which psychiatry emerged. "He had studied medicine diligently in all its branches," notes Mrs. Thrale, "but had given particular attention to the diseases of the imagination."[2] Boswell and Hawkins mention several projects of Johnson's self-analysis, among them a kind of case history of his melancholy, which Dr. Samuel Swynfen, physician of Lichfield and Birmingham and Johnson's godfather, admired for its "extraordinary acuteness, research, and eloquence."[3] Johnson's library contained a respectable collection of ancient and modern medical volumes, including many psychiatric,[4] and he maintained close friendships with several practicing physicians, including the noted Dr. Robert James. With James, an old Lichfield schoolmate, he studied "physick," and he contributed the Dedication and the "Life of Boerhaave," revised from an earlier form in the *Gentleman's Magazine* (1739), to James's vast *Medicinal Dictionary* (1745).[5] Johnson received many tributes from late eighteenth-century and early nineteenth-century physicians: from Thomas Arnold, Robert Anderson, William Perfect, and John Haslam, who were struck by his accurate descriptions of mentally disturbed patients they found in their own clinical practices.[6] Finally, Johnson himself pays tribute, if grudgingly, to his age, when "human nature became the fashionable study, . . . sometimes with nice discernment, but often with idle subtlety." But he heartily approves the purpose "to analyze the mind, to trace the passions to their sources, to unfold the seminal principles of vice and virtue, or sound the depths of the heart for the motives of action."[7] In this respect, his champion was physician and philosopher John Locke.

The influence of Locke on Johnson has been often remarked, from affinities in empiricist epistemology on many topics: education, government, historical and scientific research, language, moral philosophy, and the like. Indeed, Johnson's Lockean assumptions are frequently the starting point for discussion of the various facets of his career: as literary critic, lexicographer, political writer, historian, moralist.[8] While it would be simplistic to argue for a direct or exclusive influence—a plurality of orientations, from St. Augustine, to Robert Burton, to William Law, seems more likely—it is nonetheless evident that the analytic methods Johnson used to investigate mental disturbance are firmly anchored in and develop largely from Locke's empiricist principles.

By emphasizing not only an active organic theory of knowledge but also the degrees of its certainty and uncertainty, Locke's philosophy of experience bears closely on eighteenth-century medical psychology. His inferences about the mind's liability to imbalance are particularly enhanced by his training as a physician, his studies under Thomas Willis and his friendship with Thomas Sydenham, two foremost seventeenth-century researchers in mental anatomy, and his direct clinical contact with psychiatric patients. In his early medical journals, Locke records some observations about madness, which he calls "nothing but a disorder in the imagination, and not in the discursive faculty," and further, "Any sober man may finde it in himself in twenty occasions."[9] His remarks that deranged mental states are defects in the imagination or image-producing faculty, and not in reason or judgment, and that every man is subject to them, are a significant departure from more traditional seventeenth-century psychiatric attitudes. By contrast to earlier views of demonic possession, physiological imbalance, judgment for sin, and the like, Locke studies mental disease on a more purely naturalistic basis. He recognizes the inadequacy of older authoritarian and rationalist systems and replaces them with principles about the mental apparatus and the pervasive play of experience in the shaping of mind.

The celebrated chapter in *An Essay Concerning Human Understanding* (1690, 1700), "Of the Association of Ideas," over and above its explicit theme, presents a distillation of Locke's findings on medical psychology. In the discussion of common failures of ideation, the formation of ideas in the mind, he probes the mind's inner recesses beyond immediate awareness and urges its historical reconstruction. Thus false, hidden associations leading to madness, that is, "this strong Combination of *Ideas*, not ally'd by Nature," whose influence brings on pain and suffering, might be examined in the light of scientific truth, to lose their sovereign power. In an unprecedented exhortation, Locke calls for an informed and assiduous attention to a principled inwardness: "This wrong Connexion in our Minds of *Ideas* in themselves, loose and independent one of another, has such an influence, and is of so great force to set us awry in our Actions, as well Moral as Natural, Passions, Reasonings, and Notions themselves, that, perhaps, there is not any one thing that deserves more to be looked after."[10] In other words, madness could be explained by the postulation of a covert causal nexus, and so regarded, it would seem to have prompted Johnson's radical direct inspection of an inner life.

Evidently, Johnson's attraction to Locke's work on madness was strong and enduring, with abundant examples in his own writings of Locke's concept of the mental apparatus and its tendency to go awry. Likewise a student of medical science, with special attention to what he called the "diseases of the imagination," he adopted and built upon Locke's understanding of deranged mental states. Following Locke's argument that madness is a fragility of common life, a fate that could seize anyone at any time, Johnson distinguishes between sanity and insanity not by kind but by degree: "Disorders of intellect . . . happen much more often than superficial observers will easily believe. Perhaps, if we speak with rigorous exactness, no human mind is in its right state."[11] Pre-eminently on Locke's authority, Johnson blazes trails of the mental landscape to seek the underlying internal mechanism and the chains of causality running by irresistible association. Thus he views mental aberration from the standpoint of psychodynamics, stressing a train of fluctuating mental processes, so-called normal or abnormal, as a matter of relative function.

By conceiving of the mind psychodynamically, Johnson, with Locke, necessarily contravenes the eighteenth-century medical establishment.

Medical historians note the dominantly rationalist *mentalité* of psychiatric theory in an age which peculiarly yielded to daring social and scientific experiments, yet feared the darkly subjective aspects of the mind. The "Age of Reason" still thrived in the domain of "mad-doctors," whose quasi-psychiatry without psychology took root in the literature of the period. Their routine catalogue of organic impairments—"animal spirits," "humours," and later "nerve fibers"—obviated any critical inquiry into emotions or experience. Dismally hampered by metaphysical speculation and authoritarian error, the Enlightenment, with its acclaimed promotion of the "new science," made few advances when it came to understanding mental processes.[12]

Foucault's general insight that the history of reason is a necessary condition to the history of madness invites a welter of associations to eighteenth-century medical psychology. "Moral management," as it was frequently dubbed, when not descended from a last stronghold of scholasticism based upon Aristotle, Hippocrates, and Galen, or from a casebook for so-called Christian exempla, chimes with prolific choruses of the sentimentalist tradition in eighteenth-century society.[13] All have in common a casuistry and evasion of the very problems they were supposed to explore. Infatuated by syllogism and intricacy, they skimmed the surfaces of a smoldering inner life. Johnson resisted these popular modes, chiefly by his thoroughgoing empiricism. He describes the ethic, with its converse, rationalism, in the "Life of Boerhaave" (1739), when vigorously endorsing the great Dutch physician's pursuit of scientific truth:

> He declares himself in the strongest terms, a favourer of experimental knowledge, and reflects with just severity upon those arrogant philosophers who are too easily disgusted with the slow methods of obtaining true notions by frequent experiments; and who, possessed with too high an opinion of their own abilities, rather choose to consult their own imaginations, than inquire into nature, and are better pleased with the delightful amusement of forming hypotheses, than the toilsome drudgery of amassing observations. . . .
> He examined systems by experiments, and formed experiments into systems. . . . He examined the observations of other men, but trusted only to his own.[14]

Incidentally, Johnson suggests that Boerhaave first began to study medicine much as he did, prompted by his own unrelieved affliction.[15]

It cannot be the purpose here to rehearse, let alone solve, the enormously complex debate over Cartesian dualisms of mind and body, which touted rationalist models from the mid-seventeenth century forward.[16]

Suffice it to say that Johnson disparaged the sprawling influence of mechanist philosophies, and he spurned the fashionable cults of natural morality
and natural theology in which they generally were issued. The call to
Nature and Right Reason sounded a preachy religiosity to the ears of the
cultural elite. Thus Robert Whytt, for example, Professor of Medicine at
Edinburgh and chief developer of the physiological concepts of sensibility
and sympathy, waxes out and out rhapsodic in a scientific treatise, when he
describes God as the embodiment of the rational order. With heady enthusiasm, the otherwise sober clinician traverses a slippery slope in the con-
cluding pages of his most important work, *An Essay on the Vital and other
Involuntary Motions of Animals* (1751). He takes the tone of those natural
theologists, who divine the perfection of Nature:

> If . . . the motions and actions of our small and inconsiderable bodies, are all to
> be referred to the active power of an immaterial principle [sentience]: how
> much more necessary must it be, to acknowledge as the Author . . . of the
> universal system, . . . one who conducts the motions of the whole, by the most
> consummate and unerring reason.[17]

Moreover, rationalism, with its rage for abstract system over experience, drives the principal apparatus in the works of such renowned figures
as Anthony Ashley Cooper, third Earl of Shaftesbury, whose *Characteristics
of Men, Manners, Opinions, Times* (1711) had an immense vogue; the great
Deist theologian Dr. Samuel Clarke (1675–1729?)—whom Johnson nonetheless held in special regard; Henry St. John, Viscount of Bolingbroke, the
guiding light for Pope's very popular *An Essay on Man* (1733–34); Archdea-
con William Paley (1734–1805) of "Paley's watch" fame; Thomas Paine, who
entitled his most famous political tract *The Age of Reason* (1793). And the
celebrated Adam Smith, political economist and Professor of Moral Philosophy at Glasgow, would seem to have based his whole system on natural
theology. In two highly influential texts, *The Theory of Moral Sentiments*
(1759) and *The Wealth of Nations* (1776), he introduces the popular notions
of the "impartial spectator," the judicious person's general rules for self-
appraisal, and the "invisible hand," the providential plan in economic self-
interest. They reinforce each other in their almost sole reliance on human
reason as the guide for moral action. True to the mold, Smith had little
interest, it would appear, in the causes of human behavior, in specific
motives or instincts as the impetus for feeling: "Sympathy . . . does not arise
so much from the view of the passion, as from the situation which excites
it." Beyond the impartial spectator it is useless to inquire: "To examine

from what contrivance or mechanism within those different notions or sentiments arise [i.e., the passions], is a mere matter of philosophical inquiry."[18] With its cool logic and imperious speculation, Smith's work is a paragon of rationalist discourse.

If Johnson rejected Enlightenment pedagogy on the theory of the mind, he also must have looked askance at the practice of psychiatry in his day.[19] Medical historians suggest that incarceration in madhouses in the seventeenth and eighteenth centuries was not all that unusual. In addition to the major public asylums, numerous handbills called attention to private madhouses run by "mad-doctors," some of whom were reputable physicians, others no more than advertising quacks with no proper medical training. Respectable or not, the "mad-business" seemed to be booming by the mid-eighteenth century and gave rise to a burgeoning literature on the subject, which included some fascinating well-publicized controversies. The polemics which flared about the cause, symptoms, and cure of madness provide an important context for Johnson's psychological theory. Perhaps the debate reached its climax in the famous dispute between two eminent rival "mad-doctors," John Monro of Bethlem Hospital and William Battie of St. Luke's. While each competed for official endorsement by colleagues as well as the public at large, Monro and his dogmatic views had long-standing sanction in a variety of disciplines. But it is Battie, as we shall see, who, surely having studied Locke as a student at Cambridge, stands as Johnson's powerful intellectual ally.

John Monro, chief physician to Bethlem Hospital from 1751 to 1791, was the second of five generations of Monros who achieved eminence as "mad-doctors," of whom four held this office in succession, and he advocated the standard eighteenth-century approach to madness. This was imprisonment under harsh coercion and restraint, and a variety of physical punishments, including vomits, purges, blows, stripes, surprise baths, copious bleedings, electric shock, and meager diet. Such outright cruelty was justified by the attitude that madness was caused by "vitiated judgment," whereby, Monro states, "every quality which distinguishes a man from a brute, except a few unconnected, incoherent words, seems totally obliterated."[20]

As "vitiated judgment," madness was traditionally associated with sin or departure from God-given reason. Even in the eighteenth century, this concept was not entirely differentiated from the medieval Christian notion of demonic possession. Indeed, the notorious *Malleus Malificarum*, much of which contained painstaking pictures of so-called madness and was devoted to the thesis that mental illness was the devil's inspiration, went through ten editions before 1669 and nine more before the mid-eighteenth century.[21] Like the cure for heresy, the cure for insanity lay in a "moral physick," a treatment aimed at scourging the body as well as the soul. The madder the patient, the more severe the punishment. Johann Christian Reil (1759–1813), one of the more advanced psychiatrists of the period, remarks on the dreadful lot of the insane in Europe:

> We incarcerate these miserable creatures as if they were criminals in abandoned jails, near to the lairs of owls in barren canyons beyond the city gates, or in damp dungeons of prisons, where never a pitying look of a humanitarian penetrates; and we let them, in chains, rot in their own excrement.[22]

As a lapse in reason, mental illness became the symbol of a fall from grace, and often in literature a polemic against sin and evil, a faded version of the old morality play.[23] Imaginative writers and physicians alike represent the torture and punishment associated with madhouses as justifiable, even mandatory. Victims of emotional disturbance are seen as base, vice-ridden creatures, physically as well as mentally repulsive. Thus they are condemned to a symbolic hell to suffer the disfiguring symptoms of Pride, Wrath, Envy, Lust, and so on. They are not unlike victims of satire: indeed, the premises that shaped both in the popular imagination were mutually reinforcing. Pope and Swift, for example, are not content merely to expose their enemies' wrong-doing, but must besmear them with excrement and curse them with mental disease and perversion. The scurrilous reports in *The Dunciad* (1728; 1742), *A Tale of a Tub* (1704), *Gulliver's Travels* (1726), and other pamphlets of abuse imitate in various ways the horrendous procedures, the physical agents and techniques, used to punish people in madhouses.[24] The eighteenth-century satiric novelist, likewise, used madness as a form of moral propaganda to show the odious effects of deviating from the great Christian virtue, Reason. Stock characters and stock situations frequently derive from paradigms of good and evil, according to prevalent notions of physiognomy, organic imbalance, and symptom-formation. Much like the old Renaissance "humour" characters, these characters in novels were assigned grotesque punishments to fit their mental aberrations—as they would be in madhouses.[25] Just as psychiatric practice during the eighteenth century made superfluous the study of the patient's mind, so many novelists made superfluous the need for real character analysis. To treat mental problems was to recover reason through a variety of severe physical trials, and for doctors and writers alike the individual's mind entered into this only for an ad hoc assessment of symptoms before, during, and after treatment. And if a more tolerant attitude toward madness set in by the late eighteenth century, it was still very much conditioned by rationalism, often a crude moral-didacticism, as the best authorities on the sentimentalist tradition have confirmed.[26]

Psychiatric medical treatises through most of the eighteenth century noted in careful detail the latest refinements of physical agents and techniques. One such notorious method is described in the following excerpt from a case history by Patrick Blair, physician in Lincolnshire. It shows the physician's standard lack of psychological insight. But more important, this strange narrative of the refractory housewife forced to undergo her doctor's abhorrent torture machine reflects the moral-punitive ordeals, the punishments and forms of physical abuse, undergone by fictional characters in many eighteenth-century literary works. Thus they are chastised before they recover—if indeed they ever do—their proper Reason.

> A married Woman . . . became mad, neglected every thing, would not own her husband nor any of the Family, kept her room, would converse with nobody but kept spitting continually, turning from any that turn'd from her and chiding any who put their hand in their sides, telling them she was not a whore.

After prescribing the usual "frequent bleedings, violent Emeticks, strong purgatives and potent Sudorificks and Narcoticks," Blair reports:

> She began to enquire more seriously into the state of domestic affairs at the servants who came to see her, spoke more kindly to them, shew'd a desire to be at home, quitted much of her former gestures, speeches and behavior, was obedient when reprov'd because of them and gave all signs of recovery except that of the dislike to her husband.

At this lattermost obstinacy and sure sign of lingering madness, Blair resigns her to the ordeal of his "cold bathing engine," a sort of shower with the double shock of surprise plus quantities of cold water poured on the patient's head from measured heights:

> I ordered her to be blindfolded. Her nurse and other women stript her. She was lifted up by force, plac'd in and fixt to the Chair in the bathing Tub. All this put her in an unexpressable terrour especially when the water was let down. I kept her under the fall 30 minutes, stopping the pipe now and then and enquiring whether she would take to her husband but she still obstinately deny'd till at last being much fatigu'd with the pressure of the water she promised she would do what I desired on which I desisted.

But the next day she became "obstinate" again, so that the entire treatment had to be repeated the next week, in fact, over a period of weeks, during which she would "promise to take to her husband," to "love him as before," but she would renege the next day. Finally, explains Blair:

> I gave her the 3rd Tryal of the fall and continued her 90 minutes under it, [she] promised obedience as before but she was as sullen and obstinate as ever the next day. Being upon resentment why I should treat her so, after 2 or 3 days I threatened her with the fourth Tryal, took her out of bed, had her stript, blindfolded and ready to be put in the Chair, when being terrify'd with what she was to undergo she kneeld submissively that I would spare her and she would become a Loving obedient and dutiful Wife for ever thereafter. I granted her request provided she would go to bed with her husband that night, which she did with great chearfullness.[27]

By contrast to the violent therapies of Blair, Monro, and others, based upon madness as "vitiated judgment," William Battie, who helped found St. Luke's Hospital, the only other public asylum in London, believed that "deluded imagination" was the essential disturbance: "That man [is mad] who is fully and unalterably persuaded of the existence or of the appearance of any thing, which either does not exist or does not actually appear to him, and who behaves according to such erroneous persuasion."[28] This progressive view took the focus away from refinements of physical agents, religious superstition, and moral propaganda and opened the door to psychological investigation. Battie taught (he was the first psychiatrist to take on students) more humane methods of "Regimen," aimed at the mind and fallacious perceptions of the sufferer, and he censured the standard physical treatment as "shocking" and "destructive," even calling madhouses "loathsome prisons." Battie's opposition to Monro's regime at Bedlam seems to have been something of a *cause célèbre* during the mid-century. After the publication of Battie's *Treatise on Madness* in 1758, Monro fired off an immediate reply with his *Remarks on Dr. Battie's Treatise on Madness*, the first publication to come out of Bedlam for over two hundred years. On the title page, Monro took as his motto a quote from Horace, "*O Major, tandem parcas, Insane, minore*" (O greater madman, pray have mercy on a lesser one), and he proceeded to justify his standard procedures. Defending himself against Battie's charges of backwardness and secrecy, Monro emphatically states, "Madness is a distemper of such a nature, that very little of real use can be said concerning it."[29] The rest of the book follows this unfortunate dictum: madness is too difficult to understand, too unpleasant to go into deeply, and after all, purging, bleeding, and vomiting are the

most effective treatments. So widespread was the Monro gospel that Battie
was covered with ridicule as a result of the *Remarks*, and henceforward
known as "Major Battie." Nevertheless, Battie's pioneering example seems
to have inspired a different, if less popular attitude toward mental illness in
eighteenth-century culture, one clearly adopted and developed by Johnson.

Coincidentally, *Rasselas* was published in 1759, one year following the
appearance of Battie's and Monro's treatises in 1758, when their conflict
became public. Very likely Johnson was familiar with the issues, as the
controversy was widely promoted by journalists, Tobias Smollett, for one,
analyzing both books in *The Critical Review*.[30] With his strong interest in
"diseases of the imagination," Johnson would have followed the debates
closely and discussed them with his acquaintances, many of whom were
practicing physicians. Moreover, when his young friend, the poet Christopher Smart, suffered a mental breakdown, he was fortunate to be admitted
to St. Luke's rather than to Bethlem Hospital (i.e., Bedlam) from May 1757
to May 1758 under Dr. Battie's humane care.[31] Surely Johnson would have
been aware of the difference. Indeed, *Rasselas*'s theme of "the dangerous
prevalence of imagination," the high insignia of Johnson's psychological
theory, takes on a new wealth of meaning in the light of this radical
controversy. Discarding Monro's injunction against unreason and denying
its legion of suppression—in Blake's chilling phrase, the "mind-forged
manacles"—Johnson defends Battie's Lockean liberating vistas. Thus he
upsets the balance of long-held assumptions, as he presses forward in the
direction of insight and understanding.[32] No "mere moralist"—Sir John
Hawkins's words about his lifelong friend—Johnson helps to re-define
mental affliction when he repudiates its heretofore moral-punitive stigma.
Far from the savage indictment of the Tory satirists and eighteenth-century
novelists, the rigid fundamentalism of the orthodox middle class, the hor-
rific scourge of the mad-doctors, or the later honey-tongued encomia of the
votaries of sensibility, his exhortation most resembles Locke's: that ignorance breeds suffering, while knowledge puts us in greater prospect of
happiness. Imlac, that foremost Lockean spokesman, describes it purely in
terms of the mental constitution:

> Knowledge is certainly one of the means of pleasure, as is confessed by the
> natural desire which every mind feels of increasing its ideas. Ignorance is mere
> privation, by which nothing can be produced; it is a vacuity in which the soul
> sits motionless and torpid for want of attraction; and, without knowing why,
> we always rejoice when we learn and grieve when we forget. I am therefore
> inclined to conclude, that, if nothing counteracts the natural consequence of
> learning, we grow more happy as our minds take a wider range.[33]

*   *   *

It is broadly correct to argue that components of empirical philosophy, aided by William Battie and others' emancipatory instruction, provided the groundwork for building a theory of the dynamic unconscious. At bottom, they worked together to lend direction to the basic tenet, in the terms of modern psychoanalysis, to make the unconscious conscious. Although Locke, to be sure, gives little credence to the possibility of unconscious mentation, per se, he nonetheless prepares the way for such a principle. His question, "Can another man perceive, that I am conscious of any thing, when I perceive it not my self?"[34] was soon answered in the affirmative by Johnson. Penetrating the mystique of hitherto irreducible experience, Johnson avows the existence of a hidden mental domain. "This invisible riot of the mind," the "secret infusions," "accidental impulses," "silent and invisible inroads," etc. are part of the lexicon he uses to describe its buried functions, as we shall see. In this way he lays open the intrusive and destructive effects of latent mental content, which become the subject of his exclusive study. If Johnson feared insanity, as the case has been variously made, then these fears seem to collect around the traps of subjectivity and the remote and unsuspected meanings he dredged up from the psychical deep. "The first corruption that entered my heart," he told Mrs. Thrale, "was communicated in a dream," and he was distinctly referring to these meanings, when he spoke "with much violence, and walked away in apparent agitation."[35]

Johnson's fears were shared by a community also in dread of that raw, untrammeled world of appetite, the wicked wishes and discreditable acts lurking beneath consciousness. As Freud was to do more than a century later, Johnson fathomed strange seas of thought alone. But for him, few provisions existed to identify and manage his struggle. Unlike Freud, the heir of the Enlightenment philosophes, he did not become the founder of an iconoclastic movement, nor did he advocate militant atheism; he presumably remained an Anglican Christian his entire life. Accordingly, he made religion and morality into useful resources, as they offered familiar contexts for imparting primal perceptions and heightened feelings. They provided a conventional sphere of discourse for self-discipline and consolation on the one hand and for devastating self-torment on the other. On these latter grounds, many of Johnson's friends associated his melancholia with religious chastisement, and doubtless he utilized this powerful idiom to express anguish and deep spiritual perturbation. In his experience of himself as a sinner, he voices lacerating guilt and poisonous convictions of worthlessness. Warrant numerous examples from his private papers, where time and again he brandishes harrowing accusations of religious terrorism.[36] Or take the famous conversation with Dr. Adams of Oxford:

> *Johnson*: As I cannot be *sure* that I have fulfilled the conditions on which salvation is granted, I am afraid I may be one of those who shall be damned (looking dismally).
> *Adams*: What do you mean by damned?
> *Johnson*: (Passionately and loudly) Sent to hell, Sir, and punished everlastingly.[37]

Mrs. Thrale, who more than anyone witnessed Johnson convulsed with bitter grief, was convinced that his suffering stemmed from religion:

> No one had . . . higher notions of the hard task of true Christianity than Johnson, whose daily terror lest he had not done enough, originated in piety, but ended in little less than disease. Reasonable with regard to others, he had formed vain hopes of performing impossibilities himself; and finding his good works ever below his desires and intent, filled his imagination with fears that he should never obtain forgiveness for omissions of duty and criminal waste of time. These ideas kept him in constant anxiety concerning his salvation.[38]

And Boswell, who suppressed many of Johnson's black thoughts, records in his *Journal* a striking anecdote by James Beattie. A professor of moral philosophy at Aberdeen, Beattie recalls confessing to Johnson his being troubled with "shocking impious thoughts," whereupon Johnson responded, "If I were to divide my life in three parts, two of them have been filled with such thoughts."[39] The point is not to belabor issues of religious and moral integrity—perhaps no aspect of Johnson has been so thoroughly regarded, with varying results.[40] But it is to argue that these issues do not suffice to animate the full record of Johnson's mental travail, his journey into little known realms of consciousness. If he professed traditional values and affiliations, he also ventured into the darkness all alone. Unflinching in his honesty and uniquely committed to the scientific pursuit of truth, he braved dreaded forces and interpreted them with compelling originality. As he once wrote to young Bennet Langton about the cruel impact we feel at the death of others, "Whether to see life as it is will give us much consolation I know not, but the consolation which is drawn from truth, if any there be, is solid and durable, that which may be derived from errour must be like its original fallacious and fugitive."[41] Whether ethics, biography, literary criticism, and all the rest, this passion for knowing pervades his every topic.

If religion and morality gave Johnson some provision for exploring mental life, there were also other more fashionable uninhibited resources from which to choose, as we have seen. But he mistrusted their frantic reductionism and peered suspiciously at the high-flying preoccupation with "human nature" among the literati of his age.[42] No rationalist apologetic could appease the demons of imagination; real affliction could never be addressed by giddily pandering to the status quo. Those popular creeds of natural morality and theology—deism, stoicism, and laissez faire—were especially offensive for their smug rhetoric and sheer obliviousness to human suffering. "Life must be seen before it can be known," he writes in a scathing denunciation of Soame Jenyns's placative tract on "natural evil." "The author and Pope perhaps never saw the miseries which they imagine thus easy to be born," and he proceeds to list some ghastly images of anguish and misfortune, to wit, the "madman [who] is either arrogant and irascible, or gloomy and suspicious, or possessed by some passion or notion destructive to his quiet. He has always discontent in his look, and malignity in his bosom."[43]

At every opportunity, Johnson condemns the sanctimony and the foolish optimism boasting to palliate human ills. The exaltation of Right Reason, austere self-command, the slippery sentiments of the "man of feeling"—all evaded the private and potent reality of experience. As his friend Elizabeth Carter, noted translator of Epictetus, wrote of alleged impassivity to pleasure and pain: "The Stoic philosophy insults human nature, and discourages all our attempts, by enjoining and promising a perfection in this life of which we feel ourselves incapable."[44] It is the looming specter of this "perfection," in its many styles and embellishments, which presumably helped to generate the "great confinement," Foucault's now-prevalent charge of "blind repression" of the mentally ill in eighteenth-century Europe. Or, similarly, "the age of reason . . . put all forms of unreason . . . under lock and key."[45] The theme is crucial in recognizing how cold Rationality gave rise to absolute regulatory systems; as the argument goes, the asylum gave visible form to the deadlock between Reason and Unreason, ever frozen in fatal antithesis. Thus psychiatric practice in the eighteenth century was chiefly designed to anathematize and quarantine subjectivity, with its horrifying secrets burrowing deeper into the psyche. But not for Johnson, who undertook unique excavations in so many provinces and was never one to back away from or coolly rationalize his findings. He forged his own passage fiercely, heroically, and through difficult routes, discerning the royal road of the future.

Notes

1. The phrase, "the great confinement," was coined in Foucault's highly influential *Madness and Civilization*, which argues that eighteenth-century rationalism, with its diffusive principles of order and dread authority, initiated a movement of "blind repression" of the insane in Europe:

> From the creation of the Hôpital Général, from the opening, in Germany and in England, of the first houses of correction, and until the end of the eighteenth century, the age of reason confined. It confined the debauched, spendthrift fathers, prodigal sons, blasphemers, men who "seek to undo themselves," libertines. . . . But in each of these cities, we find an entire population of madness as well. One-tenth of all the arrests made in Paris for the Hopital General concern "the insane," "demented" men, individuals of "wandering mind," and "persons who have become completely mad." Between these and the others, no sign of a differentiation. Judging from the registries, the same sensibility appears to collect them, the same gestures to set them apart. (p. 65)

See also Doerner, *Madness and the Bourgeoisie*, passim, and Michael MacDonald *Mystical Bedlam: Madness, Anxiety and Healing in Seventeenth-Century England* (Cambridge: Cambridge University Press, 1981), p. 230 and passim.

2. *Johnsonian Miscellanies*, 1: 199.

3. Boswell, *Life*, 1: 64. Hawkins, *Life*, p. 122.

4. See Donald J. Greene, *Samuel Johnson's Library: An Annotated Guide*, English Literary Studies, no. 1 (Victoria, B.C.: University of Victoria, 1975), p. 20.

5. For information on Johnson's medical acquaintances, see Richard B. Schwartz, *Samuel Johnson and the New Science* (Madison: University of Wisconsin Press, 1971), pp. 35–38. For Johnson's contributions to James's *Medicinal Dictionary*, see O M Brack, Jr. and Thomas Kaminski, "Dr. Johnson, Robert James, and the *Medicinal Dictionary*," *Modern Philology* 81 (1984): 378–400.

6. For example, Thomas Arnold, M.D. in *Observations on the Nature, Kinds, Causes and Prevention of Insanity* (1782; 2nd ed., London: R. Phillips, 1806), 1: 136–37, illustrated cases of megalomaniac patients with Johnson's astronomer in *Rasselas*, praising the accurate description and insight, while Robert Anderson, M.D., in *The Life of Samuel Johnson, with critical observations on his works* (London: J. and A. Arch, 1795), believed Johnson was a "master of all the recesses of the human mind . . . possessed of a corrosive to eradicate, or a lenitive to assuage the follies and sorrows of the heart" (p. 209). William Perfect, M.D. began his Preface to *Annals of Insanity, Comprising a selection of Curious and Interesting Cases* (1787; 5th ed., London: Chalmers, 1800) with a quotation from *Rasselas*, and John Haslam, M.D., used the same quotation on the title page of his *Observations on Madness and Melancholy* (London: J. Callow, 1809). For more details on Johnson's recognition by eighteenth-century physicians, two essays by Kathleen Grange should be consulted: "Samuel Johnson's Account of Certain Psychoanalytic Concepts," *Journal of Nervous and Mental Disease* 135 (August 1962): 93–98, rpt. in *Samuel Johnson: A Collection of Critical Essays*, ed.

Donald J. Greene (Englewood Cliffs, N.J.: Prentice-Hall, 1965), pp. 149–57; and "Dr. Johnson's Account of a Schizophrenic Illness in *Rasselas* (1759)," *Medical History* 6 (April 1962): 162–69.

7. *Works*, 7: 88 ("Preface to Shakespeare").

8. See, for example, the arguments in Jean H. Hagstrum, *Samuel Johnson's Literary Criticism* (Minneapolis: University of Minnesota Press, 1952), pp. 3–20; Robert Voitle, *Samuel Johnson the Moralist* (Cambridge, Mass.: Harvard University Press, 1961), pp. 2–21; Paul K. Alkon, *Samuel Johnson and Moral Discipline* (Evanston, Ill.: Northwestern University Press, 1967), pp. 85–108; William Edinger, *Samuel Johnson and Poetic Style* (Chicago: University of Chicago Press, 1977), pp. 31–77 and passim; John H. Middendorf, "Ideas vs. Words: Johnson, Locke, and the Edition of Shakespeare," in *English Writers of the Eighteenth Century*, ed. John H. Middendorf et al. (New York: Columbia University Press, 1971), pp. 249–72; Claudia L. Johnson, "Samuel Johnson's Moral Psychology and Locke's 'Of Power,'" *Studies in English Literature* 24 (1984): 563–82. Significantly, most of the papers on the *Dictionary* presented at the Oxford Conference in 1984, commemorating the two hundredth anniversary of Johnson's death, noted the Lockean resonances of Johnson's linguistic theory. Locke's influence on the new science of the mind, of which Johnson kept eminently apprised, is stressed by Ernst Cassirer: "On all questions of psychology, Locke's authority remained practically unchallenged throughout the first half of the eighteenth century" (*The Philosophy of the Enlightenment*, trans. Fritz C. A. Koelln and James P. Pettegrove [Princeton, N.J.: Princeton University Press, 1951], p. 99). For similar views, see Basil Willey, *The Seventeenth-Century Background* (Garden City, N.Y.: Doubleday, 1953), pp. 264–65; Perry Miller, *Errand into the Wilderness* (New York: Harper, 1954), p. 168; Donald Greene, "Augustinianism and Empiricism: A Note on Eighteenth-Century English Intellectual History," *Eighteenth-Century Studies* 1 (1967–68): 52; and Christopher Fox, *Locke and the Scriblerians: Identity and Consciousness in Early Eighteenth-Century Britain* (Berkeley: University of California Press, 1988), pp. 7–24 and passim.

9. As quoted in Kenneth Dewhurst, *John Locke (1632–1704), Physician and Philosopher* (London: Wellcome Institute for the History of Medicine, 1963), p. 89.

10. *An Essay Concerning Human Understanding*, ed. Peter H. Nidditch (Oxford: Clarendon Press, 1975), p. 397 (2:33:9).

11. *Works*, 16: 150 (*Rasselas*, Chapter 44).

12. See in particular the probing discussions by Rousseau, *The Ferment of Knowledge*, pp. 143–210; Deporte, *Nightmares and Hobbyhorses*, pp. 3–53; and Porter, *Mind-Forg'd Manacles*, passim. Also of great value are studies written by eminent practicing analysts: Gregory Zilboorg, *A History of Medical Psychology* (New York: W. W. Norton, 1941), pp. 245–305; and Franz G. Alexander and Sheldon T. Selesnick, *The History of Psychiatry: an Evaluation of Psychiatric Thought and Practice from Prehistoric Times to the Present* (London: George Allen & Unwin, 1967), pp. 89–132; as well as professor of pathology and medical historian William B. Ober, "Eighteenth-Century Spleen," in *Psychology and Literature in the Eighteenth Century*, pp. 225–58. An indispensable collection of original sources, together with excellent historical introductions, is Richard Hunter and Ida Macalpine, *Three Hundred Years of Psychiatry, 1535–1860* (London: Oxford University Press, 1963),

passim. Needless to say, many of the facts and arguments in this chapter are greatly indebted to these pacesetting studies.

13. See R. F. Brissenden, *Virtue in Distress: Studies in the Novel of Sentiment from Richardson to Sade* (London: Macmillan Press, 1974), pp. 11–55, which traces the scientific background of eighteenth-century sentimentalism.

14. *The Oxford Authors Series: Samuel Johnson*, ed. Donald J. Greene (New York: Oxford University Press, 1984), pp. 62, 68. Hereafter cited in notes and text as *Oxford Authors*. Johnson's empiricist ethic runs through his writings and is to be found in many trenchant remarks. See, for example, his comment to Boswell that "Human experience, which is constantly contradicting theory, is the great test of truth. A system, built upon the discovery of a great many minds, is always of more strength, than what is produced by the mere workings of any one mind, which, of itself, can do little" (*Life*, 1: 454). In *Rambler* 154, he regrets, by contrast to observation and experiment, the "mental disease" of those who "rely wholly upon unassisted and natural sagacity" and who expect to "solve difficulties by sudden irradiations of intelligence, and comprehend long processes of argument by immediate intuition" (*Works*, 3: 230).

15. *Oxford Authors*, p. 55.

16. For views of the manifold scientific, theological, political, literary implications of this theme, see *The Languages of Psyche: Mind and Body in Enlightenment Thought*, ed. G. S. Rousseau (Berkeley and Los Angeles: University of California Press, 1990). The introduction offers an invaluable guide to the controversies generated over this most ubiquitous and puzzling problem in the history of ideas.

17. *An Essay on the Vital and other Involuntary Motions of Animals*, 2nd ed. (Edinburgh: Hamilton, et al., 1758), pp. 436–37.

18. *The Theory of Moral Sentiments*, ed. D. D. Raphael and A. L. Macfie (Oxford: Clarendon Press, 1976), pp. 12 (1: 1: 1: 10), 315 (7: 3, Intro.). For additional views on Smith's complex rationalism, see Herbert W. Schneider, *Adam Smith's Moral and Political Philosophy* (New York: Hafner, 1948), and R. F. Brissenden, "Authority, Guilt, and *The Theory of Moral Sentiments*," *Texas Studies in Language and Literature* 11 (1969): 945–62.

19. The conversation with Dr. Burney on the poet Christopher Smart's confinement is a telling reminder of Johnson's disagreement, and he is not being altogether sardonic when he associates Smart's harmless quirks with his own: "I did not think he ought to be shut up. His infirmities were not noxious to society. He insisted on people praying with him; and I'd as lief pray with Kit Smart as any one else. Another charge was that he did not love clean linen; and I have no passion for it" (*Life*, 1: 397).

20. John Monro, *Remarks on Dr. Battie's Treatise on Madness* (London: Clarke, 1758), p. 6.

21. Zilboorg, *A History of Medical Psychology*, pp. 151–52.

22. Quoted in Franz Alexander, *The History of Psychiatry*, pp. 115–16, from E. Kraeplin, *Hundert Jahre der Psychiatrie* (1918).

23. See discussions of the "moral" explanation for madness in DePorte, *Nightmares and Hobbyhorses*, pp. 3–53; Max Byrd, *Visits to Bedlam*, pp. 1–87; Lillian Feder, *Madness in Literature*, pp. 147–202. These studies of original sources stress a ra-

tionalist tradition from Aristotle to Burton, which quelled the impulse toward psychological understanding during most of the eighteenth century: "Echoes of Aristotle's concept of the faculties of the soul from the Middle Ages to the eighteenth century reiterate his emphasis on the soul's inherent capacity for rationality. . . . The widespread preoccupation with the subject of madness in medical, philosophical, and literary works generally reveals one primary concern: suppression of its symptoms and effects. The metaphors of madness so pervasive in Pope and Swift reflect the prevailing avoidance of any empathic exploration of the mind designated as mad" (*Madness in Literature*, pp. 151–52).

24. For a learned account of the far-reaching tradition of the physician-satirist, see Mary Claire Randolph, "The Medical Concept in English Renaissance Satiric Theory, " *Studies in Philology* 38 (April 1941): 125–57; rpt. in *Satire: Modern Essays in Criticism*, ed. Ronald Paulson (Englewood Cliffs, N. J.: Prentice-Hall, 1971), pp. 135–70. Its vestiges are apparent in Swift's *A Tale of a Tub*. Other examples abound through the mid-eighteenth century on the subject of insanity as the object of moral disapprobation. A popular poem about Bedlam surveys the spectacle of depraved creatures and ends with a vague caveat against moral transgression:

> . . . on These reflect with kind Concern
> And hence this just, this useful Lesson learn:
> If arbitrary Passions sway thy Soul,
> If Pride, if Envy, if the Lust of Gain,
> If wild ambition in thy Bosom reign
> Alas! thou vaunt'st thy sober Sense in vain.
> (Thomas Fitzgerald, *Bedlam*, in *Poems on several occasions* [London: Watts,
>   1733], pp. 10–11; rpt. in *Three Hundred Years of Psychiatry*, pp. 356–57)

Much the same, Richard Mead, physician to George II, quoting Richard Hale, Monro's predecessor at Bethlem Hospital, remarks on Hale's experience during the South-Sea Bubble in 1720: "He had more patients committed to his care, whose heads were turned by the immense riches . . . than of those, who had been completely ruined," and he readily moralizes, "Such is the force of insatiable avarice in destroying the rational faculties!" (*Medical precepts and cautions . . . Translated from the Latin, under the author's inspection, by Thomas Stack, M.D., F.R.S.* [London: Brindley, 1751]; rpt. in *Three Hundred Years of Psychiatry*, p. 387). More potently, Thomas Willis, whose classic *Cerebri anatome* (1664), a pioneering study in the structure of the brain, was illustrated by Christopher Wren, also believed in devils and in severe treatment for the mentally ill. He recommends "discipline, threats, fetters, and blows. . . . By this method, the mind held back by restraints, is induced to give up its arrogance and wild ideas and it soon becomes meek and orderly" (quoted in Zilboorg, *A History of Medical Psychiatry*, p. 261, from *Two discourses concerning the soul of brutes* [1683]). And Nicholas Robinson, physician and teacher of medicine in London and a governor of Bethlem Hospital, blamed the lack of response to physical treatments on their half-hearted use. He advocated "a Course of Medicines of the most violent Operations; and if that be not sufficient to bring down the Spirit of these Stubborn Persons, we must endeavour to reduce their artificial Strength by compulsive Methods" (*A New System of the Spleen, vapours, and hypochondriack melancholy* [London: Bettesworth, 1729]; rpt. in *Three Hundred Years of Psychiatry*, p. 347).

25. A good example is the "strait-waistcoat" or straitjacket, used to restrain persons in a violent state, which appeared in Tobias Smollett's *Sir Launcelot Greaves* (1760). An original account of the contrivance is excerpted in Hunter and Macalpine, *Three Hundred Years of Psychiatry*, pp. 449–50. Apparently, Smollett adopted a good many episodes in his novels from the theory and practice of psychiatry. See arguments on the medical contexts of Smollett's thought, together with its satiric impetus, in G. S. Rousseau, *Tobias Smollett: Essays of Two Decades* (Edinburgh: T. & T. Clark, 1982), in particular, "Towards Maturity and Mental Collapse," pp. 1–9; "Beef and Bouillon: Smollett's Achievement as a Thinker," pp. 80–123; "Quackery and Charlatanry in Some Eighteenth-Century Novels, Especially in Smollett," pp. 124–37; "Smollett's Wit and the Traditions of Learning in Medicine," pp. 160–83. On Laurence Sterne's medical imagery mixed with satire, about which there is some critical controversy, see Arthur Cash, "The Birth of Tristram Shandy: Sterne and Dr. Burton," in *Studies in the Eighteenth Century*, ed. R. F. Brissenden (Canberra: A. N. U. Press, 1968), pp. 133–54; Michael DePorte, *Nightmares and Hobbyhorses*, pp. 107–35; Max Byrd, *Tristram Shandy* (Boston: George Allen & Unwin, 1985), pp. 47–68, and passim. For a corresponding discussion of the eighteenth-century novelist's moral and rationalist view of penal institutions, see John Bender, *Imagining the Penitentiary: Fiction and the Architecture of Mind in Eighteenth-Century England* (Chicago: University of Chicago Press, 1987), especially the two chapters on Henry Fielding, pp. 139–98.

26. See J. M. S. Tompkins, "Didacticism and Sensibility," in *The Popular Novel in England 1770–1800* (Lincoln: University of Nebraska Press, 1961), pp. 70–115; R. F. Brissenden, *Virtue in Distress*, pp. 11–15, and passim. Writing on the English Moral Sense philosophers, Brissenden sums it up: "Although 'sentiment' and 'sensibility' could be taken, and indeed were taken, to refer to the feelings they still carried with them strong connotations of rationality, and were thus invested with some of the authority with which the Reason was traditionally endowed. . . . 'Sentiment' ultimately comes to mean—a *reasonable* feeling," (pp. 53–54). Just as George Rosen sums it up from the medical perspective: "For the seventeenth and eighteenth centuries, the touchstone was reason and its right use. Reason provided the norm. . . Endowed with reason, man was expected to behave rationally, that is, according to accepted social standards" (*Madness in Society*, pp. 164–65).

27. *Some observations on the cure of mad persons by the fall of water*, 1725; rpt in *Three Hundred Years of Psychiatry*, pp. 325–29.

28. *A Treatise on Madness* (London: J. Whiston, 1758), p. 6.

29. Monro, *Remarks on Dr. Battie's Treatise on Madness* (London: Clarke, 1758), "Advertisement."

30. *The Critical Review* (1757), vol. 4, p. 509; (1758), vol. 5, p. 224.

31. Christopher Devlin, *Poor Kit Smart* (London: Rupert Hart-Davis, 1961), p. 129.

32. See Keener's discussion of *Rasselas* in *The Chain of Becoming*, which observes the psychological dynamics of the eighteenth-century philosophical tale: "The fact is that experience and Imlac have taught Rasselas a certain amount of

psychology. Rasselas has come to understand some central truths about psychological mechanisms common to mankind, and about particular manifestations of them peculiar to himself" (p. 228).

33. *Works*, 16: 49 (*Rasselas*, Chap. 11).

34. *An Essay Concerning Human Understanding*, p. 115 (2: 2: 19).

35. *Johnsonian Miscellanies*, 1: 159.

36. See *Works*, 1, "Diaries, Prayers, and Annals" for those extant. Charles E. Pierce, *The Religious Life of Samuel Johnson* (Hamden, Conn.: Archon Books, 1983), pp. 84–110; Bate, *Samuel Johnson*, pp. 448–60; and Porter, "The Hunger of Imagination" in *The Anatomy of Madness: Essays in the History of Psychiatry* offer provocative discussions of Johnson's religious belief relative to his troubling mental symptoms. The controversy over whether religion drove him mad lies more in their purview than in mine, as well as in that of students of theology and theological history. Even so, it is recommended that the somewhat radical views presented in the studies mentioned above should be weighed against the evidence of a more conservative bent in, for example, Jean H. Hagstrum, "Dr. Johnson's Fear of Death," *ELH* 14 (Dec. 1947): 308–19; Donald J. Greene, "Johnson's 'Late Conversion': A Reconsideration," in *Johnsonian Studies*, ed. Magdi Wahba (Cairo: Privately printed, 1962), pp. 61–92; and Owen Chadwick, "The Religion of Samuel Johnson," *Yale University Library Gazette* 60 (April 1986): 119–36.

37. *Life*, 4: 299.

38. *Johnsonian Miscellanies*, 1: 224.

39. Boswell's *Journal* (12 Aug. 1782) as quoted in Frank Brady, *James Boswell: The Later Years 1769–1795* (New York: McGraw-Hill, 1984), p. 567.

40. In addition to the studies mentioned in note 33, see Maurice J. Quinlan, *Samuel Johnson: A Layman's Religion* (Madison: University of Wisconsin Press, 1964); Chester F. Chapin, *The Religious Thought of Samuel Johnson* (Ann Arbor: University of Michigan Press, 1968); James Gray, *Johnson's Sermons: A Study* (Oxford: Clarendon Press, 1972); Nicholas Hudson, *Samuel Johnson and Eighteenth-Century Thought* (Oxford: Clarendon Press, 1988).

41. *Letters*, 1: 111 (no. 116). For a variety of contexts for Johnson's insistence on veracity, see J. D. Fleeman, "Johnson and the Truth," in *Johnsonian Studies*, pp. 109–13.

42. Johnson's conservatism is often misconstrued despite the best efforts to explain his intellectual attitudes, beginning with Bronson's pioneering "Johnson Agonistes" to Hudson's *Samuel Johnson and Eighteenth-Century Thought*. Unfortunately, one still encounters the old stereotype, even in the most reputable of sources: "that bigoted Anglican, Dr. Johnson" (Lawrence Stone, *The Family, Sex, and Marriage in England, 1500–1800* [New York: Harper and Row, 1977], p. 573). And because of his alleged traditionalism, Johnson tends to be largely avoided by social historians of a revisionist bent, Porter being the distinguished exception.

43. "Review of [Soame Jenyns], *A Free Inquiry into the Nature and Origin of Evil*," *Oxford Authors*, pp. 527–28.

44. Elizabeth Carter, trans., *The Moral Discourses of Epictetus* (1758; London: Dent, Everyman's Library, 1910), xix.

45. K. Doerner, *Madmen and the Bourgeoisie*, p. 14.

3. "A Child is Being Beaten": The Early Career

JOHNSON'S MOURNFUL STATEMENT that he "had never sought to please till past thirty years old, considering the matter as hopeless"[1] becomes ever the more poignant in the light of his earliest recollections. His autobiographical writing entitled "Annals," surviving in fragments as a kind of stream-of-consciousness narrative, yields a wealth of meaning behind its apparent simplicity.[2] As he recreates enigmatic scenes from childhood—ones obscurely remembered or evidently absorbed from descriptions of others—we detect powerful feelings of fear, shame, love, pain, anger, pride, emerging with all their original strength and clarity. In well-preserved detail, we see the exalted picture of his father on horseback as the Sheriff of Lichfield, riding the boundaries of the city and feasting its citizens on the day after his birth. And the tender images of his mother, visiting her infant son every day at the nurse's house, tending him on the long journey to London and back to "cure" his scrofula, encouraging him in his lessons when he was in danger of failing. " 'We often,' said she, dear mother, 'come off best when we are most afraid.' These little memorials soothe my mind" (*Works*, 1: 14). But for all these benefits, we also note a strained and afflictive atmosphere:

> I was born almost dead, and could not cry for some time. . . . It was discovered that my eyes were bad; and an issue was cut in my left arm. . . . In ten weeks I was taken home, a poor, diseased infant, almost blind. I remember my aunt Nath. Ford told me . . . that she would not have picked such a poor creature up in the street. (*Works*, 1: 1–5)

Even worse, the dominant impression of Johnson's childhood was his parents' characterological depression and marital difficulties, which could not but lower his self-image:

> My father and mother had not much happiness from each other. They seldom conversed; for my father could not bear to talk of his affairs; and my mother, being unacquainted with books, cared not to talk of any thing else. Had my

mother been more literate, they had been better companions. She might have sometimes introduced her unwelcome topick with more success, if she could have diversified her conversation. Of business she had no distinct conception; and therefore her discourse was composed only of complaint, fear, and suspicion. (*Works*, 1: 7)

Likewise to Mrs. Thrale he describes his mother's morbid dejection, voiced in nagging disapproval, "always telling me that I did not behave myself properly; that I should learn behavior, and such cant: but when I replied, that she ought to tell me what to do, and what to avoid, her admonitions were commonly, for that time at least, at an end."[3] And he depicts his father's inconvertible gloom, practiced in dismal rituals and escapism. When the old man's workshop had half fallen down for lack of money to repair it, "[he] was not less diligent to lock the door every night, though he saw that any body might walk in at the back part, and knew that there was no security obtained by barring the front door. 'This (says his son) was madness.'"[4] As a last resort, "my father . . . could always take his horse and ride away for orders when things went badly."[5] Boswell confirms that Johnson attributed to his father that "vile melancholy, . . . [which] made him mad all his life, at least not sober."[6]

Doubtless Johnson's troubled beginnings left ineradicable traces in his mind and, as his biographers argue, these experiences in large directed and influenced the pathogenic course of anxiety and depression he suffered as an adult. Themes of Johnson's intrapsychic life, moreover, pervade his writing and lie at the core of many recurrent images to be found with remarkable consistency. One of these is suggested in the chapter title above, "A Child is Being Beaten," which comes from a landmark study by Freud of the same name. The image refers to a common fantasy of childhood, explaining the complex history by which individuals acquire sadistic and masochistic tendencies. It is closely associated with Freud's research into the unconscious sense of guilt, the mechanisms of self-reproach and self-punishment taken on through the child's earliest relationships. For Johnson, it conveys experiences of retaliation and persecution, conceived out of his parents' blame and despondency, in effect, another casualty of their far from amicable match. Here is the salient feature of his intrapsychic life, expressed in the quick resentment and easy provocation we recognize as characteristically Johnsonian. Of this archaic impression of being victimized by figures in authority, Freud writes: "People who harbour phantasies of this kind develop a special sensitiveness and irritability toward anyone whom they can put among the class of fathers. They allow themselves to be easily offended by a person of this kind, and in that way (to their own sorrow and cost) bring about the realization of the imagined situation of being beaten."[7]

In the harsh, anonymous world of Grub Street, Johnson apparently employed such a fantasy, so as to console himself with a familiar picture of rankling adversity. Howsoever consonant with problems in real life, his creation exaggerates the sense of being afflicted and being victimized.[8] From the standpoint of psychical reality—largely unconscious, infantile meaning and how it is used to construct current painful experience— Johnson's early career in London reenacts a dreary emotional history. Plainly lacking is the deference to conventional reality, the sustained objectivity and clearheaded analysis that distinguishes his later work. The principal writings of this period were undertaken in the throes of bitter disgrace and injustice, more imaginary than real. Thus works as diverse as *London*, *Marmor Norfolciense*, *A Complete Vindication of the Licensers of the Stage*, *Irene*, the *Parliamentary Debates*, as well as the pivotal *Life of Savage*, are shaped by virtually the same cast of mind. Under various guises, they represent painful studies of defeat and degradation, replete with images of being brought low, to fulfill the legacy of archaic moral aims.[9]

Appearing in May 1938, *London* is a belligerent poem about the corruption and vileness of the big city, and its message conveys the impossibility of enjoying life under a manifest reign of terror. Even more agitating than Juvenal's original *Third Satire*, Johnson's "imitation" takes on an emotional tone of its own, in which images of being hurt and abused continually intrude:

> Here malice, rapine, accident, conspire,
> And now a rabble rages, now a fire;
> Their ambush here relentless ruffians lay,
> And here the fell attorney prowls for prey;
> Here falling houses thunder on your head,
> And here a female atheist talks you dead.
>
> (*Works*, 6: 48, ll. 13–18)

Atrocities of statesmen and courtiers, foreign parasites, and street criminals likewise contribute to the effect of overwhelming defeat and damage: the "groaning nation" indeed seems battered and broken by an overpowering enemy. Clearly, it is the angry young man's obligatory protest as he enters the world, but even more relevant to Johnson's psychical reality, it is a seduction to utter loss and abandonment. In this connection, the poem, for all its fury, contains a curious passivity.[10] As "injured" Thales quits the city out of failure and disappointment, he describes how people are spiritually depleted and lulled into insensibility:

> For arts like these preferred, admired, caressed,
> They [foreign parasites, etc.] first invade your table, then your
>   breast;
> Explore your secrets with insidious art,
> Watch the weak hour, and ransack all the heart.
>
>   (*Works*, 6: 55, ll. 152–55)

Calamity strikes worst when we sleep, resigned to a narcotic stupor. The house burns down when we are least aware:

> Raised from some pleasing dream of wealth and power,
> Some pompous palace, or some blissful bower,
> Aghast you start, and scarce with aking sight
> Sustain the approaching fire's tremendous light.
>
>   (*Works*, 6: 57, ll. 184–87)

And in perhaps the most menacing image of all, he watches us succumb to the deadly infestations of wickedness:

> Cruel with guilt, and daring with despair,
> The midnight murderer bursts the faithless bar;
> Invades the sacred hour of silent rest,
> And leaves, unseen, a dagger in your breast.
>
>   (*Works*, 6: 59–60, ll. 238–41)

Thrilled by this elaborate panorama of danger and suffering, Johnson is true to the wishes of his unconscious life. The poem *London*, for all its seeming partisan vigor, projects a fantasy of prodigious ruin.

Two political satires of the same period, *Marmor Norfolciense* and *A Complete Vindication of the Licensers of the Stage*, published within a couple weeks of each other in May 1739, continue Johnson's hysterical attack on contemporary affairs. Both in the Swiftian vein, they employ the Scriblerian device of mock-reverence for authority, through the voice of an obtuse commentator. Viewed psychologically, *Marmor* is the more provocative, for it most resembles *London*, striking a similar chord of disaster and unhappiness. Johnson lets the mask drop rather too earnestly in several places, particularly when his bumbling narrator comes to interpret the prophesy about "scarlet reptiles," that is to say, the red-coated soldiers of the Whig standing army. Stepping out of character with less than subtlety, Johnson launches into a litany of wrongs, set off by extravagant fantasies of brutality and humiliation:

> I shall content myself with collecting, into one view, the several properties of this pestiferous brood, with which we are threatened, as hints to more sagacious and fortunate readers, who, when they find out any "red animal" that ranges uncontrolled over the country, and devours the labours of the trader, and the husbandman; that carries with it corruption, rapine, pollution, and devastation; that threatens without courage, robs without fear, and is pampered without labour, they may know that the prediction is completed. . . . The serpent, a wretched animal that crawls upon the earth, is proper emblem of low views, self-interest, and base submission, as well as of cruelty, mischief, and malevolence. (*Works*, 10: 36)

Depicted as mad terrorists, the reptiles extort a surrender of the will, creating a passive condition not unlike that in *London*. People are victimized for a kind of somnambulism, as they allow themselves to be beaten and enslaved:

> These serpents . . . will threaten, indeed, and hiss, and terrify the weak, and timorous, and thoughtless, but have no real courage or strength. . . . We are therefore to remember whenever the pest here threatened shall invade us, that submission and tameness will be certain ruin, and that nothing but spirit, vigilance, activity, and opposition can preserve us from the most hateful and reproachful misery, that of being plundered, starved, and devoured by vermin and reptiles. (*Works*, 10: 37)

Once more Johnson appears to savor and dwell upon metaphors of wreckage as he pursues suffering as a fixed and necessary mode of living. The *Complete Vindication*, while less attentive to the role of victim, creates an even more ghastly image of the adversary, as the demagogic speaker argues for unlimited authority: "Unhappy would it be for men in power, were they always obliged to publish the motives of their conduct. What is power but the liberty of acting without being accountable" (*Works*, 10: 63). The other side of Johnson's idealization of suffering, the ruthless, sneering "vindicator" exhibited here is another remnant of archaic morality, a monster baying from the psychical deep.

Johnson began writing the blank verse tragedy *Irene* in 1736 and hoped to make his reputation by it, though the play was not to be performed until more than twelve years later, and then only through David Garrick's special influence.[11] The frantic emotionalism of heroic tragedy in the early and middle eighteenth century allowed Johnson an exquisite medium for relaying the obsessive drama of his inner life. The story he chose of a woman seduced by worldly pleasure and thereby punished, must have appealed to his own pervasive fears of dissolution and all too costly gratification. Apart from its moral and religious implications, the play illustrates the emotional axiom that every enjoyment must be paid for with painful guilt and self-destruction. It opens on a note of atonement for the excess which brought on retribution, in effect, a primitive reckoning of crime and punishment. Constantinople has fallen to the Turkish army, its government chiefly to blame for the usual indiscretions of affluence, and its citizens now bewail their loss in a flood of humiliating associations:

> What e'er our crimes, our woes demand compassion.
> Each night, protected by the friendly darkness,
> Quitting my close retreat, I range the city
> And weeping, kiss the venerable ruins:
> . . . How chang'd, alas!—Now ghastly Desolation,
> In triumph sits upon our shatter'd spires;
> Now Superstition, Ignorance, and Error,
> Usurp our temples, and profane our altars.
>
> (*Works*, 6: 115–16, I. i, 58–61; 66–69)

If that were not enough, the women are marked for prey by cruel and violent despoilers:

> From ev'ry palace bursts a mingled clamour,
> The dreadful dissonance of barb'rous triumph,
> Shrieks of affright, and wailings of distress.
> Oft when the cries of violated beauty
> Arose to heav'n, and pierc'd my bleeding breast,
> I felt thy pains, and trembled for Aspasia.
> . . . Aspasia! spare that lov'd, that mournful name:
> Dear, hapless maid—tempestuous grief o'erbears
> My reasoning pow'rs—Dear, hapless, lost Aspasia!
> . . . I see the helpless maid,
> Behold the monsters gaze with savage rapture,
> Behold how Lust and Rapine struggle round her!
>
> (*Works*, 6: 116, I. i, 70–78, 80–82)

Evidently, Johnson knew the egregious conventions of "she-tragedy," shaping what here approaches bathos after the popular set pieces by Nathaniel Lee, John Banks, Nicholas Rowe, etc. Following their heavy didacticism, the heroine Irene, having yielded to the Turkish Sultan's embraces and renounced her faith to become his Queen, has an obligatory scene of rabid remorse. Shame and contrition wring her soul:

> . . . Unutterable anguish!
> Guilt and Despair! pale spectres, grin around me,
> And stun me with the yellings of damnation!
> O, hear my pray'rs! accept, all-pitying Heaven,
> These tears, these pangs, these last remains of life,
> Nor let the crimes of this detested day
> Be charg'd upon my soul. O, mercy! mercy!
>
> (*Works*, 6: 209, V. x, 49–55)

For all its show of rack and ruin, Johnson's *Irene* little avails to capture the quality of real grief and suffering at the heart of the tragic plot. Johnson himself was embarrassed by the play in later life, partly, it is believed, on account of the unskillful technique, even more, one suspects, by the naive self-indulgence.[12] Floundering through postures of regret, abasement, alienation, and loss, he never manages to interpret these profoundly interior emotions. He never reaches the guilt that injures the soul, the inwardly festering wounds and the concealed forces of stricken conscience, that he earnestly grapples with in his mature works. *Irene* is another thinly disguised exercise in woe and self-pity, even if we have a hint of the perspicacity to come in Aspasia's sharp rebuke to the heroine's feeble pleading. At one point, when faint-heartedness and frailty are tediously invoked, Aspasia counters with a glimpse into coercive mental agencies:

> The weakness we lament, our selves create;
> Instructed from our infant years to court
> With counterfeited fears the aid of man;
> We learn to shudder at the rustling breeze,
> Start at the light, and tremble in the dark;
> Till, Affectation rip'ning to belief,
> And Folly, frighted at her own chimeras,
> Habitual cowardice usurps the soul.
>
> (*Works*, 6: 134, II. i, 26–33)

Here is the stuff of future endeavor, as Johnson turns analytically to the deeper structures of the psyche.

Johnson's work as a literary drudge for Edward Cave on the *Gentleman's Magazine* afforded him many more contests with the malevolence he projected onto the world around him. If Grub Street reeked with the stench of beggary and broken dreams, it only triggered matching convictions of his own appalling worthlessness. In 1738, he became involved in compiling the "Debates in the Senate of Magna Lilliputia," an allegorical account of the sessions in Parliament, since the government made it illegal to report them openly. The "Debates," which made the fortune of the *Gentleman's Magazine*, ran from 1738 to 1746, during which time Johnson was first helper, reviser, then sole writer.[13] Some of the most famous episodes feature a diabolical Walelop (Sir Robert Walpole), a kind of jeering executioner, doubtless an analogue to the malicious authorities in *Marmor* and the *Complete Vindication*, who lay waste to civilization. Vitally linked to Johnson's intrapsychic life, the figure broods over much of the "Debates," to wit, the great series on Walpole's impeachment. Wreaking abuse upon abuse, he is described as stupendously evil:

> His most masterly attempt for the establishment of universal slavery, on which he laid out all his interest and all his subtlety, in which he laboured with incessant application and defended with the most tenacious obstinacy was the scheme of extending the laws of excise. By this he would have put a stop to all farther opposition of ministerial power; by this he would have secured himself from future trouble of corrupting and seducing individuals; he would have crushed the constitution at once, and as the tyrant of old wished to destroy mankind at a blow; our Minister, not less heroically wicked, endeavoured by one fatal vote to oppress liberty for ever.[14]

This half-wild rhetoric continues until the mysterious figure rises to answer the charges. The following speech, which has been suggested as Johnson's most dramatic writing,[15] also looks ahead to his future work. For deliberately and adeptly, he undercuts at once the whole protracted denunciation. In a flash of understanding, he discovers the enemy to inhere in maniacal delusion. Echoing the speech of rebuke and the sudden lucidity in *Irene*, Johnson coolly delineates a monstrous psychological charade. Now miraculously transformed, Walelop becomes the spokesman for sober reality:

> Of the exorbitant power with which I am invested, of the influence which I extend to all parts of the nation, of the tyranny with which I oppress those that oppose, and the liberality with which my followers are rewarded, no instance

has been produced, as indeed no effects have been felt. . . . They carry on the fiction which has once heated their imaginations, and impute to me an unpardonable abuse of that chimerical authority which only they have thought it necessary to bestow.

If their dream has really produced in them the terrors which they express, if they are really persuaded that the army is annually established by my authority, that I have the sole disposal of posts and honours, and that I employ this power to the destruction of liberty and the diminution of commerce, compassion would direct us to awaken them from so painful a delusion, to force their eyes open and stimulate them to a clear view of their own condition and that of the publick to show them that the prerogative has made no encroachments, that every supply is granted by the Senate, and every question debated with the utmost freedom, as before that fatal period in which they were seized with this political delirium that has so long harassed them with the loss of trade, the approach of slavery, the power of the crown, and the influence of the Minister.[16]

It is this method of conveying furious internal commotion, tempered by dispassionate insight, that Johnson employs in the dazzling *Life of Savage* as if to redeem what could only come to grief.

The *Life of Savage* which has intrigued readers since its first appearance in 1744 and later inclusion in the *Lives of the Poets* (1779–81),[17] would seem to call into strongest relief Johnson's masochistic *idée fixe*. At its core lies the pervasive, infantile wish of being crippled, of being crushed by malignant forces. But at the same time, we note active efforts to explain such misery and now to challenge more figments of its dread authority. Richard Savage was, or claimed to be, the illegitimate son of the Countess of Macclesfield by her lover, Earl Rivers, and was also a notorious debauchee—a drunkard, wencher, possibly a murderer—who died in a Bristol debtor's prison. His unsavory reputation, his repeated acts of imposture and radical shifts in mood, are faithfully recorded by Johnson, who appears to take Savage purely on Savage's own terms. Indeed, subjective mental states are a main feature of this often melodramatic tale of a lost soul, Johnson's late lamented friend, with whom he profoundly identified. As fellow "injustice-collectors,"[18] they courted similar failure and unhappiness, typically in their walks "round Grosvenor-square till four in the morning; in the course of their conversation reforming the world, dethroning princes, establishing new forms of government, and giving laws to the several states of Europe, till, fatigued at length with their legislative office, they began to feel the want of refreshment; but could not muster up more than four pence halfpenny."[19] But along with Johnson's identification goes a sharp new awareness, as he smokes out the evidence of self-created calamity. Drawing upon his own experience, he creates a dynamic mental picture of another, a technique to be embellished in future biographies, which lends the finest edge to his insights. Not through a conventional historical reality, but through a psychical one, Johnson understands the cause and symptoms of Savage's devastating mental disease.

Johnson's most amazing record of subjective mental states in the *Life of Savage* concerns the picture of Savage's mother, a consummate fiend, out to brutalize and destroy a poor, innocent child. With little evidence to corroborate Savage's story in the real world, he amplifies the fantasy of relentless persecution, in effect, the child being beaten.[20] The soul of innocence and purity is stalked by a hideous demon. Channeling his emotions into the lurid tale, Johnson is stupefied

> that she would look upon her son from his birth with a kind of resentment and abhorrence; and, instead of supporting, assisting, and defending him, delight to see him struggling with misery; or that she would take every opportunity of aggravating his misfortunes, and obstructing his resources, and with an implacable and restless cruelty continue her persecution from the first hour of his life to the last. (*Lives*, 2: 323–24)

So it appears that he is into it with same thrills and chills of *London*, *Irene*, and the early political writings: he pursues his topic with similar frenzy, opening the floodgates to more humiliating associations. With Gothic dimensions, Savage is resurrected as a sacrificial victim, and Johnson analogizes from the atrocities of parents who murder their children to Savage's mother, who

> forbears to destroy him only to inflict sharper miseries upon him; who prolongs his life only to make it miserable; and who exposes him, without care and without pity, to the malice of oppression, the caprices of chance, and temptations of poverty; and who rejoices to see him overwhelmed with calamities; and, when his own industry or the charity of others, has enabled him to rise for a short time above his miseries, plunges him again into his former distress. (*Lives*, 2: 338)[21]

And again, describing the time Savage's mother prejudices the Queen against him when, under sentence of death, he pleads for clemency, Johnson brandishes a full-fledged histrionics, his style out-and-out declamatory, as he burns to know

> upon what motives his mother could persecute him in a manner so outrageous and implacable; for what reason she could employ all the arts of malice and all the snares of calumny, to take away the life of her own son, of a son who never

injured her, who was never supported by her expenses nor obstructed any prospect of pleasure or advantage; why she should endeavour to destroy him by a lie—a lie which could not gain credit, but must vanish of itself at the first moment of examination, and of which only this can be said to make it probable, that it may be observed from her conduct that the most execrable crimes are sometimes committed without apparent temptation.

No sooner is he struck by this prodigious iniquity than he quakes with righteous indignation:

> This mother is still alive, and may perhaps even yet, though her malice was so often defeated, enjoy the pleasure of reflecting, that the life which she often endeavoured to destroy, was at least shortened by her maternal offices; that though she could not transport her son to the plantations, bury him in the shop of a mechanick, or hasten the hand of the public executioner, she has yet had the satisfaction of imbittering all his hours, and forcing him into exigencies, that hurried on his death. (*Lives*, 2: 353)

It would seem that this picture of Savage's mother expresses the same anguish and colossal outrage to be found in Johnson's earlier works, but the intellectual and artistic integrity of the *Life of Savage* makes it far and above prior renderings of the familiar theme. For instead of an incomprehensible horror brooding apart from the action, here is a figure which holds horror's key. The "enemy implacably malicious, whom nothing but his blood could satisfy" (*Lives*, 2: 357), marks the center of disturbance, as Johnson delves to his subject's inward turbulent ordeal. In effect, he has reified a conviction of unconscious life, a primordial image of unappeasable rage. As he shows Savage repeatedly inviting disaster, insulting his benefactors, and provoking disgrace and rejection, Johnson discovers the tyranny of a wholly mental agency that demands suffering to satisfy its claims. While Savage attributes his difficulties to outside sources, Johnson recognizes the quality of self-created defeat, as he assiduously follows the course of a vicious masochistic circle. Apparently, Savage's fatal liability caused him to generate the distress he promptly forgot in a rush of ensuing euphoria, which led him to generate distress once again. In ways suggested by the narrative, he pays a fearsome psychical entity, making punishment an excuse for further licentiousness.[22] Thus Johnson closely documents a series of compulsive acts bringing on distress, then euphoria, then distress, in exhaustive accounts of Savage's misfortunes. Over and over, he reviews virtually identical chains of events, making it clear that Savage fully directs them.

The most obvious example of Savage's cruel compulsions was his gaining, then giddily losing, the help of others. If given money after long indigence, he would immediately squander it in extravagant schemes of amusement, readily to impoverish himself anew: "To supply him with money was a hopeless attempt, for no sooner did he see himself master of a sum sufficient to set him free from care for a day, than he became profuse and luxurious. When once he had entered a tavern, or engaged in a scheme of pleasure, he never retired till want of money obliged him to some new expedient" (*Lives*, 2: 400–01). If given lodging, he would sabotage custom and propriety in the interest of perpetual merriment, shortly to be back on the streets as before. With studied insurrection, he turns all offers of help into hindrance, zealous in his wish to upset every possible kindness.[23] His being subjected to bourgeois sobriety in the homes of friends, Johnson puts temptingly in the terms of institutionalization, which is likely the way Savage perceived it. In Johnson's pregnant phrase, he was "a very incommodious inmate," laboring to break down the existing regime: "He could not confine himself to any stated hours, or pay any regard to the rules of a family, but would prolong his conversation till midnight, without considering that business might require his friend's application in the morning; and, when he had persuaded himself to retire to bed, was not, without equal difficulty, called up to dinner." He was a sworn enemy to work and the duties of collective life: "It was, therefore, impossible to pay him any distinction without the entire subversion of all oeconomy, a kind of establishment which, wherever he went, he always appeared ambitious to overthrow" (*Lives*, 2: 400). His principal striving to get thrown out once he gets in, he is the dark embodiment of a Lord of Misrule: "Wherever Savage entered, he immediately expected that order and business should fly before him, that all should thenceforward be left to hazard, and that no dull principle of domestick management should be opposed to his inclination, or intrude upon his gaiety" (*Lives*, 2: 401).

Thus Savage is shown to invite the rejection he craved, with the idea that all providers must be changed into refusers; by this maxim, "he scarcely ever found a stranger whom he did not leave a friend; but it must likewise be added that he had not often a friend long, without obliging him to become a stranger" (*Lives*, 2: 369). What is more, Savage is given to fits of violent temper, necessarily brought on by his rejection. Johnson observes this process by the acts of provocative beggary, how Savage repeatedly solicits "loans" with little if any compunction: "He appeared to think himself born to be supported by others, and dispensed from all necessity of providing for himself" (*Lives*, 2: 431). Driven by ferocious need, he behaves at best casually toward his patrons, "without the least submission or apparent consciousness of dependence" (400); at worst, he is insolent and rude. As if to reenact the rampant claims entangled with his mother, the unscrupulous sense of entitlement gives vent to a cankerous rage: "A refusal was resented by him as an affront, or complained of as an injury: nor did he readily reconcile himself to those who either denied to lend, or gave him afterwards an intimation that they expected to be repaid" (*Lives*, 2: 400).

Johnson comes still closer to the festering rage when he describes his subject's sudden crazed outbursts. Always the one to feel an offense, Savage explodes in a volley of rancor and abuse: at previous supporters whom he names persecutors and oppressors, at his former chief benefactor, Lord Tyrconnel, who, related to the Countess, tried to hold Savage off by a pension, even a reception into his home, until their inevitable breach. But what for any other man would be pangs of remorse, for Savage, turn into pathological hate:

> He very frequently demanded that the allowance which was once paid him should be restored; but . . . he never appeared to entertain for a moment the thought of soliciting a reconciliation, and . . . he treated [Lord Tyrconnel] at once with all the haughtiness of superiority and all the bitterness of resentment. He wrote to him not in a style of supplication or respect, but of reproach, menace, and contempt; and appeared determined, if he ever regained his allowance, to hold it only by the right of conquest." (*Lives*, 2: 401–02)

Stressing this virulence, Johnson further notes that Savage was impetuous and haphazard, typically prone to more wild compulsions, now loving, now despising, whoever came his way. If he imagined himself crossed, he turned viperous, seething "with the most violent agonies of rage" and "the utmost vehemence of indignation"[24]: "His temper was, in consequence of the dominion of his passions, uncertain and capricious; he was easily engaged, and easily disgusted; but he is accused of retaining his hatred more tenaciously than his benevolence. . . . When he was provoked (and very small offenses were sufficient to provoke him), he would prosecute his revenge with the utmost acrimony till his passion had subsided" (*Lives*, 2: 431). His friendship, moreover, could be treacherous, for though a fast and ardent ally, he could switch abruptly into an implacable foe, since "he considered himself discharged by the first quarrel from all ties of honour or gratitude." As would be expected, "This practice drew upon him an universal accusation of ingratitude" (431). Indeed, Johnson implies that the fever which eventually killed him, as he awaited assistance in the Bristol debtor's prison, was brought on by charges of that same "atrocious ingratitude" (428). A misunderstanding, which Johnson for good reason leaves ambiguous,[25] provokes a rupture with Pope, until now a loyal supporter. Savage, "much disturbed at the accusation" that he was the cause, was seized by fatal illness a few days later. It was evidently a shock of recognition he could not bear.

The heart of Johnson's analysis of Richard Savage occurs about midway through the narrative, where, after a long list of his subject's rationalizations about failure and suffering, he brilliantly encapsulates the dominant idea that "the blame was laid rather on any person than the author." Here follows the cool penetration of work to come, as he warns against the "danger of this pleasing intoxication"—of creating imaginary wrongs and enjoying them to boot. He describes a syndrome, amply documented in the "Life," in effect, a perpetual orgy of self-affliction and manic relief. The phases are both the causes and effects of one another, and thus a vicious circle is inscribed. "By imputing none of his miseries to himself" and "never made wiser by his sufferings," Savage "proceeded, throughout his life, to tread the same steps on the same circle; always applauding his past conduct, or, at least, forgetting it to amuse himself with phantoms of happiness, which were dancing before him" (Lives, 2: 380). What is more, Savage's invention of imaginary wrongs hardly touched his real guilt; rather it momentarily slowed down the relentless sway of his crimes and punishment: "After having lulled his imagination with those ideal opiates, of having tried the same experiment upon his conscience; and having accustomed himself to impute all deviations from the right to foreign causes, it is certain that he was, upon every occasion, too easily reconciled to himself, and that he appeared very little to regret those practices which had impaired his reputation" (Lives, 2: 380).

In this piercing analysis is the brinkmanship so integrally linked to Johnson's own deepest beliefs and assumptions about himself. Flirting with disaster, living in dread of an unexplained, uncontrollable enmity, while courting its strange excitement, Savage ran a grim, unremitting course of self-destruction. In "the same experiment upon his conscience" lie the submerged clues to Savage's torturous compulsions, which Johnson stunningly brings to light.[26] Here was the source, the sustenance, and the bitter end of a life ravaged by mental disease. Toward the end of the narrative, Johnson gives many instances of Savage's deterioration, one of the most poignant being a letter he reprints, written after the poet's confinement for debt: "'The whole day,' says he, 'has been employed in various people's filling my head with their foolish chimerical systems, which has obliged me coolly (as far as nature will admit) to digest, and accommodate myself to, every different person's way of thinking; hurried from one wild system to another till it has quite made a chaos of my imagination, and nothing done—promised—disappointed—ordered to send, every hour, from one part of the town to the other'" (*Lives*, 2: 421). Like Savage's confinement in the bourgeois family, or any of the manifold confinements proposed throughout the "Life"—to moral amendment, social duty, indeed, to "the light of reason" (430) itself—Johnson grasps their futility and passes them over, intent as he is on a far different design. In another early project for the *Gentleman's Magazine*, the "Life of Boerhaave" (1739), Johnson is also profoundly affected by his subject's pain, here a certain physical affliction, which had at the time no known remedy. What better explanation can he offer for his pioneering contributions to a newly emerging science of the mind, than the one which is couched in his praise for the great Dutch physician: "His own anguish taught him to compassionate that of others, and his experience of the inefficacy of the methods then in use incited him to attempt the discovery of others more certain."[27]

Notes

1. *Johnsonian Miscellanies*, 1: 318.
2. Regrettably, only a fragment of Johnson's private papers remain, filling the first volume of the Yale *Works*, and, to my knowledge, there has been no extended study of his personal writings, in and of themselves. For a rare appraisal of what survives of his autobiography, see Donald Greene, "The Uses of Autobiography in the Eighteenth Century," in *Essays in Eighteenth-Century Biography*, ed. Philip B. Daghlian (Bloomington: Indiana University Indiana Press, 1968), pp. 67–95. For an account of Johnson's formative years, which uses the autobiography as a primary source, see Bate, *Samuel Johnson*, pp. 1–36.
3. *Johnsonian Miscellanies*, 1: 161.
4. *Johnsonian Miscellanies*, 1: 148.
5. *Johnsonian Miscellanies*, 1: 154.
6. *Life*, 1: 35.
7. Freud, *Standard Edition*, 17: 195.
8. As Thomas Kaminski has shown in his recreation of the early years in London, Johnson was not in the dire straits, at least financially, that we were often led to believe: "Johnson was not living a life of plenty, nor was he in distress. His limited funds—we cannot say income, for he was probably living off capital—were not cause for reproach; nor did they indicate poverty, that is, the want of necessities. He lived as a gentleman of slender means, but he lived among gentlemen" (*The*

Early Career of Samuel Johnson [New York: Oxford University Press, 1987], p. 7, and passim).

9. For more detailed psychological insights into the early writings, see Clifford, *Young Sam Johnson*, pp. 175–221, and Greene, *The Politics of Samuel Johnson* (New Haven, Conn.: Yale University Press, 1960), pp. 81–111 on Johnson's sense of wounded merit, as well as Isobel Grundy, *Samuel Johnson and the Scale of Greatness* (Leicester: Leicester University Press, 1986), pp. 34–61 on his Swiftian technique of "diminishing" characters, which, I suggest, accords with the bitterness and frustration of his personal life at the time. Greene's "psychological reconstruction" is especially penetrating:

> One must imagine the young Johnson newly arrived in London, sore at the neglect of the world, repelled by the ugliness of city life, and homesick for the gentler scenes of the Midlands. Through the instrumentality of Savage, or Hervey, or Guthrie, or the *Craftsman*, there is revealed to Johnson the appalling wickedness of Walpole's regime, which is responsible for the sad state of a world in which "slow rises worth." The young man's eyes are opened. He eagerly seizes on the Walpolian iniquities and uses them as pegs on which to hang his own griefs: bribery and castrati and masquerades become projections and symbols of the Johnsonian dissatisfaction with the world. (p. 91)

10. See T. F. Wharton's explication of *London*, which also discusses elements of passive fantasy, in *Samuel Johnson and the Theme of Hope* (New York: St. Martin's Press, 1984), pp. 29–42.

11. Johnson's former pupil at the failed Edial school, David Garrick, was by 1749 England's most famous actor and the manager of Drury Lane.

12. According to Boswell, "When one was reading his tragedy of "Irene," to a company at a house in the country, he left the room; and somebody having asked him the reason of this, he replied, "Sir, I thought it had been better" (*Life*, 4: 5). See also Bronson's discussion, "Johnson's 'Irene': Variations on a Tragic Theme," in *Johnson Agonistes*, pp. 100–155.

13. Greene, *The Politics*, pp. 92–95, 112–40.

14. *Oxford Authors*, p. 106. This and the speech to follow are from *Gentleman's Magazine*, where the debate in the Commons over Walpole's impeachment was printed February, March, and April 1743.

15. Greene, *Politics*, p. 128.

16. *Oxford Authors*, p. 110.

17. Possibly no work of Johnson's, intended for publication, is so tantalizing. For some well-informed views, see: Benjamin Boyce, "Johnson's *Life of Savage* and its Literary Background," *Studies in Philology* 53 (October 1956): 576–98; William Vesterman, "Johnson and the *Life of Savage*," *ELH* 36 (1969): 659–78; John A. Dussinger, "Johnson's *Life of Savage*: The Displacement of Authority," in *The Discourse of the Mind in Eighteenth-Century Fiction* (The Hague: Mouton, 1974), pp. 127–47; Paul K. Alkon, "The Intention and Reception of Johnson's *Life of Savage*," *Modern Philology* 72 (1974): 139–50; Robert W. Uphaus, "The 'Equipoise' of Johnson's *Life of Savage*," in *The Impossible Observer: Reason and the Reader in Eighteenth-*

Century Prose (Lexington: University of Kentucky Press, 1979), pp. 89–107; Robert Folkenflik, *Samuel Johnson, Biographer* (Ithaca, N.Y.: Cornell University Press, 1978), pp. 195–213; Martin Maner, *The Philosophical Biographer: Doubt and Dialectic in Johnson's Lives of the Poets* (Athens: University of Georgia Press, 1988), pp. 57–73; Donald Greene, "Samuel Johnson's *The Life of Richard Savage*," in *The Biographer's Art: New Essays*, ed. Jeffrey Meyers (London: Macmillan, 1989), pp. 11–30. Still the most analytically satisfying study, albeit not of Johnson but of the character of Savage, is by the eminent psychoanalyst Edmund Bergler, "Samuel Johnson's 'Life of the Poet Richard Savage'—A Paradigm for a Type," *American Imago* 4 (December 1947): 42–63.

18. Edmund Bergler first coined the phrase as a practicing psychoanalyst and used it in his stunning analysis of Savage's character pathology.

19. *Johnsonian Miscellanies*, 1: 371.

20. As Boswell says, the story was never corroborated (*Life*, 1: 170–74), and, to this day, that remains so. See Clarence Tracy, *The Artificial Bastard: A Biography of Richard Savage* (Cambridge, Mass.: Harvard University Press, 1953), preface, p. vii: "As to the great question of the genuineness of Savage's claim to be the illegitimate son of the fourth Earl Rivers by the Countess of Macclesfield, I have not been able to settle it finally."

21. In a *Rambler* article on parental tyranny, Johnson embellishes a similar tale of darkness in the parent who "may wanton in cruelty without controul," who

> may please himself with exciting terror as the inflicter of pain; he may delight his solitude with contemplating the extent of his power and the force of his commands, in imagining the desires that flutter on the tongue which is forbidden to utter them, or the discontent which preys on the heart in which fear confines it; he may amuse himself with new contrivances of detection, multiplications of prohibition, and varieties of punishment. (*Works*, 5: 23–24, *Rambler* 148)

22. In a classic formulation of the need for punishment and suffering in psychological disorders, the noted psychoanalytic theorist Franz Alexander explains how pain relieves emotional tension and becomes in itself one source of morally unrestrained behavior:

> One of the most common defense mechanisms is based on this deeply rooted emotional syllogism, that suffering atones for guilt. According to this peculiar equation conscience accepts suffering as currency by which its claims can be satisfied. . . . This explains why persons who have been subjected to intense suffering feel that their turn has come to do what they want and that they can therefore disregard convention. (*Fundamentals of Psychoanalysis* [1948], 2nd ed. [New York: W.W. Norton, 1963], p. 119)

23. On the subject of Savage's kindness—the word which appears most often in the *Life* is *compassion*—Bergler notes that Savage selectively forgave those who wronged him, in particular, disreputable women. He analyzes this as the "magic

gesture," also crediting Johnson for seeing through the hoax: "'Magic gestures' have little to do with being a 'saint or a hero,' as Johnson assumes. It is an unconscious technique of psychic masochists who express their complaints in dramatizing the superficial defense: 'I show you how I wanted to be treated—kindly.' Behind that palimpsest, the deeper repressed layer is hidden: 'Look, bad mother, how cruel *you* were'" ("Samuel Johnson's 'Life of Savage,'" pp. 59–60).

24. Note the incident Johnson reports on Savage's reaction to a gift of clothes, for which he was not first consulted:

> It had scarcely deserved mention had it not, by affecting him in an uncommon degree, shewn the peculiarity of his character. Upon hearing the design that was formed he came to the lodging of a friend with the most violent agonies of rage, and being asked what it could be that gave him such disturbance, he replied with the utmost vehemence of indignation, "That they had sent for a taylor to measure him." (*Lives*, 2: 411)

25. The dispute involved all sorts of mischief instigated by three highly volatile parties, Pope, Savage, and John Henley, the inflammatory orator and apparently a mutual enemy. See Hill's documentation of the incident in *Lives*, 2: 428, footnotes 1–5. Johnson was careful not to take sides, but by stating that "Mr. Savage returned a very solemn protestation of his innocence," we, knowing Savage, may suspect the worst.

26. Johnson's use of the word *conscience* is vitally linked to the inward life, to the views of *conscious* and *unconscious*, a concept which Jean Hagstrum illustrates in "Towards a Profile of the Word *Conscious* in Eighteenth-Century Literature," in *Psychology and Literature in the Eighteenth-Century*, pp. 23–50. Reviewing the etymologies of these words, he explains: "So deeply did self-examination become involved with self-evaluation, that the two cannot easily be separated. . . . For [Johnson] merely to recall in solitude his inner state, present or past, was inevitably to judge it" (pp. 26–27).

27. *Oxford Authors*, p. 55.

4. The Physician of the Soul

IF WE TRY TO IMAGINE Johnson meditating on the celebrated inscription at the gates of the Ptolmaean library, "*Psyches iatreion*," the Physic of the Soul, our traditional view of his moral and religious authority takes a wider scope. The familiar strains of spiritual healing found in works like *The Vanity of Human Wishes* and the sermons are as much psychiatry as theology. They lead beyond the inescapable adversity of human life to a distinctive quality of restoration and well-being. They probe the mind's inner resources, together with the system of pleasure and pain, reward and punishment, which constitute a civilized society. The most psychological of religious and moral interpreters, Johnson could not rest satisfied with a collection of dry, undigested canonical precepts; he had to discover the hidden order governing the human mind.

As many have observed, Johnson's Christianity is remarkably free of other-worldliness. No legions of devils or choirs of angels inhabit his cosmos; nor do extravagant symbols and rituals appear to affect how he practiced his faith. No interminable metaphysics on the abstract nature of the soul avail him while the great problems of life remain untouched.[1] He seems not altogether satisfied, indeed he is amazed by Milton's speculative design in *Paradise Lost*, sharply to observe that "the want of human interest is always felt," and at times to censure defects in the supernatural machinery of the poem. Of the spectacular inventions of Heaven and Hell, he objects to how they baffle and overwhelm human understanding: "Poetical pleasure must be such as human imagination can at least conceive, and poetical terrour such as human strength and fortitude may combat. The good and evil of Eternity are too ponderous for the wings of wit; the mind sinks under them in passive helplessness, content with calm belief and humble adoration" (*Lives*, 1: 182). The aversion to high-flown conceit in religious literature similarly leads him to reject many forms of sacred poetry as affected, unnatural display.[2] "Religion must be shown as it is," he declares in the "Life of Waller." "Suppression and addition equally corrupt it; and such as it is, it is known already" (*Lives*, 1: 292), he writes in support of

natural feeling and the unvarnished truth. By contrast to artifice and euphu-
ism, he recommends the simplest, most immediate emotion as best suited
for pious meditation:

> Faith, unvariably uniform, cannot be invested by fancy with decorations.
> Thanksgiving, the most joyful of all holy effusions, yet addressed to a Being
> without passions, is confined to a few modes, and is to be felt rather than
> expressed. Repentance, trembling in the presence of the judge, is not at leisure
> for cadences and epithets. Supplication of man to man may diffuse itself
> through many topics of persuasion; but supplication to God can only cry for
> mercy. (*Lives*, 1: 292)

Johnson's own devotions are intensely personal and direct, just as he
required of his theology. Moreover, his frequent practice of composing
liturgical collects and formal prayers during periods of emotional crisis
sheds fresh light on his piercing self-analysis. Readers of Johnson's *Prayers
and Meditations*, heavily edited as they are by George Strahan, the young
clergyman friend to whom he gave them shortly before his death, and a self-
appointed guardian of his reputation for religious piety,[3] cannot help but
be struck by the endless recitation of grief, doubt, and self-lacerating guilt.
Let it be noted that we are not concerned here with questions of religious
orthodoxy, though, to be sure, Johnson framed many models of his religious thought from a lifetime acquaintance with the Bible, the Book of
Common Prayer, and other Christian teachings.[4] It is, however, by way of
his professed faith that we approach once more, now uncommonly open
and undisguised, a familiar scheme of intrapsychic life.

The devotions tell over and over of "terrours" (*Works*, 1: 73, 107, 125,
306), the "tyranny" of "vain imaginations" (63, 312), "scruples" (70, 84, 99,
106, 108, 368), "negligence" (48, 77), "perplexities" (73), and "disturbances
of the mind very near to madness" (264). Most of all, they describe how
Johnson created dangerous situations of seduction and assault in the continual round of vows and resolutions he bound himself to and broke. The
syndrome shows him falling in and out of disaster: confessing a wrong,
evidently lured to committing it again, and then punishing himself for it.
Not surprisingly, it recalls the streak of habitual brinkmanship, where he is
ever the hapless victim. It is astonishing to see how long and laboriously he
persevered:

> Easter Eve. 1761: "I have led a life so dissipated and useless, and my terrours
> and perplexities have so much encreased, that I am under great depression and
> discouragement. . . . I have resolved . . . till I am afraid to resolve again." (73)

Sept. 18. 1764. 7 in the Evening: "I have now spent fifty five years in resolving, having from the earliest time almost that I can remember been forming schemes of a better life. I have done nothing." (81)

Easter Day, Apr. 7. 1765. About 3 in the morning: "When I consider how vainly I have hitherto resolved at this annual commemoration of my savior's death to regulate my life by his laws, I am almost afraid to renew my resolutions. Since the last Easter I have reformed no evil habit, my time has been unprofitably spent, and it seems as a dream that has left nothing behind. My memory grows confused, and I know not how the days pass over me." (91–92)

July 22–23. "This day I found this book with the resolutions, some of which I had forgotten. . . Of the time past since those resolutions were made I can give no very laudable account. . . . My memory has been for a long time very much confused. Names, and Persons, and Events slide away strangely from me. . . The other day looking over old papers, I perceived a resolution to rise early always occurring. I think I am ashamed or grieved to find how long and how often I had resolved, what yet except for about one half year I have never done. My Nights are now such as give me no quiet rest." (157–59)

In the *Prayers and Meditations* Johnson torments and abases himself before an almighty taskmaster, and he begs *"to be loosed from the chain of my sins"* (81). Originating from the *Book of Common Prayer*—"Though we be tied and bound with the chain of our sins, yet let the pitifulness of thy great mercy loose us"—the metaphor also refers to an inveterate motif of self-enslavement. In prayer upon prayer, the vicious circle of broken pledges seduces him to would-be criminality. And heeding this critical issue of intrapsychic life we are not unprepared for the chilling diary entry in Latin, "De pedicis et manicis insana cogitatio" (140), translated "insane thought about foot-fetters and manacles." Neither are we puzzled by Johnson's pleas to be disciplined by Mrs. Thrale in the extraordinary letter in French, nor stunned by the notorious padlock entrusted to her, in view of the deep-rooted impulse to danger.[5] As medical historians have argued, public confinement in Johnson's lifetime loomed menacingly large, to wit, his friend the poet Christopher Smart's being institutionalized.[6] No doubt for Johnson, the fantasy of incarceration, as we shall see in *Rasselas*, posed various wishful as well as self-punitive unconscious meanings.

Picking up the thread of Johnson's work in the late 1740s, we understand his moral and religious teaching in the light of an intense foraging inward. Johnson's passionate Christianity, moreover, allows him to assail darkest, heretofore unsuspected reservoirs. For him the old Hebraic-Christian injunction of self-examination acquires unprecedented urgency and vast complexity. In the act of soul-searching, he confirms the vital, far-

reaching influence of the psychical apparatus. Most important, he summons his arguments of faith in accordance with dynamic mental functioning. No frigid resolve or abstract dogma could loosen the grip of instinct
and emotion. Engaged in a project on general education, he writes in the
Preface to the *Preceptor* (1748):

> The laws of mere morality are of no coercive power; and, however they may,
> by conviction, of their fitness please the reasoner in the shade, when the
> passions stagnate without impulse, and the appetites are secluded from their
> objects, they will be of little force against the ardour of desire, or the vehe-
> mence of rage, amidst the pleasures and tumults of the world. To counteract
> the power of temptations, hope must be excited by the prospect of rewards,
> and fear by the expectation of punishment; and virtue may owe her panegy-
> ricks to morality, but must derive her authority from religion.[7]

To do battle with the forces of nature, Johnson engages a prototype of
mental experience based without compromise upon nonrational sources.
He contends not with theoretical overlays, but with the very sources
themselves. The allegory he contributed to the second volume of the
Preceptor, "The Vision of Theodore, the Hermit of Teneriffe," makes many
of these known, drawing in large from the dark and painful struggle of
inner life. Johnson once called this deceptively simple piece the best thing
he ever wrote.[8]

According to the parable in "The Vision of Theodore," Habit is the
inescapable adversary who obstructs the road to the Temple of Happiness.
She often joins with Appetite and Passions, first to entice by offers of
assistance, but then to ensnare in perpetual thralldom, those not amenable
to proper guidance. Falling into her clutches, mortals are lost to various
corruptions: Ambition, Avarice, Intemperance, Indolence, Despair. By
contrast, Education, Innocence, Reason, and Religion lead rightfully to the
cherished goal. The tale is not unusual for conveying conventional wisdom,
except that Johnson appears to have amplified the description of Habit
from his principal models.[9] He makes Habit into a fearsome slave driver,
and he accentuates how it lures and constrains its victims. By contrast to
other figures, indeed in violation of his own rule that "allegorical persons . . . may produce effects, but cannot conduct actions,"[10] he gives the
frightful creatures striking agency: "It was the peculiar artifice of Habit not
to suffer her power to be felt at first. Those whom she led, she had the
address of appearing only to attend, but was continually doubling her
chains upon her companions. . . . Habit always threw new chains upon her
fugitive." Magnifying the cause makes the effects more vivid and concrete.

The chains of Habit "were so slender in themselves, and so silently fastened, that while the attention was engaged by other objects, they were not easily perceived. Each link grew tighter as it had been longer worn, and when by continual additions they became so heavy as to be felt, they were very frequently too strong to be broken" (*Works*, 16: 202, 207).

Hardly a typical allegorical abstraction, Johnson's Habit takes on a life of its own, its stratagems perceived, for the most part dimly, or perhaps not at all, until the victim tries to break away: "Nor did any escape her but those who by an effort sudden and violent, burst their shackles at once, and left her at a distance; and even of these many rushing too precipitately forward, and hindered by their terrors from stopping where they were safe, were fatigued with their own vehemence, and resigned themselves again to that power from whom an escape must be so dearly bought, and whose tyranny was little felt, except when it was resisted" (207). Rampant and dangerous, Habit ever stalks the road to Happiness and turns it to ruin. Johnson belabors the description of being driven through a foul and murky under-world:

> They wandered on from one double labyrinth to another with the chains of Habit hanging secretly upon them. . . . They proceeded in their dreary march without pleasure in their progress, yet without power to return. . . . Discontent lowered in their looks, and Sadness hovered round their shades; yet they crawled on reluctant and gloomy, till they arrived at the depth of the recess . . . where the dominion of Indolence terminates, and the hopeless wanderer is delivered up to Melancholy: the chains of Habit are riveted forever, and Melancholy, having tormented her prisoner for a time, consigns him at last to the cruelty of Despair. (211–12)

If this were not enough, the slaves of Habit are most tormented by their own slogging offensiveness: "[They] had this aggravation above all others, that they were criminal but not delighted" (211).

Evidently autobiographical, the portrayal of Habit explains an interior process of coercion and infirmity of purpose. Its dire influence corresponds to the crippling inhibition Johnson loathes and contends with in his private papers. The repeated acts of obsessive behavior and the dreadful paralysis of will come from a sense of relentless obstruction: in the terms of the allegory, "Habit" prevents the exercise of purposeful life. Remarkably, its unsparing yoke and enforced drudgery have the quality of compulsions. With increasing tenacity, Habit gains upon her prey, withholding, subduing, riveting, until the battle waged over consciousness itself is given up and lost. Desire, thus deprived and frustrated, must carry on its struggle on countless other fronts, to anticipate themes to be analyzed in future writings: the submerged and treacherous decoys, the slavish self-delusions in *The Vanity of Human Wishes*, the periodical essays, and *Rasselas*.

In "The Vision of Theodore," Reason and Religion hold a reparative course for human desire and help recover agency and consciousness. Most important, it is Religion, *not* Reason, who helps liberate the imprisoned spirit. When Habit prevails, each is called on for assistance, but with mixed results: "Habit, insolent with her power, would often presume to parley with Reason, and offer to loose some of her chains if the rest might remain. To this Reason, who was never certain of victory, frequently consented, but always found her concessions destructive, and saw the captive led away by Habit to his former slavery" (207–08). There is no question that Johnson views Reason to be fallible and lacking real potency, just as the figure earlier protests, " 'My power,' said Reason, 'is to advise, not to compel' " (204). If here and elsewhere, he sometimes enlists the "light of reason," it is no imperious deliverer, but a compliant subordinate, and flawed to boot.[11] By some contrast, Religion, once summoned, "never submitted to treaty, but held out her hand with certainty of conquest; and if the captive to whom she gave it did not quit his hold, always led him away in triumph, and placed him in the direct path to the temple of Happiness" (208). With her emissary Conscience, Religion reaches the mightiest faculties of all, those of conscious volition and the latent powers exerted in that cause. Thus the individual overmatches forces of the mind pitted against one another, his energies reclaimed and at his own disposal. Far from an exercise of preemptive rationality, the act originates in mental operations that are almost wholly nonrational. For Johnson, Religion consolidates, as it engages, deepest structures of the mind. As he once explained it in the "Life of Milton," religious belief reverts to primal impressions: "These truths are too important to be new: they have been taught to our infancy; they have mingled with our solitary thoughts and familiar conversation, and are habitually interwoven with the whole texture of life" (*Lives*, 1: 182).

On the authority of Christian ethics, *The Vanity of Human Wishes* (1749) treats the subject of impetuous worldliness. It illustrates that material goals breed disappointment and suffering, while religious faith holds the potential for human happiness. Johnson once described himself as a "straggler," who "may leave this town and go to Grand Cairo, without being missed here or observed there,"[12] and this desolate anonymity also captures a quality of the "imitation" of Juvenal's *Tenth Satire*. Characters wander alone and without identity, but for the catastrophic events that mark their downfall. They emerge from faint shadows and indefiniteness, the places of "clouded maze," "dreary paths" and "treacherous phantoms in the mist." As he examines human nature from high civilization to barbarism, "from China to Peru," Johnson finds a common inward theme: that impelled by primal instinct—"hope and fear, desire and hate," and struggling through devious mental landscapes—"fancied ills" or "airy good"— human beings plunge headlong to disaster. Inexorably their desires trace the pattern of their destruction, as the tragedies of destiny unfold:[13]

> Fate wings with ev'ry wish th' afflictive dart,
> Each gift of nature, and each grace of art,
> With fatal heat impetuous courage glows,
> With fatal sweetness elocution flows,
> Impeachment stops the speaker's pow'rful breath,
> And restless fire precipitates on death.
>
> (*Works*, 6: 92, ll. 15–20)

Thus desire is doomed to extinction, its energies wasted and depleted in useless, vicious turns. The struggle waged appears much as it did in "The Vision of Theodore," an interior contest, where compulsion likewise ended in horror and loss. With every wish, the mind veers dangerously out of control, and the experience of habitual need subjugates and wears down its victim. Insatiable ambition exacts the bitter end of once celebrated figures, such as Cardinal Wolsey, Charles XII of Sweden, Jonathan Swift, the Duke of Marlborough, Lady Vane, and Catherine Sedley. Theirs is merely one more road to ruin, as they too are circumvented by a train of unscrupulous attendants, falling captive to wealth, fame, political and scholarly aspiration, military prowess, beauty, love, and so on. We observe them in the last throes of agony and regret, before they are consigned to oblivion. Images of dissolution and insubstantiality are suffused throughout the poem. From fireworks, Johnson pictures the flitting glow of a single moment's distinction:

> Unnumber'd suppliants crowd Preferment's gate,
> Athirst for wealth, and burning to be great;
> Delusive Fortune hears th' incessant call,
> They mount, they shine, evaporate, and fall.
>
> (*Works*, 6: 95, ll. 73–76)

He shows how Wolsey's pageantry of fame and fortune abruptly expires, soon to be followed by his life:

At once is lost the pride of aweful state,
The golden canopy, the glitt'ring plate,
The regal palace, the luxurious board,
The liv'ried army, and the menial lord.
With age, with cares, with maladies oppress'd,
He seeks the refuge of monastic rest.
Grief aids disease, remember'd folly stings,
And his last sighs reproach the faith of kings.

(Works, 6: 96, ll. 113–20)

And in the lines so admired by T.S. Eliot,[14] he renders the futile shocking death of the young swashbuckling king of Sweden:

His fall was destin'd to a barren strand,
A petty fortress, and a dubious hand;
He left the name, at which the world grew pale,
To point a moral, or adorn a tale.

(Works, 6: 102, ll. 219–22)

The Vanity of Human Wishes, with its remorseless theme of vagary and of motives gone astray, was the first of Johnson's works to bear his name. More than likely, he identified with its tragic cast and restive conflict, now acutely to be owned. In the character of the straggler, he was soon to write to Thomas Warton: "I have ever since [my wife's death] seemed to myself broken off from mankind a kind of solitary wanderer in the wild of life, without any certain direction, or fixed point of view. A gloomy gazer on a world to which I have little relation."[15] This tenor of emotional numbness explains one response in the poem to the daemonic forces within us. It is an alternative not unlike the Stoical repression of all emotion: "Where then shall Hope and Fear their objects find? / Must dull Suspense corrupt the stagnant mind?" (*Works*, 6: 107, ll. 343–44). The unedifying spectacle of suffering and defeat freezes the very current of purposeful life:

Must helpless man, in ignorance sedate,
Roll darkling down the torrent of his fate?
Must no dislike alarm, no wishes rise,
No cries attempt the mercies of the skies?

(Works, 6: 107–08, ll. 345–48)

But the sinking desperation of these lines is not Johnson's final word. In the Stoical answer, he senses the danger of drastic impairment to the psyche, referring to displacement and inhibition of emotion as even bleaker prospects. In effect, he casts off the straggler's identity and, as antidote to its stuporous isolation, he calls upon divine assistance. The act of prayer may tame the wild excesses of nature and the scourge of Fate, as well as rescue man from chilling solitude. The ending of *The Vanity of Human Wishes* speaks directly to an internalization of the great Christian paradigm—*love, patience, faith*—in accordance with those same "truths," as he stated, "interwoven with the whole texture of life." By contrast to the defensive repression of emotion, we note its full engagement in the stirring coda:

> Pour forth thy fervours for a healthful mind,
> Obedient passions, and a will resign'd;
> For love, which scarce collective man can fill;
> For patience sov'reign o'er transmuted ill;
> For faith, that panting for a happier seat,
> Counts death kind Nature's signal of retreat.
>
> (*Works*, 6: 108, ll. 359–64)

Invoking these most elevated moral states, Johnson shows how chaotic and disruptive trends may be taken at last under the jurisdiction of a "healthful mind," etc., that is to say, subdued by the very power that made them. This transformation, which the "laws of heav'n ordain," is amply explained as a psychological event, an act which draws upon compelling inner persuasions.[16] Thus inherent in "celestial wisdom" Johnson finds vital links to the mental apparatus. Through the intricate workings of mental life, he presents the agency by which we become moral and social beings. He has not far to go in designating the function of the superego.

*   *   *

The rolling baroque rhythms of Johnson's sermons continue his piercing inroads into the mystique of mind. While they were written for others, chiefly the Reverend John Taylor, and defy chronological ordering,[17] the sermons present nonetheless stimulating facets of Johnson's religious thought. Heeding the standard of his other religious and moral writings, they affirm basic convictions with vigorous arguments modelled in strong-textured prose. Most interesting is the view of religion as the means to ascertain and make tolerable our helplessness in the face of nature's crushing superiority. The homiletic style frees Johnson to invoke awesome catalogues of injury and suffering, at bottom, the effect of powers which he frequently relates to internal sources.[18] Once more, the urgent claim of human wishes runs dangerously out of control, here resonating in tones of advancing catastrophe. Anxiety is generated by the cadences of the periodic sentence, throwing the mind frantically forward. We are propelled through experiences of imminent disaster and held in suspense over long emphases of intimidation and conflict: only at the end do we repose in assurance of the motive of the whole.[19] By implicit analogy to the psychical sphere, labors rest and impulses accomplish their aim under the sanction, as it were, of a higher mental agency. Thus we press on in the quest for purposeful life. One such passage serves to illustrate how Johnson structures this adaptation of lower to higher energies in the frame of religious ideas, how, as he puts it, we "direct our desires to a better state":

> When we know, that we are on every side beset with dangers; that our condition admits many evils which cannot be remedied, but contains no good which cannot be taken from us; that pain lies in ambush behind pleasure, and misfortune behind success; that we have bodies subject to innumerable maladies, and minds liable to endless perturbations; that our knowledge often gives us pain, by presenting to our wishes such felicity as is beyond our reach, and our ignorance is such, that we often pursue, with eagerness, what either we cannot attain, or what, if we could attain it, disappoints our hopes; that in the dead calm of solitude we are insufficient to our own contentment, and that, when weariness of our selves impels us to society, we are often ill received; when we perceive that small offenses may raise enemies, but that great benefits will not always gain us friends; when we find ourselves courted by interest, and forsaken by ingratitude; when we see ourselves considered as aliens and strangers by the rising generation; it seems that we must by necessity turn our thoughts to another life. (*Works*, 14: 253, Sermon 15)

For Johnson, the crucible of faith is in the dynamism of inward life, which keeps nature at bay: here appointed are the powers to curb the mind's devouring need and compensate its suffering privation. It is an admirable self-regulatory process, argued from Lockean naturalism, as the theory was earlier presented in *An Essay Concerning Human Understanding*:

> Good and evil . . . are nothing but Pleasure or Pain, or that which occasions, or procures Pleasure or Pain to us. *Morally Good and Evil* then, is only the Conformity or Disagreement of our voluntary Actions to some Law, whereby Good or Evil is drawn on us, from the Will and Power of the Law-maker; which Good and Evil, Pleasure or Pain, attending our observance, or breach of the Law, by the Decree of the Law-maker, is that we call *Reward and Punishment*.[20]

Explaining the practical duties of human beings in a political state, Johnson likewise delves to the heart of elemental instinct: "The general employment of mankind is to increase pleasure, or remove the pressure of pain. These are the vital principles of action" (*Works*, 14: 195, Sermon 18). Here also are the facts and conditions of a knowledge, ascertained by radical direct inspection. No less circumspect in religious matters than in any other, Johnson punctures the flimsy fabric of contrivance and arrives at his verities by palpable experience. "We cannot make the truth; it is our business only to find it. . . . To believe obstinately without grounds of belief, and to determine without examination, is the last degree of folly and absurdity" (*Works*, 14: 223, Sermon 20). In these terms, Johnson's proofs of Christianity reinstate his scientific views of the mind: for him, the confirmation of God takes place beneath the polished surfaces of rationality, that is to say, in hidden motives and subtle turns of the mental apparatus. Sensed through deepest cloaked meanings, He "searches the secrets of the heart" and "sees the force of every passion, knows the power of every prejudice, attends to every conflict of the mind." Akin to Locke's "Law-maker," who is also attested to psychologically,[21] He is represented as an inner critical judge and active agency: "He only, that knows every circumstance of life, and every motion of the mind, can tell how far the crimes, or virtues, of each man are to be punished or rewarded" (*Works*, 14: 178, Sermon 16).

If the dynamism of inward life is the measure of Johnson's religious conviction, he also understands how the analysis of deep-seated mental content may be evaded and resisted, despite the most scrupulous inquiry. Moreover, he recognizes that there is no single knowable reality as the final test of truth. In human experience there is no court of last resort in settling questions of fact versus fantasy. Aptly, the sermons explore versions of knowing through subjective emotional experience which is related to the dynamic unconscious. Johnson's sermons are often astonishing records of happenings in the mind, involving the struggle with "resistless impulse"—his own striking expression—which, being unconscious, leaves only fragmentary, barely legible traces. He accounts for seeming discontinuities in mental life by making clear the unyielding mechanism, the causal chain of impulse and action:

> It is frequently observed in common life, that some favourite notion or inclination, long indulged, takes such an entire possession of a man's mind, and so engrosses his faculties, as to mingle thoughts perhaps he is not himself conscious of with almost all his conceptions, and influence his whole behavior. It will often operate on occasions with which it could scarcely be imagined to

have any connection, and will discover itself, however it may lie concealed, either in trifling incidents, or important occurrences, when it is least expected or foreseen. It gives a particular direction to every sentiment and action, and carries a man forward, as by a kind of resistless impulse, or insuperable destiny. (*Works*, 14: 173, Sermon 16)

With utmost vigilance, Johnson monitors this mechanism which develops in response to experience and along the lines laid down by its inherent nature. It sets its own aims and moreover works covertly beyond the reach of normal awareness. Cutting to the very thick of the unconscious, he describes "insensible deviations" (*Works*, 14: 41, Sermon 4), and "secret tendencies, and all those lurking inclinations, which operate very frequently without being attended to even by ourselves" (*Works*, 14: 80, Sermon 7). He remarks ideas of a "subtle insinuating kind . . . [which] are suffered to approach unregarded, and gain ground imperceptibly upon minds directed to different views; and to fix themselves at leisure in the heart, where perhaps they are scarcely discovered" (*Works*, 14: 87, Sermon 8). He uncovers the old compulsion of "habits . . . [that] may be suppressed and lie dormant for a time, and resume their force, at an unexpected moment" (*Works*, 14: 114, Sermon 10), as well as "inordinate desires [that] remain, not only unsubdued, but unsuspected, under the splendid cover of some specious practice, with which the mind delights itself too much, to take a rigorous survey of its own motions" (*Works*, 14: 144, Sermon 13).

Given the laws of psychical agency thus brought to light, Johnson appears to have championed a belief in a thoroughgoing psychological determinism, that is, in forces of the mind, known or unknown, dedicated to preserving their own function. But to whatever measure he played the determinist, Johnson was no fatalist. If he postulates an uncompromising mental apparatus, its terms differ significantly from other determinist paradigms so prevalent in the eighteenth century. From Shaftesburians to Deists, Stoics, and votaries of Sensibility, even to fundamentalist Christians, many invoked Lockean assumptions about the mind's rigid causality, engrossed as they were in caveats about the "association of ideas," and the potent effects of latent mental content.[22] But in fact it is Johnson who stresses the more purely experiential mode, and, to use the parlance of our century, an existential humanist conception of self-mastery. His stubborn arguments on choice and vital experience sharply oppose the juggernaut of early modern rationalism, to mire its victims in fatal passivity. His common polemic against the "ruling passion" exemplifies this distinctive point of view.

In the "Annotations to Crousaz, *Commentary* on Pope's *Essay on Man*" (1739), Johnson repudiates the popular Deist notion of the ruling passion, a kind of inborn determinism, on the grounds that it is a product of "reason" instead of "fact and experience." While granting that the phenomenon may occur, he believes its source is *not* logically and innately predestined; rather, he suggests, with purer Lockean intent, it derives from primary impressions received in early childhood: "Men, indeed, appear very frequently to be influenced a long time by a predominant inclination . . . but perhaps if they review their early years and trace their ideas backwards, they will find that those strong desires were the effects either of example or instruction, the circumstances in which they were placed, the objects which they first received impressions from, the first book they read, or the first company they conversed with."[23] Over forty years later in the "Life of Pope," he amplifies the debate over the ruling passion, which he describes, following Pope, as "an original direction of desire to some particular object, an innate affection which gives all action a determinate and invariable tendency, and operates upon the whole system of life either openly or more secretly" (*Lives*, 3: 173–74). But again he denies that the passions are "innate or irresistible," and he deliberately refutes superstition and established opinion: "Men are directed not by an ascendent planet or predominating humour, but by the first book which they read, or some early conversation which they heard, or some accident which excited ardour and emulation" (*Lives*, 3: 174). Moreover, he censures those who would encourage the passivity of emotion entailed by the theory. He argues along lines of his regular antipathy to a priori thinking, in order to expose its fallible edicts:

> This doctrine is in itself pernicious as well as false; its tendency is to produce the belief of a kind of moral predestation, or overruling principle which cannot be resisted: he that admits it is prepared to comply with every desire that caprice or opportunity shall excite, and to flatter himself that he submits only to the lawful dominion of Nature, in obeying the resistless authority of his "ruling Passion." (*Lives*, 3: 174.)[24]

Finally, and with some bold assurance, he dismisses the much-touted dogma by pointing out its famous apostle's poor grasp of psychological terminology: "Pope has formed his theory with so little skill that, in the examples by which he illustrates and confirms it, he has confounded passions, appetites, and habits" (*Lives*, 3: 174–75). If, as seems likely, Johnson sensed an affinity to his own determinist views of the mind, he at the same time demanded clear and well-founded scientific accuracy, in accordance with his own hard-won expertise.[25]

What offends Johnson in the mechanist scheme he grudgingly acknowledges is the nihilistic potential of forces inherent in the mind. Unconditional and unchecked, impulse commands its own blind purpose, wasting and despoiling the integrity of self. But for all its ferocity, the essential militia of the internal world also holds the bulwark against primary chaos, and by this overriding principle, Johnson finds the triumph of man's intelligence over the hostile, pitiless forces of nature. In the sermons, the internal world puts forth not only what is lowest, but what is highest, too, in the course of human development. It harbors ethical values and, through its intricate agency, observes, judges, and approves or condemns human conduct. Johnson often denotes this interiorization of higher principles in the traditional idiom of worship of God. Explaining the motives of holy devotion, he lays open a complicated skein of mental events. His focus squarely on dynamics of mind, he views the means by which man endeavors to transform his inner compulsions:

> All ideas influence our conduct with more or less force, as they are more or less strongly impressed upon the mind; and they are impressed more strongly, as they are more frequently recollected or renewed. . . . By dwelling upon, and indulging any idea, we may increase its efficacy and force, make it by degrees predominant in the soul, and raise it to an ascendant over our passions, so that it shall easily overrule those affections or appetites which formerly tyrannized within us. (*Works*, 14: 101, Sermon 9)

Thus man struggles to "imprint upon himself an habitual attention to the laws of God" (102). In this way the mind seizes upon the most excellent representative of its resistless authority. If he is to be driven, man may, at best, be driven by the highest duties. He may mobilize, just as he yields, to a superior ideal:

> As this unbounded dominion of ideas, long entertained by the fancy, and naturalized to the mind, is a very strong argument against suffering ourselves to dwell too long upon pleasing dreams, or delightful falsehoods, or admitting any inordinate passion to insinuate itself, and grow domestick; so it is a reason, of equal force, to engage us in a frequent, and intense meditation on those important and eternal rules, which are to regulate our conduct, and rectify our minds; that the power of habit may be added to that of truth, that the most useful ideas may be the most familiar, and that every action of our lives may be carried on under the superintendence of an over-ruling piety. (*Works*, 14: 174, Sermon 16)

The consummate guardian of human impulse and its vicissitudes, the prototype of God in Johnson's religion bestows powers of self-discipline, frequently engaged through prayer, "No man can . . . reconcile himself to an action, by which he shall displease him, to whom he has been returning thanks for his creation and preservation, and by whom he hopes to be still preserved. He therefore, who prays often, fortifies himself by a natural effect" (*Works*, 14: 34, Sermon 3); and through grace, "By grace alone can we hope to resist the numberless temptations that perpetually surround us; by grace only can we reject the sollicitations of pleasure, repress the motions of anger, and turn away from the allurements of ambition" (*Works*, 14: 236, Sermon 22). Of consoling and protective offices, this quality of God provides security and self-possession, though not to forget the redoubtable sway of the almighty taskmaster. As the morbid anxiety of his private devotions ever testifies, as well as the stark terrorism he embroiders in other works we have and shall continue to explore, Johnson never omitted from mind the oppressive fear of an archaic heritage. But above all, he affirms man's power to refine and to sublimate the bedlam of primitive instinct perpetually to be borne. Alluding to the duties of the governed in a political state, he imagines how what was the lowest part of mental life is converted to the highest: "The first duty . . . of subjects is obedience to the laws; such obedience as is the effect, not of compulsion, but of reverence; such as arises from a conviction of the instability of human virtue, and of the necessity of some coercive power, which may restrain the exorbitancies of passion, and check the career of natural desires" (*Works*, 14: 258–58, Sermon 24). This monumental conversion of *compulsion* into *reverence*, which takes place in the mind's deepest reservoirs, unlocks the portentous meaning of the superego.

Despite the acrimonious war against religion waged by Voltaire, Holbach, Hume, and other philosophes, a campaign which culminated in Freud, Johnson stubbornly stuck to his Christian guns.[26] But ironically he shared a common idealism with these radical disciples of the Enlightenment, even if he liked to brandish the weapons of the opposition. Foraging into the darkness alone, he also sought the illuminate principles of scientific truth. To whatever extent his religious temperament was joined with his relentless explorations of mental life, he put this coalition to invaluable analytic use. In his private devotions, not intended for publication, he often undergoes an excoriating census of guilt and self-doubt, by the lash of a divine taskmaster. But in the subdued public voice of "The Vision of Theodore," *The Vanity of Human Wishes*, and the sermons, he enlists a higher prerogative, an exercise of principled intelligence. The primacy of intelligence over instinct—a desideratum as much Johnsonian as Freudian—may help to dispel the fallacious perceptions of the mind. Thus the "tyranny" and "terrours" of "vain imaginations" at last are driven from their lair. Giving no ground, Johnson does battle with the enemy that eludes understanding: "We must banish every false argument, every known delusion from our minds, before our passions can operate in its favour; and forsake what we know must be forsaken, before we have endeared it to ourselves by long possession. . . . But let those who have hitherto neglected this great duty, remember, that it is yet in their power, and that they cannot perish everlastingly but by their own choice!" (*Works*, 14: 26, Sermon 2). The indomitable conviction echoes the famous advice to Boswell, one sorely infatuated individual, steeped in delusion and ridden by despair. It is the recourse to self-mastery, uniquely founded in the dynamism of *this* world and no other, that Johnson recommends. As he exquisitely reads the tapestries of unconscious life, the healing intelligence is nothing less than a psychology of freedom:

> There lurks, perhaps, in every human heart a desire of distinction, which inclines every man first to hope, and then to believe, that Nature has given him something peculiar to himself. This vanity makes one mind nurse aversions, and another actuate desires, till they rise by art much above their original state of power; and as affectation, in time, improves to habit, they at last tyrannise over him who at first encouraged them only for show. Every desire is a viper in the bosom, who, while he was chill, was harmless; but when warmth gave him strength, exerted it in poison. . . . Let all such fancies, illusive and destructive, be banished henceforward from your thoughts for ever. Resolve, and keep your resolution; choose, and pursue your choice.[27]

Notes

    1. An excellent introduction to Johnson's religious thought is Gray, *Johnson's Sermons*, pp. 131–82:

> In most things, certainly, Johnson insisted on systematic, empirical observation. The mystical heights to which Law, for instance, attained, were beyond Johnson's range. In ordering his own thoughts on religious belief and dogma, therefore, Johnson naturally avoided matters that seemed to him to go beyond believable, demonstrable evidence, and sought a systematic creed that could be contained within the bounds of human reason and credulity. (p. 131)

    2. Mrs. Thrale recalls how "he would inveigh against devotional poetry, and protest that all religious verses were cold and feeble, and unworthy the subject, which ought to be treated with higher reverence, he said, than either poets or painters could presume to excite or bestow." (*Johnsonian Miscellanies*, 1: 284)

3. See *Works*, 1: xvi–xviii for the sources of these, as well as J.D. Fleeman, "Some Notes on Johnson's Prayers and Meditations," *Review of English Studies*, n.s. 19 (May 1968): 172–79, for conjectures on the editorial mind Strahan brought to bear upon them. See also John B. Radner, "Samuel Johnson and the Vanity of Human Resolutions," *Enlightenment Essays* 4 (Fall–Winter 1973): 9–14, who interprets the diaries as Johnson's attempt to establish control over his habitual idleness.

4. The grounds of Johnson's religious thought have been well represented and, at times, hotly disputed by Hagstrum, "Dr. Johnson's Fear of Death," Greene, "Johnson 'Late Conversion,'" Chapin, Quinlan, Gray, Pierce, Chadwick, and Hudson, cited earlier, as well as by Katharine C. Balderston, "Doctor Johnson and William Law," *PMLA* 75 (September 1960): 382–94.

5. *Letters*, 1: 307–08 (no. 307.1). The original and still most satisfying analytic treatment of Johnson's alleged masochism is Katharine C. Balderston, "Johnson's Vile Melancholy." See also the trenchant discussions by Bate, *Samuel Johnson*, pp. 384–89, 439–41; Wain, *Samuel Johnson: A Biography*, 286–92; Peter Newton, "Samuel Johnson's Breakdown," pp. 101–06; and William B. Ober, *Bottoms Up! A Pathologist's Essays on Medicine and the Humanities*, pp. 186–89.

6. See the stimulating account, "Confinement and its Rationales," in Porter, *Mind-Forg'd Manacles*, pp. 110–68. Although Porter basically disputes Foucault's charge of the "great confinement" in England, he finds an encroaching social stigmatization of the mentally ill, which sometimes indeed led to their being put away:

> Already in the eighteenth century, the availability of private madhouses was leading to the confinement of people who were essentially just social nuisances or embarrassments—provoking Dr. Johnson's heartfelt defence of Kit Smart's liberty. Johnson feared that his own abnormal mannerisms might one day cascade into the kind of derangement which would lead to confinement; hence his celebrated delivery of a padlock to Hester Thrale. (p. 168)

7. *The Works of Samuel Johnson* (London: William Pickering, 1825), 5: 243–44.

8. *Life*, 1: 192, 537. It should be noted that Johnson said this sometime before 1760, the year of Bishop Percy's letter, which is the source of the statement.

9. For an exploration of Johnson's sources and variations, see Gwin J. Kolb, "*The Vision of Theodore*: Genre, Context, Early Reception," in *Johnson and His Age*, ed. James Engell, Harvard English Studies 12 (Cambridge, Mass.: Harvard University Press, 1984), pp. 107–24. See also Lawrence Lipking, "Learning to Read Johnson: *The Vision of Theodore* and *The Vanity of Human Wishes*," *ELH* 43 (1976): 517–37; and Bernard L. Einbond, *Samuel Johnson's Allegory* (The Hague: Mouton, 1971), pp. 56–64.

10. *Lives* 3: 233 ("Life of Pope"). See also the "Life of Milton": "To give them any real employment or ascribe to them any material agency is to make them allegorical no longer, but to shock the mind by ascribing effects to non-entity" (*Lives*, 1: 185). The "shock," intentional or unintentional, is fairly well evinced by "Theodore's" Habits.

11. In Sermon 18, Johnson also detects the limitations of Reason: "To subdue passion, and regulate desire, is the great task of man, as a moral agent; a task, for which natural reason, however assisted and enforced by human laws, has been found insufficient, and which cannot be performed but by the help of religion" (*Works*, 14: 193). Likewise in Sermon 4, he stresses "the errours of bewildered reason" and "fallible reason" (*Works*, 14: 40). The much-abused rubric of the eighteenth century as an "Age of Reason" has been chiefly dispelled, thanks to the valiant efforts of Donald Greene and others, who point out that not all were enamored of triumphant logic and symmetry. See "Augustianism and Empiricism: A Note on Eighteenth-Century English Intellectual History," *Eighteenth-Century Studies* 1 (1967): 33–68, as well as *The Age of Exuberance* (New York: Random House, 1970), pp. 86–126. To be sure, Johnson frequently recommends reason as a guide through difficult spiritual straits. The introduction to the *Yale Sermons* by Jean Hagstrum and James Gray clarifies what he means: "'Reason' used in connection with SJ's religion refers, not primarily to stoical or ethical reason, to *a priori* reason, to scientific reason, or to the reason that perceives the truth of philosophical systems (see Voitle, ch. 1), but to a sensible desire for preservation that chooses life and safety here and hereafter" (li, n. 8). The chapter cited is from Robert Voitle, *Samuel Johnson the Moralist* (Cambridge, Mass.: Harvard University Press, 1961), pp. 1–46, which reviews the various and complex definitions of reason in the eighteenth century.

12. *Life*, 3:306. According to Boswell, the remark was made in 1778, but it is echoed in many of Johnson's personal reflections, such as in the mournful letter to Thomas Warton, quoted above.

13. Many interpretations of *The Vanity of Human Wishes* focus on its tragic elements, from Ian Jack's chapter in *Augustan Satire* (Oxford: Clarendon Press, 1952), pp. 135–45, to Leopold Damrosch, Jr., *Samuel Johnson and the Tragic Sense* (Princeton, N.J.: Princeton University Press, 1972), 139–59. See also the lively critical debate generated in Donald Greene, review of *Samuel Johnson and the Tragic Sense* by Leopold Damrosch, Jr., *Modern Philology* 71 (1974): 443–49; Leopold Damrosch, "On Misreading Eighteenth-Century Literature: A Defense," *Eighteenth-Century Studies* 8 (1974–75): 202–06; Donald Greene, "On Misreading Eighteenth-Century Literature: A Rejoinder, " *Eighteenth-Century Studies* 9 (1975): 108–18. On a related note, see the thorough repudiation of Johnson's alleged Stoicism in Donald Greene, "Johnson, Stoicism, and the Good Life" in *The Unknown Johnson*, ed. John J. Burke, Jr. and Donald Kay (Madison: University of Wisconsin Press, 1983), pp. 17–38. On the subject of Johnson's personal revelations in the poem, W. J. Bate's discussion in *Samuel Johnson*, pp. 277–89, is moving and incisive.

14. See Eliot's introduction to *London: A Poem and The Vanity of Human Wishes* (London: Etchells and Macdonald, 1930).

15. *Letters*, 1: 59 (no. 56).

16. Chester Chapin also suggests the psychological bent of Johnson's religious proofs, that he often sought and supported his findings by concrete empirical arguments. See "Johnson and Pascal," in *English Writers of the Eighteenth-Century*, ed. John Middendorf (New York: Columbia University Press, 1971), pp. 3–16; as

well as Charles Hinnant, *Samuel Johnson: An Analysis* (London: Macmillan Press, 1988), p. 22.

17. For background of their composition, sources, main themes, and style, Gray, *Johnson's Sermons* is the standard monograph.

18. Paul Alkon's view of the sermons' lack of concern with the mental anatomy is perhaps too severe. As he states in *Samuel Johnson and Moral Discipline*, "Nowhere in the sermons does Johnson explain in significant detail the nature of our mental anatomy. . . . Morally proper and improper modes of thought are described without any searching attention to the mental mechanisms which circumscribe the channels in which thoughts are inclined to flow" (p. 208). On the contrary, Johnson had no reason to abandon his work on the mental anatomy in his homiletic writing. Indeed so intimate a subject as man's relation to God calls forth some of his most strenuous powers of psychological discernment.

19. See W.K. Wimsatt's detailed analysis of the dynamism inherent in Johnson's periodic sentences in *The Prose Style of Samuel Johnson* (New Haven, Conn.: Yale University Press, 1941), pp. 13–41 and passim; as well as Gray, *Johnson's Sermons*, pp. 200–31.

20. ed. Nidditch, p. 351 (2: 28: 5).

21. Gray also cites Locke's passage on the "Law-maker," referring to Johnson's seeking support for his religious beliefs "in the evidence of the senses":

> . . . . In this respect he was again a child of the Age of Reason, in which philosophers sought, for instance, to explain morality in terms of observable natural phenomena. Locke's endeavour to enunciate a psychological theory of happiness, it will be remembered, was partly related to the Christian emphasis on rewards and punishments—another example of the rational desire to wed science and apologetics. (*Johnson's Sermons*, p. 138)

22. The influence of Locke's "association of ideas" on eighteenth-century thought is so well known as to need little explanation. Some useful references include: Ernest Tuveson, *Imagination as a Means of Grace: Locke and the Aesthetics of Romanticism* (Berkeley and Los Angeles: University of California Press, 1960), pp. 33–41 and passim; Deporte, *Nightmares and Hobbyhorses*, pp. 19–25; Keener, *The Chain of Becoming*, pp. 24–29 and passim. See also Christopher Fox, *Locke and the Scriblerians: Identity and Consciousness in Early Eighteenth-Century Britain* (Berkeley and Los Angeles: University of California Press, 1988), for insights into Locke's theory of the "self." For a discussion of the doctrine of predestination in Anglican, Lutheran, and Calvinist theology, see Gregory F. Scholtz, "Anglicanism in the Age of Johnson: The Doctrine of Conditional Salvation," *Eighteenth-Century Studies* 22 (1988/89): 203–04. See also Gray, *Johnson's Sermons*, p. 68 on Johnson's interest in empiricist applications of natural law to the study of human morality.

23. *Oxford Authors*, p. 92. See also *Rambler* 43, where Johnson, now sardonic, discredits the ruling passion:

> Some that imagine themselves to have looked with more than common penetration into human nature, have endeavoured to persuade us, that each man is

born with a mind formed peculiarly for certain purposes, and with desires unalterably determined to particular objects, from which the attention cannot be long diverted, and which alone, as they are well or ill persued, must produce the praise or blame, the happiness or misery, of his future life. . . . This position has not, indeed, been hitherto proved with strength proportionate to the assurance with which it has been advanced, and, perhaps, will never gain much prevalence by a close examination. (*Works*, 3: 232)

24. This section appears to echo the earlier one in the Crousaz commentary:

It is not proper to dwell too long on the resistless power and despotic authority of this tyrant of the soul, lest the reader should, as it is very natural, take the present inclination, however destructive to society or himself, for the Ruling Passion, and forbear to struggle when he despairs to conquer. (*Oxford Authors*, p. 92)

25. See *Rambler* 49 (*Works*, 3: 263–68), where Johnson creates a developmental scheme of human desire from infancy to adulthood, defining terms such as appetites, instincts, passions, and so forth. The first half of the essay is almost purely devoted to nomenclature, as if Johnson were reciting a scheme of the mind he familiarly utilized, which was probably the case. See Alan T. McKenzie, "The Systematic Scrutiny of Passion in Johnson's *Rambler*," *Eighteenth-Century Studies* 20 (1986/87): 129–52, which reviews the tradition Johnson inherited.

26. For a masterly exposition of this ferocious contest during the eighteenth century, which also probes its antecedents in Western thought, see Peter Gay, *The Enlightenment: An Interpretation* (New York: Knopf, 1966–69), especially Book Two, Chapter Six, "In Dubious Battle." See also Gay's uncompromising study of Freud's anti-religion in *A Godless Jew: Freud, Aetheism, and the Making of Psychoanalysis* (New Haven, Conn.: Yale University Press, 1987).

27. *Letters*, 1: 165–66 (no. 163).

5. "Wrecked by Success": Approaching Fame and Fortune

IT IS ONE OF THE GREAT IRONIES of human affairs to observe that success often brings with it many problems, not the least being deep-rooted internal conflict. The glow of success, for all its accompanying fanfare and exhilaration, is also liable to produce intense anxiety, inhibition, and even despair. From an analytic point of view, this conflict arises from instincts working at cross purposes: from fantasies of aggressive conquest and subjugation of one's enemies on the one hand, and fears of retaliation on the other. An approach from the inside might reveal any number of subjective, largely unconscious meanings of success, which are not always what common sense would dictate nor what would ordinarily meet the eye. In his famous essay, "Some Character Types Met with in Psychoanalytic Work: Those Wrecked by Success" (1916), Freud underscored the Oedipal triumph in some forms of worldly success and the guilty self-punishment in the subsequent personal and occupational wreckage. He spoke of individuals who fall ill after realizing a deeply cherished ambition, and he attributed the illness to longstanding "internal frustration" and "forces of conscience which forbid the subject to gain the long hoped-for advantage from the fortunate change in reality."[1] Thus Freud establishes a model of unconscious mental life which clarifies the conflict between ascendancy and guilt, related to many difficulties and threats posed by conventional success. He identifies peculiar hostile and punishing trends as primitive moral aims stemming from forbidden wish fulfillment, and he discovers a chain of circumstance which could only come to grief.

In his struggle for worldly success, to be a great man at the center of literary society, Johnson was no stranger to the conflict between aggressive ambition and guilty self-punishment. He knew from personal experience the tumultuous feelings associated with being a have-not: "Ah, Sir, I was mad [rude] and violent,"[2] he describes to Boswell his brief residence at Oxford as a young man. Led on by a confusion of bravado and suffering, he explains, "It was bitterness which they mistook for frolick. I was miserably poor, and I thought to fight my way by my literature and my wits; so I disregarded all power and all authority."[3] To Fanny Burney, he represents the same: "When I was beginning the world, and was nothing and nobody, the joy of my life was to fire at all the established wits . . . to vanquish the great ones was all the delight of my poor little dear soul!"[4] Contention and envy are not surprising in one who early lavished his highest commendation on "starving merit," and lived by the plaintive motto, "SLOW RISES WORTH BY POVERTY DEPRESSED." As he approached middle life, Johnson saw many of his boyhood friends comfortably established in one or another of the professions,[5] not to mention the meteoric rise of his former pupil of the failed Edial school, David Garrick. What bitter consolation was to be found in the message from his old mentor, Gilbert Walmsley, himself a prosperous lawyer and Registrar of the Ecclesiastical Court of Lichfield, who wrote in 1746 to Garrick, asking him to tell the dissolute protégé, "I esteem him as a great genius—quite lost both to himself and the world."[6] At the lack of a settled profession, Johnson was always to bristle, even as late as his sixties, and he seems to have regretted missing, at least by his own standards, a certain heady ambition: for all he had won as a celebrated writer, Sir William Scott's compliment that he might have been Lord Chancellor and thus attained the peerage was taken so amiss that "Johnson, upon this, seemed much agitated; and, in an angry tone, exclaimed, 'Why will you vex me by suggesting this, when it is too late.'"[7]

More to the matter of Johnson's heated striving are copious illustrations by friends and acquaintances of how he "talked for victory," how he "tossed and gored" whatever contenders entered the ring.[8] Perhaps Sir Joshua Reynolds best captures this quality of willful belligerence, in a well-honed character sketch:

> The most light and airy dispute was with him a dispute on the arena. He fought on every occasion as if his whole reputation depended upon the victory of the minute, and he fought with all the weapons. If he was foiled in argument he had recourse to abuse and rudeness. . . . But what appears extraordinary is that a man who so well saw, himself, the folly of this ambition of shining, of speaking, or of acting always according to the character [he] imagined [he] possessed in the world, should produce himself the greatest example of a contrary conduct.[9]

But Sir Joshua also stresses a wholly different side of Johnson's "natural disposition," known best to his intimate circle. By all reports, his friends picture a dissonant set of emotions, as he is shown repeatedly begging pardon for a variety of reckless and unseemly affronts: of Boswell, whom he humiliated in company for interrupting him—"Well, I am sorry for it. I'll make it up to you twenty different ways, as you please"[10]; of Reynolds, in a quarrel at General Paoli's over taking too much wine—"(Drawing himself in, and, I really thought, blushing,) 'Nay, don't be angry, I did not mean to offend you.'";[11] of Bishop Percy, the unfortunate target of reprisal for an imagined insult, the gentleman first having to beg Johnson's pardon—"Dr. Percy rose, ran up to him, and taking him by the hand, assured him affectionately that his meaning had been misunderstood; upon which a reconciliation instantly took place";[12] of Dr. Burney, whom he contradicted with such apparent vehemence that "Mr. Johnson asked his pardon generously and genteelly, and when he had left the room rose up to shake hands with him, that they might part in peace."[13] Frances Reynolds recalls how, after roundly rebuking a dignitary of the Church at a dinner party, Johnson abjectly apologized to the lady of the house, and as soon as he could, "When the ——— [Reverend] came up into the Drawing-Room, Dr. Johnson immediately rose from his seat, and made him sit on the sophy [sic] by him, and with such a beseeching look for pardon, and with such fond gestures—literally smoothing down his arms and his knees—tokens of penitence, which were so graciously received by the ——— as to make Dr. Johnson very happy."[14] Mrs. Thrale frankly enumerates Johnson's stinging attacks on visitors of all sorts, quickly to be followed by remorse: "He did not wish to inflict the pain he gave, and was sometimes very sorry when he perceived the people to smart more than they deserved."[15] And Fanny Burney records the following colloquy between her hostess and Johnson:

> Dr. J.—Madam, I am always sorry when I make bitter speeches, and I never do it but when I am insufferably vexed.
>   Mrs. T.—Yes Sir; but you suffer things to vex you, that nobody else would vex at. I am sure I have had my share of scolding from you!
>   Dr. J.—It is true, you have; but you have borne it like an angel. . . . Mrs. Thrale is a sweet creature, and never angry; she has a temper the most delightful of any woman I ever knew.[16]

Obviously, the compliment is meant to make up for what would appear to be longstanding rudeness, but this is not to pull the wool over anyone's eyes. Mrs. Thrale's droll rating of her intractable guest as zero on "good humour"[17] certainly jibes with Boswell's amusing anecdote of riding one evening to dinner with Johnson, who observes: "It is wonderful, Sir, how rare a quality good humour is in life. We meet with very few good humoured men." Upon Boswell's offering several candidates, Johnson dismisses them all. "Then," according to the storyteller, "shaking his head and stretching himself at ease in the coach, and smiling with much complacency, he turned to me and said, 'I look upon *myself* as a good humoured fellow.'"[18] Boswell says he was highly diverted but soon struck with wonder, as well he might be. Though Johnson apparently made jest of his rankling temper, to what extent did he fathom his clear culpability and guilty struggles to make amends?

The ferocity of Johnson's "burning to be great," so sharply at variance with his self-reproach, can never be underestimated as a distraught modus vivendi. Despite the indulgence of his friends, he often appears to suffer the consequences of this especially painful disorientation. Nowhere does the problem crop up more dramatically than in the famous scene of penance at Uttoxeter, where he recreates a profound Oedipal crisis of his life. Fifty years after he had refused to help his ailing father by attending the old man's bookstall in a neighboring marketplace, Johnson returned to Uttoxeter and stood bareheaded in the rain, as if to atone for the sin. Undoubtedly he grieved for what he had done, but might his suffering not obscure still powerful feelings of defiance and vindictive triumph, in heightened repetition of a familiar conflict. In the past, and to an even greater degree, in the present, he held ascendancy over the impoverished bookseller: then he was an aspirant to fame and fortune; now he was the pre-eminent literary man of his day. Explaining the cruel spurn to his father's request, Johnson says, "My pride prevented me from doing my duty, and I gave my father a refusal." Unquestionably he felt remorse, but might his contrition not cover up, on the deeper level, still festering wounds, not to mention a vainglorious conquest over a contemptible foe. Certainly the scene he describes has strangely mixed undertones of effrontery as well as of mourning: "Going into the market at the time of high business, [I] uncovered my head, and stood with it bare an hour before the stall which my father had formerly used, exposed to the sneers of the standers-by and the inclemency of the weather."[19] Johnson's act seems to convey much of the exhibitionist frenzy of those "wrecked by success," the quality of the self-destructive poseur, whose unconsciously influenced ordeal brings him to pursue failure and unhappiness.

In the decade between the writing of *The Vanity of Human Wishes* (1749) and *Rasselas* (1759), Johnson consolidated his views on the discovery of hidden conflicts and invisible pressures bearing on the making of men's minds. He developed one of the most remarkable schemata before Freud on problems rooted in hitherto unperceived mental acts and agencies. Johnson's early middle-life was the period of his greatest productivity, notably the completion of the *Dictionary* (1755) after nine exhausting years as a "harmless drudge" and the extended project of the periodical essays through the 1750s. Indeed, he turns the latter into a vital medium for the interpretation and clarification of mental processes, and one suspects that the Johnson who recommends keeping a journal to record "the state of your own mind,"[20] is wrestling in these dutifully consigned pieces with his own deepest preoccupations. As Boswell suggests, "Notwithstanding his constitutional indolence, his depression of spirits, and his labour in carrying on his *Dictionary*, he answered the stated calls of the press twice a week from the stores of his mind."[21] A kind of psychopathology of everyday life, the periodical essays are garnered out of Johnson's intimate experience, out of the struggle for understanding which caused him frequently to jot down a record of his thoughts and activities. His Proustian autobiography and *Prayers and Meditations* are the purest remaining evidence of this monumental self-analysis, not to mention the large masses of private papers he destroyed shortly before his death. For Johnson, these writings must have been important vehicles for identifying and managing a tumultuous inner life. By the same token, the periodical essays, written at the threshold of middle life, launch into depths of persistent, often elusive themes of human desire, gratification, and frustration. Whatever their professed moral or religious design, they have the power of a moving personal testament.[22] Pervaded by motifs of discord and suffering, particularly the *Rambler*, which was written during his wife Tetty's protracted illness leading to her death, the periodical essays contain a world of unconscious meaning, of underlying metaphors and dramatizations played out in the mode of everyday reality.

Viewed for their deeper content, the periodical essays explore feelings of severe anxiety, with allusions to injury, betrayal, seduction, threat, loss, and other forms of dismal privation. But however laden with these familiar issues, they also counteract a compulsion to despair by their bold and aggressive intelligence. They hold the possibility for insight and readiness for change, staunchly to resist the age's fashionable contagions, spawned of rationalism and helpless passivity. Significantly, it was during the 1750s that Johnson's reputation was becoming assured. He was achieving his dream of being a great man at the center of literary society. As if to efface the youthful

memory of neglect and affliction, he attained a position of national eminence, crowned by the award in 1762 of an annual pension. But for all the
trappings of prosperity, he seems at the same time to have typified the
person who is "wrecked by success," who snatches defeat, as it has been put,
out of the jaws of victory. Certainly the *Rambler*, *Idler*, and *Adventurer*
essays of the 1750s reflect this profound ambivalence, arguably the prevailing quality of Johnson's emotional state during the still relatively obscure
middle years.[23]

Tracking elusive psychological landscapes, the periodical essays need
to be viewed through an analytic spectrum. How, for example, does Johnson escape the deeply embedded emotional squalor to become a worldly
man? How does he find alternatives to the internal world of bad objects, all
but indelibly impressed during childhood and early adulthood? In the
personal references scattered through the Preface to the *Dictionary*, he
conveys some sense of this vast subterranean toil, to be appraised alongside
the magnitude of his professional achievement. As he dedicates the com-
pendious volumes "to the honour of my country," we catch a glimpse of
him dramatically poised between vaunting ambition and self-pity:

> Whether I shall add any thing by my own writings to the reputation of English
> literature must be left to time: much of my life has been lost under the pressure
> of disease; much has been trifled away; and much has always been spent in
> provision for the day that was passing over me; but I shall not think my
> employment useless or ignoble, if by my assistance foreign nations, and distant
> ages, gain access to the propagators of knowledge, and understand the teachers
> of truth; if my labours afford light to the repositories of science, and add
> celebrity to Bacon, to Hooker, to Milton, and to Boyle.
>
> When I am animated by this wish, I look with pleasure on my book,
> however defective, and deliver it to the world with the spirit of a man that has
> endeavoured well.[24]

If flushed with victory, he squares off against all rivals. He notoriously
trounces Lord Chesterfield, a fitting image of the Oedipal father, deathless
and forever the object of reckoning. Spurning the ancient prerogative of his
Lordship, who offered (belatedly) to sponsor the *Dictionary*, he, in effect,
challenges the "lordship" of many others: fond and foolish old Michael
Johnson; the mentors, Cornelius Ford and Gilbert Walmsley, however well-
inclined; his employers, Sir Wolstan Dixie, a boorish, ill-tempered man,
and Edward Cave, that taciturn, "penurious pay-master";[25] and very likely
more. In all too telling and provoking ways have they exacted compliance,
emulation, servility, much the same.[26] But progressively he establishes a

difference. Johnson now takes the measure of his own accomplishment, and, in doing so, he stands apart from the conflagration of grandiose wishes, to be warded off by envy and guilt. With keen irony and perhaps more self-awareness than is commonly accorded him in the famous letter,[27] which Thomas Carlyle called "the death-knell of patronage," he exposes the dangerous kernel of vindictive aims: "I was overpowered like the rest of Mankind by the enchantment of your address, and could not forbear to wish that I might boast my self Le Vainquer du Vainquer de la Terre, that I might obtain that regard for which I saw the world contending."[28] From this bondage to infantile fantasy, to fixed and pervasive ideas of assault and subsequent ruin, Johnson struggles to be free. He explores how it is to be thrown on one's own resources, beginning with the *Rambler*.

*   *   *

Embarking on a new course of his career with the first printing of the *Rambler* in March 1750, Johnson means to settle old scores. He seeks the hidden arsenal of psychological defenses that man deploys to hold off intolerable wishes and overpowering anxieties. Using the example of his own risky enterprize, he inaugurates the series by inquiring into experiences of impending disaster, of feeling at the mercy of doubtful, if not malignant, forces. Aside from the obvious external difficulties that are common enough, he appears more interested in the inward obstacles that bedevil the newly launched author. *Ramblers* 1, 2, and 3 present a striking picture of jeopardy, of being bombarded on the one side by ardent wishes for success, on the other, by oppressive forebodings of failure. Evidently this most interesting battle takes place between warring factions of the mind, pitting motives against their constraints, the ubiquity of impulse against its obstruction. The arena is fraught with unresolved tension, where Johnson delves to deeper levels of contradiction and concealment. In *Rambler* 1, a sardonic wit overlays feelings of disruption and qualms about putting oneself forward as a candidate for literary fame. He pictures himself in the queasy role of a would-be suitor: "Since the world supposes every man that writes ambitious of applause, as some ladies have taught themselves to believe that every man intends love, who expresses civility, the miscarriage of any endeavour in learning raises an unbounded contempt, indulged by most minds without scruple, as an honest triumph over unjust claims, and exorbitant expectations." To ward off this unpleasing ambivalence, he must resort to subterfuge: "The artifices of those who put themselves in this hazardous state, have therefore been multiplied in proportion to their fear as well as their ambition; and are to be looked upon with more indulgence, as they are incited at once by the two great movers of the human mind, the desire of good, and the fear of evil." But for now, he dismisses it all as a silly charade, and his irreverence purely smacks of those novitiate years in London: "For who can wonder that, allured on one side, and frightned on the other, some should endeavour to gain favour by bribing the judge with an appearance of respect which they do not feel, to excite compassion by confessing weakness of which they are not convinced, and others to attract regard by a shew of openness and magnanimity, by a daring profession of their own deserts, and a publick challenge of honours and rewards?" (*Works*, 3: 6).

Dropping the snide cover and in earnest in the next essay, he shows how the most potent of human strivings never seem to ripen into reward, but are merely self-perpetuating:

> This quality of looking forward into futurity seems the unavoidable condition of a being, whose motions are gradual, and whose life is progressive: as his powers are limited, he must use means for the attainment of his ends, and intend first what he performs last; as, by continual advances from his first stage of existence, he is perpetually varying the horizon of his prospects, he must always discover new motives of action, new excitements of fear, and allurements of desire. The end therefore which at present calls forth our efforts will be found, when it is once gained, to be only one of the means to some remoter end. The natural flights of the human mind are not from pleasure to pleasure, but from hope to hope. (*Rambler* 2, *Works*, 3: 10)

As he will elucidate in *Ramblers* to come, this orchestration of human desire entails a monumental struggle. It opposes anticipated success to a self-punishing pursuit of failure, an archaic moral aim from within, that strives to counteract the positive, triumphant experience. Here in these early essays, the "fears," "doubts," and "terrours," which Johnson carefully balances against "hopes," wishes," and "ambition," indicate primitive wreckage dictated by darker impulses of the psyche. With increasing tenacity, he understands these impulses and endeavors to describe them analytically. What are in *Rambler* 3 external persecutors—rabid critics, spewing malevolence and causing him to dread "the united attacks of this virulent generation" (*Works*, 3: 16)—become in following essays treacherous enemies from within. Much as he converted his personal experience to the use of psychological insight in the *Life of Savage* and other early works, Johnson recognizes familiar metaphors of wreckage, which engage his own deepest beliefs and assumptions about himself. His analysis of the old seduction to rack and ruin helps diminish its power over him, while he educates others who are plagued alike.

Adopting the persona of a paranoid author in *Rambler* 16, Johnson shows how delusions of grandeur and persecution are set in counterpoint, one against the other, in an exaggerated picture of a success-wrecker. A haughty young man parades his accomplishment with all manner of pert and supercilious airs. His first publication, which he anticipated with "raptures" and "defiance" (*Works*, 3: 87), was met with prodigious acclaim, this, according to him, and only after he elicited profuse flattery from his friends, whom he treated to a week-long drunk, "a kind of literary revel" (89). But he soon finds that celebrity invites hostility and believes he sees others "raging with envy," that he can discover "the secret rancour of their heart" (89). Feeling increasingly beset by villains, he at first attempts to face them down but soon shrinks in terror at their very gaze. They dog him pitilessly in order to steal his portrait as well as his papers. He takes precautions by keeping an iron chest and a padlock on his door and moving five times a week, always in the dead of night. By the terms of his matchless superiority, the more he stews, the more his fortunes fly:

> I live, in consequence of having given too great proofs of a predominant genius, in the solitude of a hermit, with the anxiety of a miser, and the caution of an outlaw; afraid to shew my face, lest it should be copied; afraid to speak, lest I should injure my character, and to write lest my correspondents should publish my letters; always uneasy lest my servants should steal my papers for the sake of money, or my friends for that of the publick. Thus it is to soar above the rest of mankind. (91)

Miscellus (in Latin, poor, little) exhibits, albeit in caricature, the process by which self-punishing behavior may follow on the heels of conquest and presumed overthrow of one's rivals. The dread and intimidation he feels are projections of internal self-contempt, a retaliation for vaunting ambition and a mask for worthlessness and deficiency. His self-importance shoots up at the cost of more deeply submerging his faults. By tracking the flow of accolades to its core of weakness and inferiority, Johnson exposes this character's defensive security. "I . . . am condemned, irreversibly condemned, to all the miseries of high reputation," (88) Miscellus exults with apparent illogic. But his victory makes sense in the realm of mental happenings, that it exists in ever-present ironic tension with crushing inadequacy and defeat.

Another instance of the wrecking action Johnson often associates with success is to be found in two *Rambler* articles analyzing "bashfulness." The condition is described by one sufferer, aflame with grand intent, as he enters a large assembly and gets stampeded by little more than his own vagaries:

> The whole company rose at my entrance; but when I saw so many eyes fixed at once upon me, I was blasted with a sudden imbecility, I was quelled by some nameless power which I found impossible to be resisted. My sight was dazzled, my cheeks glowed, my perceptions were confounded; I was harassed by the multitude of eager salutations, and returned the common civilities with hesitation and impropriety; the sense of my own blunders encreased my confusion, and before the exchange of ceremonies allowed me to sit down, I was ready to sink under the oppression of surprize; my voice grew weak, and my knees trembled. (*Rambler* 157, *Works*, 5: 72–73)

Once more, Johnson sets up the antithesis of irreconcilable emotions, as he views the restraints imposed by bashfulness not only as social discomfiture but as a "disease of the mind" (*Rambler* 159, *Works*, 5: 83). Inquiring into the disturbance for its deeper causes, he finds that bashfulness slyly tallies with reckless deeds, i.e., the fierce convictions which many "have panted to advance at the hazard of contempt and hatred, when they found themselves irresistibly depressed by a languid anxiety, which seized them at the moment of utterance, and still gathered strength from their endeavours to resist it" (81). The essay abounds in pictures of vehement reaction: "To excite opposition and influence malevolence is the unhappy privilege of courage made arrogant by consciousness of strength" (82). No sooner does an aggressive wish rear up, than it is countered by furious forces of the opposite direction. The bolder the aim, the angrier the retaliation, and in these terms, the bashful individual has his courage almost wholly subverted. He feels a "frigorific power . . . [and is] impeded by a timidity which he himself knows to be vitious, and must struggle long against dejection and reluctance" (82). What brings on such numbing disability is construed by Johnson as a response to intolerable inner demands. He shows how wishful anticipation of overmatching others sabotages performance and achievement. He detects how grandiose wishes cohabit with anxieties of being exposed and rendered worthless: "No cause more frequently produces bashfulness than too high an opinion of our own importance. He that imagines an assembly filled with his merit, panting with expectation, and hushed with attention, easily terrifies himself with the dread of disappointing them, and strains his imagination in pursuit of something that may vindicate the veracity of fame, and shew that his reputation was not gained by chance" (84). It is another kind of brinkmanship, where "renown or infamy are suspended upon every syllable," where one hazards all in frantic derring-do or die. Despair is the consequence of being thus driven by stresses and strains that derive their influence from inward persecution: "Under such solicitude, who can wonder that the mind is overwhelmed, and by struggling with attempts above her strength, quickly sinks into languishment and despondency" (84).[29]

Other pretenders to fame and fortune in the *Rambler* are similarly inclined to radical inconsistencies outside the domain of normal awareness. *Ramblers* 144, 145, and 146 are a sagacious threesome that show how aspiring authors risk vicious onslaught and incite the enmity of others. They are besieged by "armies of malignity" and "invisible assailants." Duly noted is the peculiar contrariety, the defiance and hurt, with which they meet the attack. No sooner does a man achieve success, does he "emerge from the crowd, and fix the eyes of the publick upon him, than he stands as a mark to the arrows of lurking calumny, and receives, in the tumult of hostility, from distant and from nameless hands, wounds not easily to be cured" (*Rambler* 144, *Works*, 5: 4). His tormentors are clearly recognized from the outside as "persecutors of merit" (5), and the havoc they create, to be sure, is externally evinced: "Such are the arts by which the envious, the idle, the peevish, and the thoughtless, obstruct that worth which they cannot equal, and by artifices thus easy, sordid, and detestable, is industry defeated, beauty blasted, and genius depressed" (7). Sizing up the objective situation, Johnson urges that "the common interest of learning requires that her sons should cease from intestine hostilities, and instead of sacrific-ing each other to malice and contempt, endeavour to avert persecution from the meanest of their fraternity." (*Rambler* 145, *Works*, 5: 12) But when he comes to analyze the wreckage from the inside, he finds wounds more deeply lodged and not so readily redressed.

"When once a man has made celebrity necessary to his happiness, he has put it in the power of the weakest and most timorous malignity, if not to take away his satisfaction, at least to withhold it" (*Rambler* 146, *Works*, 5: 13), he states in the final essay of the series. Here is an overture to the unsuspected draffs of secret malignity, which cannot be imputed merely to the florid literary rivalries noted earlier. The three essays need to be taken as a whole in order to see how Johnson develops the theme of unconsciously designed and executed self-injury. What began as external persecution now focuses upon the internal; what was evaded through plausible explanation of the wrath of others now becomes self-induced calamity by which individuals bring on their own failure and unhappiness. Like previous success-wreckers, the aspirant helplessly dangles through vacillating extremes, now buoyant, now dashed. Not unacquainted with its ludicrous side, Johnson describes how he anticipates his triumph when he first slips out incognito to simper and gloat: "When a writer has with long toil produced a work intended to burst upon mankind with unexpected lustre, and withdraw the attention of the learned world from every other controversy or enquiry, he is seldom contented to wait long without the enjoyment of his new praises. With an imagination full of his own importance, he walks out like a monarch in disguise, to learn the various opinions of his readers" (13). But meeting with ignorance and rebuffs on every side, he soon grows un-manageable, "violent and tumultuous." The impetuous author's wretched-ness increases in the same proportion as his hopes, and so must he invent excuses "to allay his vexation." In the manner of his confederacy, he dredges up the usual suspects, that "his enemies, such as superiority will always raise, have been industrious, while his performance was in the press, to vilify and blast it; and that the bookseller, whom he had resolved to enrich, has rivals that obstruct the circulation of his copies" (15). Turning solemnly at last to the underlying issue, Johnson explains, "By such arts of voluntary delusion does every man endeavour to conceal his own unimportance from himself. . . . It seems not to be sufficiently considered how little renown can be admitted in the world" (15–16). The delusion reaches to the very core of disturbance, now to be owned. It is a way of protecting against the inherent dualism of forces in the mind, the concealed and contradictory impulses, ever colliding in monstrous futility. In a brilliant reading of man's ineradi-cable ambivalence, Johnson defines the struggle in Oedipal terms. He postulates how desire and destruction coexist as natural determinants of the human lot:

> The hope of fame is necessarily connected with such considerations as must abate the ardour of confidence, and repress the vigour of pursuit. Whoever claims renown from any kind of excellence, expects to fill the place which is now possessed by another; . . . and surely he that is pushing his predecessors into the gulph of obscurity, cannot but sometimes suspect, that he must himself sink in like manner, and as he stands upon the same precipice, be swept away with the same violence. (17)

*   *   *

In a rare moment of self-dramatization, infused by some waggery, the Rambler comes alive to poke fun at his pious suffering. A "correspondent" addresses him on the subject of a delectable new grief:

Sir,

Though you seem to have taken a view sufficiently extensive of the miseries of
life, and have employed much of your speculation on mournful subjects, you
have not exhausted the whole stock of human infelicity. There is still a species
of wretchedness which escapes your observation, though it might supply you
with many sage remarks, and salutary cautions. I cannot but imagine the start
of attention awakened by this welcome hint; and at this instant see the
Rambler snuffing his candle, rubbing his spectacles, stirring his fire, locking
out interruption, and settling himself in his easy chair, that he may enjoy a new
calamity without disturbance. For, whether it be, that continued sickness or
misfortune has acquainted you only with the bitterness of being; or that you
imagine none but yourself able to discover what I suppose has been seen and
felt by all the inhabitants of the world: whether you intend your writings as
antidotal to the levity and merriment with which your rivals endeavour to
attract the favour of the publick; or fancy that you have some particular powers
of dolorous declamation, and "warble out your groans" with uncommon
elegance or energy; it is certain, that whatever be your subject, melancholy for
the most part bursts in upon your speculation, your gaiety is quickly overcast,
and though your readers may be flattered with hopes of pleasantry, they are
seldom dismissed but with heavy hearts. (*Rambler*, 109, *Works*, 4: 215–16)

Johnson's self-mocking comment on his achievement invites its own
comment. If the periodical essays descend to dank and gloomy regions of
human experience, he wryly acknowledges that effect to set his work apart
from that of countless others. No light-hearted frolic across dainty flower-
ing gardens serves the geologist of the mind. In the role of sober moral
essayist, Johnson comes into his own. If his writings bear the traces of his
life, he dares to patrol the precipices of the mental underworld, more so
than his contemporaries. Staking a territory doubtless more craggy than the
arbiter elegantarium of Addison and Steele's *Spectator* (1711–12) with its
legion of imitators,[30] and venturing outside the pale of ethical, religious,
and medical systems, dominated by a rage for Reason, as we have seen,
Johnson presses on to unexplored repositories. Their buried secrets, much
as the "unsuspected cavities" in Rasselas's palace, lie darkly hidden and
drastically shunned. But Johnson grapples with the redoubtable forces that
inhabit there: the archaic desires, unheeded motives, the concealed stratagems of mental events. He creates a psychopathology of everyday life out
of a unique engagement with irrational springs of action, where the assumption of a dynamic unconscious is not merely conjectural, it is real.
Avoiding traps of rationalist subterfuge, chiefly the inveigling guideposts
of moral-didacticism which set the tone and direction of the psychiatry of
his age, he takes the high empiricist road. He seeks the process by which

individuals are buffeted by conflict, riven by ambivalent emotion, and impelled by powers that catch them unawares. For Johnson, mental problems were accessible by exposing their delusional bases. In this respect, the *Rambler*, *Idler*, and *Adventurer* essays employ distinctively radical methods to heal the demons of the mind.

The periodical essays are pervaded by the subject of mental suffering and how it originates in various disguised and contradictory strands of experience. The "tyranny" or "dominion" of the mind, Johnson's salient idea, uncovers an arsenal of stratagems, operating through phobias, compulsive acts, inhibition, repression, and the like. He commonly traces this interior chain of command to crude and, for the most part, vaguely detectable sources, and he regards their deterministic function:

> Whoever shall review his life will generally find, that the whole tenor of his conduct has been determined by some accident of no apparent moment, or by a combination of inconsiderable circumstances, acting when his imagination was unoccupied, and his judgment unsettled; and that his principles and actions have taken their colour from some secret infusion, mingled without design in the current of his ideas. The desires that predominate in our hearts, are instilled by imperceptible communications, at the time when we look upon the various scenes of the world, and the different employments of men, with the neutrality of inexperience; and we come forth from the nursery or the school, invariably destined to the pursuit of great acquisitions, or petty accomplishments. (*Rambler* 141, *Works*, 4: 383–84)

The doctrine of psychological determinism relates integrally to Johnson's view of the mind struggling in the grips of causality. He frequently pictures a galling onslaught of action and reaction, of simultaneously wishing, anticipating, fearing, refraining. Over and again, he ferrets out dissonant enigmatic forces, operating with a secret dynamic of their own. They emerge as the anguish of unslaked desire. The theme works ubiquitously through many vivid and concrete passages: "Unnatural desires insinuate themselves unobserved into the mind, and we do not perceive that they are gaining upon us, till the pain which they give us awakens us to notice" (*Adventurer* 119, *Works*, 2: 462–63). And again: "The pleasures of fancy, and the emotions of desire are more dangerous as they are more hidden, since they escape the awe of observation, and operate equally in every situation, without the concurrence of external opportunities" (*Rambler* 8, *Works*, 3: 46). The cruel travesties of human endeavor—why people sabotage their careers, languish in seclusion, give themselves up to uncontrollable passions which in their sober moments they know to be absurd—all of these lurk in the concealed corridors of the mind. Bringing them to light, Johnson is eloquent, penetrating, moving:

> This invisible riot of this mind, the secret prodigality of being, is secure from detection, and fearless of reproach. The dreamer retires to his apartments, shuts out the cares and interruptions of mankind, and abandons himself to his own fancy; new worlds rise up before him, one image is followed by another, and a long succession of delights dances round him. . . . The infatuation strengthens by degrees, and, like the poison of opiates, weakens his powers, without any external symptom of malignity. . . . But they who are convinced of the necessity of breaking from this habitual drowsiness, too often relapse in spite of their resolution; for these ideal seducers are always near; . . . they invade the soul without warning, and have often charmed down resistance before their approach is perceived or suspected. (*Rambler* 89, *Works*, 4: 106–07)

What is more, the addictive potency of these stimuli looms large, setting off a chain of irresistible cravings:[31] "Every desire, however innocent, grows dangerous, as by long indulgence it becomes ascendent in the mind. When we have been accustomed to consider any thing as capable of giving happiness, it is not easy to restrain our ardour, or to forbear some precipitation in our advances, and irregularity in our persuits" (*Rambler* 207, *Works*, 5: 312). But like the effects of drunkenness, the excitement is quickly exhausted, giving way to a deadening stupor: "These [fond hopes], like all other cordials, though they may invigorate in a small quantity, intoxicate in a greater; these pleasures . . . become dangerous and destructive, when once they gain ascendant in the heart. . . . To lull our faculties in a lethargy, is poor and despicable" (*Adventurer* 69, *Works*, 2: 394). Speaking directly to the irrational, to the chimerical, Johnson confronts the most drastically edited of human conceptions, which are submerged, to use his thrilling phrase, in "some internal consciousness":[32] "Nothing is to be estimated by its effect upon common eyes and common ears. A thousand miseries make silent and invisible inroads on mankind, and the heart feels innumerable throbs which never break into complaint. Perhaps, likewise, our pleasures are for the most part equally secret, and most are borne up by some private satisfaction, some internal consciousness, some latent hope, some peculiar prospect, which they never communicate . . . " (*Rambler* 68, *Works*, 3: 359). He evokes the wasteful energies contending one against the other to break down volition and abridge freedom: "Every submission to our fear enlarges its dominion. . . . The case of Tantalus, in the region of poetick punishment, was somewhat to be pitied, because the fruits that hung about him retired from his hand; but what tenderness can be claimed by those who though perhaps they suffer the pains of Tantalus will never lift their hands for their own relief?" (*Rambler* 134, *Works*, 4: 347).

The continual craving for gratification, in *Rasselas*, "that hunger of imagination which preys incessantly upon life" (*Works*, 16: 118), lends a powerful incentive to many of the character sketches appearing in the *Rambler* and *Idler*. Evidently, the theme is entangled with Johnson's own private conflicts, as Mrs. Thrale recalls him telling her, the character of Sober, for one, was "intended as his own portrait"[33]: "Sober is a man of strong desires and quick imagination, . . . [which] will not suffer him to lie quite at rest, and though they do not make him sufficiently useful to others, they make him at least weary of himself" (*Idler* 31, *Works*, 2: 97). His analysis of character so rooted in self-analysis, Johnson conveys the sense of a hectic, unmanageable world, where one feels little more than subjective, ever-churning sources of agitation. He understands how the unremitting struggle for satisfaction impairs the enjoyment of living. Many of his fictional characters are embroiled in a tumult of prohibitive rituals and injunctions, by which they disavow their relation to others. Their anxious warnings and troubling defenses turn them away from reality.

In the history of Cupidus, Johnson illustrates a case of renunciation, which operates to hold strong desire at bay. Cupidus grew up in a family where "visionary opulence" was the sole occupation. The group met for years determining schemes of pleasure that depended on the inheritance of a large fortune from relatives who threatened never to die. When finally the relatives did so, they went in protracted succession, to the accompaniment of the family's exasperation and own decline, until only Cupidus is left to execute in truth what they all could only imagine. He complains, however, that he is rendered incapable of enjoying the riches, and instead, finds himself in the grips of a fateful irrationality:

> I have returned again to my old habit of wishing. Being accustomed to give the future full power over my mind, and to start away from the scene before me to some expected enjoyment, I deliver up myself to the tyranny of every desire which fancy suggests, and long for a thousand things which I am unable to procure. . . . I had formed schemes which I cannot execute, I had supposed events which do not come to pass, and the rest of my life must pass in craving solicitude, unless you can find some remedy for a mind, corrupted with an inveterate disease of wishing, and unable to think on any thing but wants, which reason tells me will never be supplied. (*Rambler* 73, *Works*, 4: 22)

Having given up all of his claims for happiness to a fantasy life, Cupidus droops behind barriers to the outside world. He is at once insatiable and living in dread of satiety, never having taken in real interests or relationships: "I had not enlarged by conceptions either by books or conversation" (19). By dint of his impossible designs, he is necessarily riven by vehement needs and dim forebodings of their consummation.

Cupidus's problem resembles that of another Johnsonian fantasist, Dick Linger, weighed down by "listlessness." Having frittered away some years as a soldier in a time of peace, he inherits a small fortune and believes through his new independence, "I had now found what every man desires" (*Idler* 21, *Works*, 2: 67). But before too long, he surrenders once more to idleness. It is clear from the story that Linger's truculent idleness is rooted in wishes made unattainable by his fears. As he pictures the first withering onslaught: "I soon perceived my spirits to subside, and my imagination to grow dark. The gloom thickened every day around me. I wondered by what malignant power my peace was blasted" (67). He had begun his narrative by describing the warring internal factions that have rendered him all but lost to life: "Those only will sympathize with my complaint, whose imagination is active and resolution weak, whose desires ardent, and whose choice is delicate; who cannot satisfy themselves with standing still, and yet cannot find a motive to direct their course" (66). And he ends with the same immobilizing tactics that seal his doom:

> Burthensome to myself and others, I form many schemes of employment which may make my life useful or agreeable, and exempt me from the ignominy of living by sufferance. The new course I have long designed but have not yet begun. The present moment is never proper for the change, but there is always a time when all obstacles will be removed, and I shall surprize all that know me with a new distribution of my time. Twenty years have past since I resolved a complete amendment, and twenty years have been lost in delays. (68)

Like Cupidus, poor Linger is chronically remote and disengaged.

Perhaps the most pitiable Johnsonian fantasist is Victoria, who was taught only to exult in her beauty, so that when she contracts smallpox she loses her sole means of happiness along with her looks. In an account which enlists our compassion, where another writer might have looked for moral disdain, Victoria tells of being for the first time without a young woman's cherished "excellence":

> She is at once deprived of all that gave her eminence or power; of all that elated her pride, or animated her activity; all that filled her days with pleasure and her nights with hope; all that gave gladness to the present hour, or brightened her prospects of futurity. . . . [Imagine] such helpless destitution, such dismal

inanity. Every object of pleasing contemplation is at once snatched away, and the soul finds every receptacle of ideas empty, or filled only with the memory of joys that can return no more. All is gloomy privation, or impotent desire; the faculties of anticipation slumber in despondency, or the powers of pleasure mutiny for employment. (*Rambler* 133, *Works*, 4: 342)

Victoria's predicament borrows from Johnson's customary model of the mind's impoverishment through rude contending forces, now to excite, now to subdue. Clearly he suggests she was diseased before the onset of smallpox. Encouraged to bask in her specialness, she was predisposed to create fantasies of a grandiose self: "I was born a beauty. From the dawn of reason I had my regard turned wholly upon myself, nor can recollect any thing earlier than praise and admiration. . . . My mother . . . contemplated me as an assemblage of all that could raise envy or desire, and predicted with triumphant fondness the extent of my conquests, and number of my slaves" (*Rambler* 130, *Works*, 4: 326–27). Early infected by megalomania, Victoria's relationships are characterized by extreme self-centeredness, coldness, ruthlessness, envy, exploitation, in short, by little pleasure other than her imagined omnipotence and the extorted tribute of others. A goddess sustained by icy forms and illusions, she never participated in sublunary affairs and is loath to do so in her present crisis: "None had any care to find amusements for me, and I had no power of amusing myself. Idleness exposed me to melancholy, and life began to languish in motionless indifference" (*Rambler* 133, *Works*, 4: 344). She thus experiences the world in a primitive and frightening way—devoid of meaning, devoid of nourishment, devoid of love.

There can be no question that Johnson discerned the covert agencies of primitive instinct and was not reluctant to portray them. By contrast, however, to the romantic primitivism of Jean-Jacques Rousseau and other influential naturalist writers, his is an expression of a radical kind. Far from the high-flying rationalist paradigms, that man desires the good and left to "follow Nature" he will discover virtue, happiness, and truth, Johnson argues trenchantly along experiential lines. In the tradition of Hobbes and Mandeville,[34] which culminated in Darwin and Freud, he depicts man as a creature aflame with irreconcilable passions: to love and to destroy. For him, human beings harbor fierce archaic impulses, the more terrifying as they are the more discoverable under multi-layered operations of the psyche. And these incitements to disaster are to be controlled by necessary cultural coercions. In effect, Johnson sees society as a mass of isolated, hostile individuals, who inflict suffering on one another as they compete for the very same goals. Cautioning, for example, youthful entrants into the world about "the depravity of mankind," he writes:

> He surely is an useful monitor, who inculcates to these thoughtless strangers, that the "majority are wicked": who informs them, that the train which wealth and beauty draw after them, is lured only by the scent of prey; and that, perhaps, among all those who croud about them with professions and flatteries, there is not one who does not hope for some opportunity to devour or betray them, to glut himself by their destruction, or to share their spoils with a stronger savage. (*Rambler* 175, *Works*, 5: 161)

Civilization and government thus become mere preventive measures: neither are they nor their converse, Nature, to be magically endowed: "The end of all civil regulations is to secure private happiness from private malignity; to keep individuals from the power of one another" (*Idler* 22, *Works*, 2: 70). In his most vitriolic polemics, Johnson is keen on unmasking for his starry-eyed adversaries the primitive unmajesty of men, when left to their own devices. Warning sympathizers with the colonists in *Taxation No Tyranny* (1775), for example, he paints a cataclysmic picture of the effects of revoking the governmental charter: "The society is dissolved into a tumult of individuals, without authority to command, or obligation to obey; without any punishment of wrongs but by personal resentment, or any protection of right but by the hand of the possessor" (*Works*, 10: 425). By suspending the power of institutions and thereby the bonds of civil authority, individuals would sink into chaos and acts of internecine slaughter.[35] These same views of the absolute antagonism between civilization and human instinct underlie basic themes in his contributions to the Vinerian lectures on law, as well as in the *Lives of the Poets*, as we shall see.

Perhaps Johnson's most dramatic example of the perils of unlicensed instinct is in the original *Idler* 22 on the vultures, suppressed when the essays were collected in book form, undoubtedly because he or his printer thought it too shocking for the general public.[36] Using the metaphor of cannibalism, he disinters the darkest origins of oral and sadistic rage. Cannibals believe in the power of magic, in the might of their own wishes, divined in words and enacted in rites, to conquer the world. If they want to possess the strength of an enemy, then they make of him a tasty morsel. They do not know guilt for this deed, only pride. Bloodshed and oral incorporation of the enemy offer triumph and the magical remission of sins.

Striking an uncharacteristically mordant pose in *Idler* 22, Johnson presents cannibalism in an ostensibly favorable light. The man-eating vultures, far from vicious or primitive, are a reasonable, eminently civilized lot. A family group is observed meeting for the last in a series of lectures on "the arts of a vulture's life," before being dismissed to the mountains and the skies. Their leader, a philosophic mother vulture, sits on a high rock with her young about her and begins a discourse on the martial arts: "My children, . . . you will the less want my instructions because you have had my practice before your eyes; you have seen me snatch from the farm the household fowl, you have seen me seize the leveret in the bush, and the kid in the pasture, you know how to fix your talons, and how to balance your flight when you are laden with your prey. But you remember the taste of more delicious food; I have often regaled you with the flesh of man" (*Idler* 22 (original), *Works*, 2: 318). Hardly an innocuous beast fable, Johnson's tale lurches into bizarre dimensions. As the mother vulture continues, he exposes the violent lust and butchery provoked in war:

> The vultures would seldom feast upon . . . flesh [of man], had not nature, that devoted him to our uses, infused into him a strange ferocity, which I have never observed in any other being that feeds upon the earth. Two herds of men will often meet and shake the earth with noise, and fill the air with fire. When you hear noise and see fire which flashes along the ground, hasten to the place with your swiftest wing, for men are surely destroying one another; you will then find the ground smoking with blood and covered with carcasses, of which many are dismembered, and mangled for the convenience of the vulture. (319)

With as gruesome an impact as Swift's *A Modest Proposal* (1729), the satire works to suggest that vulture strategies—suave, predatory, coolly rational—are in fact human strategies. Bolstered by their pseudo-dignity and unprincipled finesse, the vultures are really no different from their human counterparts on the field of battle. When a vulture-pupil naively asks, "When men have killed their prey . . . why do they not eat it? When the wolf has killed a sheep he suffers not the vulture to touch it till he has satisfied himself. Is not man another kind of wolf?" it is explained, "Man . . . is the only beast who kills that which he does not devour, and this quality makes him so much a benefactor to our species" (319). Propelled alike by ferocious instinct, vultures and humans believe they are supported and advanced by the blood-ritual of military aggression. Johnson facetiously registers even the vultures' astonishment at this ravenous need. Doubtless a sound environmentalist, the young one puzzles, "I would gladly know the reason of this mutual slaughter. I could never kill what I could not eat." (319). The grisly satire discloses the psychological meaning of warfare as the most cruel archaic sadism. As civilization regresses to the appetite of vultures, these creatures are the grotesque caricature of humankind: on the surface, polished, urbane, reasonable, but down deep, a seething mass of rapacity and rage, which, in the most barbaric enactment of primitive aggression, seeks to devour its own object. The mother vulture ends her lesson by describing to her brood the "beneficial" acts of military leaders: "There is, in every herd, one that gives directions to the rest, and seems to be more eminently delighted with a wide carnage. What it is that intitles him to such pre-eminence we know not; he is seldom the biggest or the swiftest, but he shews by his eagerness and diligence that he is, more than any of the others, a friend to vultures" (320). Thus human beings revert to the primordial condition of cannibals. They feed entire communities into the machinery of death.

Examining characters from many walks of life, Johnson articulates the deepest tensions plaguing modern society. He provides abundant examples of primitive instinct as it overtakes what decency and nobler values man develops in response to ineluctable necessity. Hostile impulses in the service of aggression are a social malady, the manifest symptom of which is a lapse in purposeful communication: "There is no crime more infamous than the violation of truth. It is apparent that men can be social beings no longer than they believe each other. When speech is employed only as the vehicle of falsehood, every man must disunite himself from others, inhabit his own cave, and seek prey only for himself" (*Idler* 20, *Works*, 2: 62). This quality of frightful alienation infests the murky caves and dens inhabited by many who labor in the dark all alone, the victim of fears of being invaded and despoiled. Ridden by paranoia, these characters must enact strange ceremonies which are often traced to delusions of grandeur and persecution. Their cold rationality and grim earnestness belie vehement defenses erected against what they experience as manifold attack:

> With Ned Smuggle all is a secret. He believes himself watched by observation and malignity on every side, and rejoices in the dexterity by which he has escaped snares that never were laid. Ned holds that a man is never deceived if he never trusts, and therefore will not tell the name of his taylor or his hatter; he rides out every morning for the air, and pleases himself with thinking that nobody knows where he has been; and when he dines with a friend he never goes to his house the nearest way, but walks up by a bye-street to perplex the scent. When he has a coach called he never tells him at the door the true place to which he is going, but stops him in the way that he may give him directions where nobody can hear him. The price of what he buys or sells is always concealed. He often takes lodgings in the country by a wrong name, and

thinks that the world is wondring where he can be hid. All these transactions he registers in a book, which, he says, will some time or other amaze posterity. (*Idler* 92, *Works*, 2: 286)

Further, tremendous anxiety about relationship and involvement weighs heavily upon the chronically guarded individual. Floundering in the grips of an unseen terror, he is arrested into non-commitment: "Sophron creeps along, neither loved nor hated, neither favoured nor opposed; he has never attempted to grow rich for fear of growing poor, and has raised no friends for fear of making enemies" (*Idler* 57, *Works*, 2: 180).

Many of Johnson's characters show telltale signs of a rupture with reality in patterns of estrangement and loss of conscious volition. The man given to fits of rage little understands "that he is mean enough to be driven from his post by every petty incident, that he is the mere slave of casualty, and that his reason and virtue are in the power of the wind" (*Rambler* 11, *Works*, 3:, 59). Suspirus the "screech-owl" is scarcely moved by his auguries of doom and gloom, just as he is locked into one invariable subject, which the Rambler observes,

> I do not perceive that his mournful meditations have much effect upon himself. He talks, and has long talked of calamities, without discovering, otherwise than by the tone of his voice, that he feels any of the evils which he bewails or threatens, but has the same habit of uttering lamentations, as others of telling stories, and falls into expressions of condolence for past, or apprehension of future mischiefs, as all men studious of their ease have recourse to those subjects upon which they can most fluently or copiously discourse. (*Rambler* 59, *Works*, 3: 317)

Lady Bustle deftly displaces her traumas and flies from life in a fierce regimen of domestic duties:[37]

> Lady Bustle has, indeed, by this incessant application to fruits and flowers, contracted her cares into a narrow space, and set herself free from many perplexities with which other minds are disturbed. She has no curiosity after the events of a war, nor the fate of heroes in distress; she can hear, without the least emotion, the ravage of a fire, or devastations of a storm; her neighbours grow rich or poor, come into the world or go out of it, without regard, while she is pressing the gelly-bag, or airing the store-room; but I cannot perceive that she is more free from disquiets than those whose understandings take a wider range. Her marigolds when they are almost cured, are often scattered by the wind, the rain sometimes falls upon fruit when it ought to be gathered dry. While her artificial wines are fermenting, her whole life is restlessness and anxiety. Her sweetmeats are not always bright, and the maid sometimes

forgets the just proportions of salt and pepper, when venison is to be baked. Her conserves mould, her wines sour, and pickles mother; and, like all the rest of mankind, she is every day mortified with the defeat of her schemes, and the disappointment of her hopes. (*Rambler* 52, *Works*, 3: 278)

And Anthea's phobic aversion to a coach ride in the country with her lover is helplessly exciting by perpetual frights and panics and rows, from which she is curiously removed. As the poor gentleman describes it:

Our whole conversation passed in dangers, and cares, and fears, and consolations, and stories of ladies dragged in the mire, forced to spend all the night on a heath, drowned in rivers, or burnt with lightening; and no sooner had a hairbreadth escape set us free from one calamity, but we were threatened by another. . . . Every man we saw was a robber, and we were ordered sometimes to drive hard lest a traveller whom we saw behind should overtake us, and sometimes to stop, lest we should come up to him who was passing before us. She alarmed many an honest man by begging him to spare her life as he passed by the coach, and drew me into fifteen quarrels with persons who encreased her fright by kindly stopping to enquire whether they could assist us. At last we came home, and she told her company next day what a pleasant ride she had been taking. (*Rambler* 34, *Works*, 3: 188–89)

Even more drastic, Gelidus (in Latin, frozen or numb) regularly locks himself away to pursue abstruse research:

He spends his time in the highest room of his house, into which none of his family are suffered to enter; and when he comes down to his dinner, or his rest, he walks about like a stranger that is there only for a day, without any tokens of regard or tenderness. He has totally divested himself of all human sensations; he has neither eye for beauty, nor ear for complaint; he neither rejoices at the good fortune of his nearest friend, nor mourns for any publick or private calamity. (*Rambler* 24, *Works*, 3: 132–33)

Reports of mortal danger encountered by his neighbors—and his own brother—hardly disturb him, except as he calibrates their problems by the "abstruser sciences." Hurricanes and fires are more interesting to him than people. More like a mechanical device than a human being, he lives "insensible to every spectacle of distress, and unmoved by the loudest call of social nature, . . . [he] has so far abstracted himself from the species, as to partake neither of the joys nor griefs of others, but neglects the endearments of his wife, and the caresses of his children, to count the drops of rain, note the changes of the wind, and calculate the eclipses of the moons of Jupiter" (133–34). Clearly Gelidus is a preliminary draft of the mad astronomer in *Rasselas*, whose massive defenses and shocking isolation reverberate through that work. The finished portrait is perhaps Johnson's most accomplished study of the concealed and contradictory forces of the mind, grinding out their implements of harrowing delusion.

*   *   *

We are back to being "wrecked by success." If the periodical essays bear the imprint of Johnson's own experience, they were his medium for exploring terrifying fantasies brimming with irrationality. He found the sources of pathological suffering to inhere in mental events, and he strove bravely to make them intelligible. Scornful of the comfortable theodicies then in vogue about the age-old problem of evil in the world, he grappled with demons in the mind. To this end, he utilized and vigorously endorsed the tenets of modern scientific empiricism:

> The writers of medicine and physiology have traced with great appearance of accuracy, the effects of time upon the human body, by marking the various periods of the constitution, and the several stages by which animal life makes its progress from infancy to decrepitude. . . . It had been a task worthy of the moral philosophers to have considered with equal care the climactericks of the mind; to have pointed out the time at which every passion begins and ceases to predominate, and noted the regular variations of desire, and the succession of one appetite to another.[38] (*Rambler* 151, *Works*, 5: 38)

Perhaps here was the stuff of Johnson's own self-analysis, regrettably lost, but the blueprint which survives suggests an arduous enterprise. For this alone, he had a settled aversion to smooth and ingratiating ways to explain human misery, which fell back upon allegedly clairvoyant systems and logic. Of these, Soame Jenyns's *A Free Inquiry into the Nature and Origin of Evil* earned his particular contempt.[39] In his notorious "Review," which repudiates the claims of conventional rationalist apologia, he once again tackles the awesome secrets of the psyche. He tests the meaning of success and failure, based upon his own disquieting observation.

The "Review" was written in response to Jenyns's popular book invoking the shopworn theory of the Great Chain of Being to account for moral evil. A wealthy, officious dilettante, Jenyns attempted to palliate human suffering in blandest tones, preaching submission to things as they are, much as Pope, through Bolingbroke, prated on in *An Essay on Man* (1733–34):

All Nature is but Art, unknown to thee
All Chance, Direction which thou canst not see;
All Discord, Harmony not understood;
All partial Evil, universal Good.
And spight of Pride, in erring Reason's spight,
One truth is clear; "Whatever Is, is Right."[40]

Johnson censures such fatuous reductionism when he publishes the "Review," which ran in three issues of the *Literary Magazine* (1757). That suffering should be endured placidly must have been an anathema to him. Jenyns typically gushes: "I am persuaded that there is something in the abstract nature of pain conducive to pleasure; that the sufferings of individuals are absolutely necessary to human happiness."[41] As the essay persists in tediously peddling its dogma, Johnson does not scruple to counter with an image of ghastly suffering. Wielding the naked truth of experience, he cuts through the tissue of empty blandishments with his memorable rebuttal:

> Life must be seen before it can be known. This author and Pope perhaps never saw the miseries which they imagine thus easy to be borne. The poor, indeed, are insensible of many little vexations, which sometimes embitter the possessions and pollute the enjoyments of the rich. They are not pained by casual incivility, or mortified by the mutilation of a compliment; but this happiness is like that of a malefactor who ceases to feel the cords that bind him when the pincers are tearing his flesh.[42]

Moreover, Johnson invents an altogether different and unique horror when he interprets Jenyns's suave theory that omnipotent beings torture humans for diversion, just as humans inflict injury upon animals of a lower sort. In effect, he works with former renderings of a familiar analytic theme: the appalling images he embroiders indicate primitive fantasies of abuse and humiliation. Once more he comes to challenge the dominion of an enmity unexplained. And sharpening the focus of his analytic lens, he exposes a monstrous charade. With high sardonic contempt, he draws out the latent features of Jenyns's insidious analogy:

> As we drown whelps and kittens, they [omnipotent beings] amuse themselves now and then with sinking a ship, and stand round the fields of Blenheim, or the walls of Prague, as we encircle a cockpit. As we shoot a bird flying, they take a man in the midst of his business or pleasure, and knock him down with an apoplexy. Some of them, perhaps, are virtuosi, and delight in the operations of an asthma, as a human philosopher in the effects of the air pump. To swell a man with a tympany is as good sport as to blow a frog. Many a merry bout

have these frolic beings at the vicissitudes of an ague, and good sport it is to see a man tumble with an epilepsy, and revive and tumble again, and all this he knows not why. As they are wiser and more powerful than we, they have more exquisite diversions; for we have no way of procuring any sport so brisk and so lasting as the paroxysms of the gout and stone, which undoubtedly must make high mirth, especially if the play be a little diversified with the blunders and puzzles of the blind and deaf. We know not how far their sphere of observation may extend. Perhaps now and then a merry being may place himself in such a situation as to enjoy at once all the varieties of an epidemical disease, or amuse his leisure with the tossings and contortions of every possible pain exhibited together.[43]

What is flaunted as rational can be profoundly irrational. Jenyns's fanatical system has doubtless hardened him to its crazed effects. The orderly and logical design belies a critical failure of reason, which Johnson at once detects. From his shrewdly penetrating vantage point, he looks into the abyss of maniacal delusion. He makes out the lineaments of a lewd archaic atrocity, where, wrapt in inscrutable causes and detached from human concerns, lower those *"hunters, whose game is man."* In Jenyns's meanderings, Johnson hears this heavy rumble of metaphysical brooding, which draws its energy from the most rank and crude regressions. And his answer takes the measure of his life's work: "The only end of writing is to enable the readers better to enjoy life, or better to endure it."[44] The famed pronouncement reaffirms his own intrepid efforts to fathom mines of buried truth. His parade of overweening authors, raging militarists, mad scientists, and escapists from the inescapable banality of life; his gallery of the rich, famous, and beautiful—all, to be sure, fell prey to a blind and resistless antagonism. But we make no intrinsic sense of their failure by lurid external projections,

> That a set of beings unseen and unheard are hovering about us, trying experi-
> ments upon our sensibility, putting us in agonies to see our limbs quiver,
> torturing us to madness that they may laugh at our vagaries, sometimes
> obstructing the bile that they may see how a man looks when he is yellow;
> sometimes breaking a traveller's bones to try how he will get home; sometimes
> wasting a man to a skeleton, and sometimes killing him fat for the greater
> elegance of his hide.[45]

Through these pictures of primitive terror, Johnson divines man's worst nightmares. He disinters the ancient memory of inexorable retaliation. He lays open the sly, submerged contrivances of self-torment and self-destruction. People who are "wrecked by success" come as no surprise to one who has plumbed the depths of his own wreckage to discover a wealth of knowledge of the human mind.

Notes

1. Freud, *Standard Edition*, 14: 318.
2. *Life*, 1: 73–74. Boswell transcribes it as "mad and violent" instead of "rude and violent" (Bate, *Samuel Johnson* p. 607, note 29).
3. *Life*, 1: 73–74.
4. *Diary and Letters of Madame D' Arblay*, ed. Austin Dobson (London: Macmillan, 1904–05), 1: 115.
5. That is, Robert James and Edmund Hector, in medicine; John Taylor in the church. Bate has sagaciously observed:

> No writer has been more aware of the frightening potentiality of envy in the human heart, its readiness to spring alive, and the range of emotions and rationalization it can immediately, and self-deceptively, twist to its purpose. His experience, not only now but also, more importantly, throughout the next twenty years, provided as strong a temptation to chronic and even bitter envy as most people are ever forced to undergo. (*Samuel Johnson*, p. 74)

6. *Garrick Correspondence* (1831), 1: 44–45, as quoted in Bate, *Samuel Johnson*, p. 231.
7. *Life*, 3: 309–10. See in the same (p. 309, n. 1) Hill's note on Hannah More's comment in her *Practical Piety*:

> That accurate judge of human life, Dr. Johnson, has often been heard by the writer of these pages to observe, that it was the greatest misfortune which could befal a man to have been bred to no profession, and pathetically to regret that this misfortune was his own.

And Boswell provokes him much as Sir William:

> I talked before him upon a topick which he had once borne patiently from me when we were by ourselves—his not complaining of the world, because he was not called to some great office, nor had attained to great wealth. He flew into a violent passion, I confess with some justice, and commanded us to have done. 'Nobody, (said he) has a right to talk in this manner, to bring before a man his own character, and the events of his life, when he does not choose it should be done. I never have sought the world; the world was not to seek me. (*Life*, 4: 171–72)

The last is so uncommonly self-deceiving as to confirm Johnson's extreme agitation.
8. *Life*, 2: 66.
9. *Johnsonian Miscellanies*, 2: 227–28.

10. *Life*, 3: 338.

11. *Life*, 3: 329.

12. *Life*, 3: 273.

13. *Johnsonian Miscellanies*, 1: 244.

14. *Johnsonian Miscellanies*, 2: 263.

15. *Johnsonian Miscellanies*, 1: 282. But see James Clifford, *Hester Lynch Piozzi (Mrs. Thrale)* (1941; 2nd ed., Oxford: Clarendon Press, 1952), pp. 267–69 on Mrs. Thrale's making Johnson look peevish and irascible: "Her over-emphasis on this querulousness, because it was serviceable in explaining their final quarrel and separation, is the most serious blot on the *Anecdotes*" (p. 268).

16. *Diary and Letters of Madame D'Arblay*, 1: 128–29.

17. *Thraliana: The Diary of Mrs. Hester Lynch Thrale (Later Mrs. Piozzi)*, ed. Katherine C. Balderston (1942; 2nd ed., Oxford: Clarendon Press, 1951), 1: 329.

18. *Life*, 2: 362.

19. *Johnsonian Miscellanies*, 2: 426–27. Boswell uses the shorter account by the Reverend Henry White (*Life*, 4: 372–73). For the dating, see Clifford, *Young Sam Johnson*, pp. 135, 339, n. 17.

20. *Life*, 2: 217: "The great thing to be recorded, (said he), is the state of your own mind; and you should write down every thing that you remember, for you cannot judge at first what is good or bad; and write immediately while the impression is fresh, for it will not be the same a week afterwards." See also Mrs. Thrale's recollection, with which she launches *Thraliana*: "It is many Years since Doctor Samuel Johnson advised me to get a little Book, and write in it all the little Anecdotes which might come to my knowledge, all the Observations I might make or hear; all the Verses never likely to be published, and in fine ev'ry thing which struck me at the Time" *Thraliana*, 1: 1. Clifford suggests that she also might have begun the "Children's Book" at Johnson's prompting (*Hester Lynch Piozzi*, p. 70).

21. *Life*, 1: 203.

22. The compelling psychological parallels between Johnson's life and works have been widely remarked, though in no particularly methodical way. As an example, Watkins puts it (sometimes overstated):

> The results of this lifelong struggle [with melancholy] are plain in his works, even when they do not emerge obviously. It is this power of emotion and imagination, so severely disciplined, which gives depth and meaning. . . . The roots [of his writings] are all deep in his own experience, even apparently serene pronouncements springing from suffering and despair. (*Perilous Balance*, p. 92)

Much the same, Arieh Sachs observes:

> Johnson's greatness lies in his ability to transform his personal distress of melancholy, guilt, and indolence into impersonal observation. The experience of a desperately neurotic man was turned into a generalized scheme of morals and religion which could claim universal validity. (*Passionate Intelligence: Imagination and Reason in the Work of Samuel Johnson* [Baltimore: Johns Hopkins University Press, 1967], p. 14)

And Bate describes it vividly and frankly:

> He could write as well as he did about grief or despair, about remorse and
> guilt, about boredom, satiety, and the hunger for novelty, about pride, aggres-
> sive competition, and the habit of arguing "for victory," because he himself
> was so susceptible to all of them and yet was constantly putting them at arm's
> length in order to see them for what they were. (*Samuel Johnson*, pp. 312–13)

23. The dedicated labors of Johnson's most recent biographers do much to
dispel the mystery of the 1750s, about which Boswell merely speculated. While not
specifically psychoanalytic, these studies offer important insights into Johnson's
mind during a critical period of his life. See particularly, Wain, *Samuel Johnson*, pp.
162–215, Bate, *Samuel Johnson*, pp. 261–340, and Clifford *Dictionary Johnson: Samuel
Johnson's Middle Years* (New York: McGraw-Hill, 1979), pp. 88–148. For an explicitly
psychoanalytic account, see Newton, "Samuel Johnson's Breakdown."
    24. *Oxford Authors*, p. 327. Johnson continues to swing through familiar
vicissitudes in most of the last paragraph of the Preface:

> It may gratify curiosity to inform it that the *English Dictionary* was written
> with little assistance of the learned, and without any patronage of the great;
> not in the soft obscurities of retirement, or under the shelter of academic
> bowers, but amidst inconvenience and distraction, in sickness and in sorrow:
> and it may repress the triumph of malignant criticism to observe that if our
> language is not here fully displayed, I have only failed in an attempt which no
> human powers have hitherto completed. (p. 328)

The final sentence is a precious bit of flummery: "I have protracted my work till
most of those whom I wished to please have sunk into the grave, and success and
miscarriage are empty sounds: I therefore dismiss it with frigid tranquillity, having
little to fear or hope from censure or from praise."
    25. *Life*, 4: 409. Despite this, as Boswell testifies, "Of his friend Cave, he
always spoke with great affection." And Johnson's "Life of Cave" is full of sympathy
and appreciation. It first appeared in *Gentleman's Magazine*, 1754, pp. 55–58 and was
revised for inclusion in the second edition of *Biographia Britannica* (1784). J.D.
Fleeman prints this revised version in his edition of *Early Biographical Writings of Dr.
Johnson* (Westmead: Gregg, 1973), pp. 407–10.
    26. Johnson's relationship to figures in authority deserves a volume of its own.
To Mrs. Thrale, he gave a revealing glimpse into his early relationship with his
father:

> The trick which most parents play with their children, of shewing off their
> newly-acquired accomplishments, disgusted Mr. Johnson beyond expression;
> he had been treated so himself, he said, till he absolutely loathed his father's
> caresses, because he knew they were sure to precede some unpleasing display
> of his early abilities; and he used, when neighbours came o'visiting, to run up a
> tree that he might not be found and exhibited. . . . An old man's child
> (continued he) leads such a life, I think, as a little boy's dog, teized with

awkward fondness, and forced, perhaps, to sit up and beg, as we call it, to divert a company. (*Johnsonian Miscellanies*, 1: 152–53)

It was said of him as a young man in Lichfield, "he has the character of being a very haughty, ill-natured gent[leman]," (*Johnsonian Gleanings*, ed. Aleyn Lyell Reade (Privately printed, 1909–52; rpt. New York: Octagon Books, 1967), 5: 30. Boswell writes of his appointment at the Bosworth School under Sir Wolstan Dixie:

> This employment was irksome to him in every respect, and he complained grievously of it. . . . His general aversion to this painful drudgery was greatly enhanced by a disagreement between him and Sir Wolstan Dixey, the patron of the school, in whose house, I have been told, he officiated as a kind of domestick chaplain, so far, at least, as to say grace at table, but was treated with what he represented as intolerable harshness; and, after suffering for a few months such complicated misery, he relinquished a situation which all his life afterwards he recollected with the strongest aversion, and even a degree of horrour. (*Life*, 1: 84–85; see also Clifford, *Young Sam Johnson*, pp. 131–34)

And examples of the insolence and pugnacity of those early years in London are legion. Witness the tactlessly presumptuous salutation of his letter to Cave, when he first sought employment: "Sir: As you appear no less sensible than your Readers of the defects of your Poetical Article, you will not be displeased, if, in order to the improvement of it, I communicate to You the Sentiments of a person, who will undertake on reasonable terms sometimes to fill a column" (*Letters*, 1: 3, no. 3). And there is of course the famous episode when, infuriated at the man's hectoring verbal abuse, he made short work of the publisher Thomas Osborne. As Boswell says, "It has been confidently related, with many embellishments, that Johnson one day knocked Osborne down in his shop, with a folio, and put his foot upon his neck. The simple truth I had from Johnson himself. 'Sir, he was impertinent to me, and I beat him'" (*Life*, 1: 154). To Mrs. Thrale, Johnson adds, one dare say, more boastfully, 'I have beat many a fellow, but the rest had the wit to hold their tongues'" (*Johnsonian Miscellanies*, 1: 304).

27. Paul J. Korshin, "The Johnson-Chesterfield Relationship: A New Hypothesis," *PMLA* 85 (1970): 247–59 discriminates the motives of Johnson's rather blind prejudice by calling attention to the way he vented his dislike of the Earl's political character.

28. *Letters*, 1: 64 (no. 61).

29. See Johnson's intriguing comment on Hamlet's most famous soliloquy, where, interpreting the hero's reluctance to act, he also looks at inner propulsions and their restraints. He singles out "fear," which "chills the ardour of 'resolution,' checks the 'vigour of enterprise,' and makes the 'current' of desire stagnate in inactivity" (*Works*, 8: 981).

30. The prototype for English periodical essays of the eighteenth century was evidently Addison's and Steele's *Spectator*, which established the structure and tone for the genre. According to Johnson, it began as a semi-serious, almost frivolous guide for decorum in everyday affairs, attempting "to teach the minuter decencies

and inferior duties, to regulate the practice of daily conversation, to correct those depravities which are rather ridiculous than criminal, and remove those grievances which, if they produce no lasting calamities, impress hourly vexation" ("Life of Addison," *Lives*, 2: 92). The *Cambridge Bibliography of English Literature* lists the sum total of periodical publication by the eighteenth century, including essay sheets, newspapers, journals, monthly miscellanies, weekly diatribes, and daily medleys, as 2,500 titles or so by 1800. See also the editor's introduction to *Studies in the Early English Periodical*, ed. R. P. Bond (Chapel Hill: University of North Carolina Press, 1957), pp. 3–48.

31. See Roy Porter, ed. Thomas Trotter, *An Essay, Medical, Philosophical, and Chemical, on Drunkenness and its Effects on the Human Body* (1894; rpt.London: Tavistock Reprint Series on the History of Psychiatry, 1988). The introductory essay reviews eighteenth-century medical attitudes toward addictive behavior, attitudes with which Johnson was doubtless familiar.

32. Jean Hagstrum argues how the unconscious lurks in the eighteenth-century word *conscious* and uses Johnson as a prime example. Though he chiefly finds Johnson's "secretly conscious" to be an escapist realm subject to ethical reclamation, and therefore not strictly the stuff of the Freudian unconscious, I think he would agree that the powerful internal workings of the two are virtually identical. See "Towards a Profile of the Word *Conscious*," pp. 41–44.

33. *Johnsonian Miscellanies*, 1: 178. Also, according to Mrs. Thrale, "he had his own outset into life in his eye when he wrote the eastern story of Gelaleddin."

34. Boswell reports Johnson's admiration of the early eighteenth-century physician and philosopher: "I read Mandeville forty, or, I believe, fifty years ago. He did not puzzle me; he opened my views into real life very much" (*Life*, 3: 292). See also *Life*, 3: 56, n. 2).

35. See Donald Greene, *Politics*, pp. 212–19, for an evenhanded discussion of this most enduringly controversial of Johnson's political tracts:

> Johnson is, in fact, in advance of most of his contemporaries in seeing and clearly stating the fact of the omnicompetence of the modern state. He is advocating nothing; but he is relentless in pulling the veil from the eyes of those who refuse to see that things do stand so. And since they do, such concepts as the "laws of nature, the rights of humanity, the faith of charters, the danger of liberty, the encroachments of usurpation," which "have been thundered in our ears, sometimes by interested faction and sometimes by honest stupidity," vanish into mist. Behind the ineffectual disguise of such comforting slogans stands the naked fact of political power." (p. 215)

36. The Seven Years War (1756–63) brought Johnson into the political fray with the publication of two essays, "An Introduction to the Political State of Great Britain" and "Observations on the Present State of Affairs," both appearing in the *Literary Magazine* in 1756. But so inflammatory was Johnson's political analysis, so vituperatively did he condemn a great international war just begun by his country as "only the quarrel of two robbers for the spoils of a passenger" (*Works*, 10: 188), that it is likely he lost his job, as Donald Greene suggests, for the series ended abruptly.

See *The Politics*, pp. 154–72, and *Works*, 10: 126–29, 184–85). But through the inoffensive mask of the Idler, he every so often published scathing anti-war protests. Such is the context of the original *Idler* 22, which first appeared 9 September 1758 and was quickly reprinted by a number of popular journals.

37. It is worth noting that Lady Bustle bears an uncanny resemblance to Dora's mother, beset by "housewife psychosis," in Freud's "Analysis of a Case of Hysteria": "From the accounts given me by the girl and her father I was led to imagine her as an uncultivated woman and above all as a foolish one, who had concentrated all her interests upon domestic affairs. . . . She had no understanding for her children's more active interests, and was occupied all day long in cleaning the house with its furniture and utensils and in keeping them clean—to such an extent as to make it almost impossible to use or enjoy them" (*Standard Edition*, 8: 20).

38. In *Rambler* 49 (*Works*, 3: 263–68), Johnson himself presents a developmental scheme of the passions, from infancy to adulthood.

39. For an account of Johnson's convictions and the rhetoric he employed in the "Review," see Richard B. Schwartz, *Samuel Johnson and the Problem of Evil* (Madison: University of Wisconsin Press, 1975). See also Charles H. Hinnant, *Samuel Johnson: An Analysis* (London: Macmillan, 1988), pp. 5–11, which uses the "Review" as the point of departure to see Johnson in the Newton-Leibniz controversy over ideas of vacuum and plenum.

40. *The Twickenham Edition of the Poems of Alexander Pope*, ed. John Butt et al. (London: Methuen, 1938–68), vol. 3, pt. 1, pp. 50–51, "An Essay on Man," Epistle 1, ll. 289–94.

41. *A Free Inquiry into the Nature and Origin of Evil* (London: R. and J. Dodsley, 1757), p. 60.

42. *Oxford Authors*, p. 527. Donald Greene annotates the passage: "This gruesome imagery, *pained, mutilation, pincers*, alludes to a recent event much in the public eye at the time, the dreadful torture and execution (with red-hot pincers tearing his flesh and molten lead poured into the wounds) of Robert-François Damiens for inflicting a superficial wound on Louis XV of France" (p. 818).

43. *Oxford Authors*, p. 535.

44. *Oxford Authors*, p. 536.

45. *Oxford Authors*, p. 536.

6. The Uses of Enchantment

ONE OF HIS FONDEST MEMORIES, Johnson once told Mrs. Thrale, was sitting on his nurse's lap while she read to him *St. George and the Dragon*. Looking back on his wonder and delight, he is convinced that such old-fashioned tales of enchantment, by contrast to contemporary good-boy and good-girl stories, are the only ones fit to please small children: "Babies do not want . . . to hear about babies; they like to be told of giants and castles, and of somewhat which can stretch and stimulate their little minds."[1] Though it may seem incongruous with the sterner stuff of the *Rambler* and other projects of requisite morality, Johnson in fact reveled throughout his life in romance and adventure tales, stories like *La Morte d' Arthur*, *Guy of Warwick*, *Don Bellianis*, and *Amadis de Gaul*. To Bishop Percy, whom he assisted in putting together the famous *Reliques of Ancient English Poetry* (1765), a collection of early English and Scottish ballads, he confesses a great relish for "romances of chivalry" from boyhood on. Percy confirms that during one summer visit in 1764, Johnson, then fifty-four, chose for his everyday reading an obscure Spanish romance, in folio, and he read it straight through.[2] And some years later, he wrote jauntily to Mrs. Thrale, "This little Dog does nothing, but I hope he will mend; he is now reading Jack the Giant Killer. Perhaps so noble a narrative may rouse in him the soul of enterprize."[3]

Other modes of literature conjuring up the remote and the exotic also held a special fascination for Johnson. Apparently, he was attracted by fictions of all sorts: allegory, fable, oriental tale, accounts of the super-natural, the incredible revelations of travel books. Indeed, it has been estimated that of the 325 essays in the *Rambler*, *Idler*, and *Adventurer*, about 143 contain a fiction of one kind or another,[4] not to mention "The Vision of Theodore" (1748), a chapter in Charlotte Lennox's *The Female Quixote* (1752), *Rasselas* (1759), and a lesser known, somewhat neglected little piece, appearing in Anna Williams's *Miscellanies in Prose and Verse* (1766), entitled "The Fountains: A Fairy Tale." These works, as well as his own avid reading, would indicate a taste for the richly imaginative, for writing that could rouse the emotions and, in the Lockean sense, leave powerful impressions on the mind. Johnson passionately believed that books could influence life, even help to mold the personality. Partly on this basis, he dismissed the stuporous theory of the "ruling passion": "Perhaps if . . . [people] review their early years and trace their ideas backwards, they will find that those strong desires were the effects either of example or instruction, the circumstances in which they were placed, the objects which they first received impressions from, *the first books they read*, or the first company they conversed with" (italics mine).[5] Thus he begins *A Journey to the Western Islands of Scotland* (1775) with childlike whimsy, "I had desired to visit the Hebrides, or Western Islands of Scotland, so long, that I scarcely remember how the wish was originally excited" (*Works*, 9: 3). But he knows it was his father who put Martin's *Description of the Western Islands of Scotland* (1703) into his hands when he was a small boy and encouraged him to read it.[6] About the same time he was given *The Whole Duty of Man* to study on Sundays, "a heavy duty to me," he recalls, for the rather tedious, too sententious book was one, "from a great part of which I could derive no instruction."[7] Later, as an undergraduate at Oxford, he picked up William Law's *A Serious Call to a Devout and Holy Life*, and its intoxicating, mystical intensity made a lasting impression on his life.[8]

Johnson's preoccupation with fantasy and the imagination has been largely understood in view of his famous warnings against its "dangerous prevalence." But for all the well-known caveats about seduction and betrayal—a dominant theme, to be sure, in his writings—it is also important to look at his more positive responses. Certainly, he was no celebrant of the poet as "maker," touched by divinity: he professed his essential *ars poetica* in less rhapsodic modes, "to enable the readers better to enjoy life, or better to endure it," as we have seen. But neither was he inaccessible to the pleasures of pure creativity. He often pays tribute to imaginative genius for its unbounded powers, its exemption from the laws of mundane necessity: "Milton's delight was to sport in the wide regions of possibility; reality was a scene too narrow for his mind. He sent his faculties out upon discovery, into worlds where only imagination can travel, and delighted to form new modes of existence, and furnish sentiment and action to superior beings, to trace the counsels of hell, or accompany the choirs of heaven" (*Lives*, 1: 177–78). Or consider his high praise for the use of the supernatural and its enhancing affinities to real life: "Shakespeare approximates the remote, and familiarizes the wonderful; the event which he represents will not happen, but if it were possible, its effects would probably be such as he has assigned;

and it may be said that he has not only shewn human nature as it acts in real exigencies, but as it would be found in trials, to which it cannot be exposed" ("Preface to Shakespeare," *Works*, 7: 65). Johnson thoroughly understands the integrity of magical agencies in such plays as *Hamlet*, *Macbeth*, *A Midsummer Night's Dream*, and *The Tempest*, and he goes to some length to frame an historical context for "witchcraft or enchantment," just as he is always tantalized by its technique.[9] Pope's otherworldly creatures likewise allure him, and he never hesitates to join the frolics in *The Rape of the Lock*: "A race of aerial people, never heard of before is presented to us in a manner so clear and easy, that the reader seeks for no further information, but immediately mingles with his new acquaintance, adopts their interests, and attends their pursuits, loves a sylph and detests a gnome" (*Lives*, 3: 233–34). And celebrating his late friend William Collins, he is much absorbed by the poet's exotic strains of invention:

> He loved fairies, genii, giants, and monsters; he delighted to rove through the meanders of inchantment, to gaze on the magnificence of golden palaces, to repose by the water-falls of Elysian Gardens. . . . The grandeur of wildness and the novelty of extravagance were always desired by him. (*Lives*, 3: 337)

While most literary critics respect the difficulty of interpreting Johnson's concept of fantasy,[10] the matter is perhaps too readily subsumed by aesthetic, religious, and moral issues. Unhappily, these often tend to represent him as severely judgmental, a kind of dour enforcer of a timeworn propriety. But from Johnson's psychological point of view, those revisions of reality imposed by the hidden order of the mind were no absolute target for either denial or indulgence. What fantasy can do positively and what fantasy can do negatively are encompassed alike by his sophisticated survey of mental events. What is more, he is wholly capable of gliding agilely from one standard to the other, and often in the same piece. A good example is his keen analysis of *Don Quixote*, a book he prized most highly,[11] where he teases out the meaning of tainted human desire. After a fond recollection of the knight's lavish ambitions, ones he stresses that are common to mankind, he indicates the implicit dilemma: "The understanding of a man, naturally sanguine, may, indeed, be easily vitiated by the luxurious indulgence of hope, however necessary to the production of every thing great or excellent, as some plants are destroyed by too open exposure to that sun, which gives life and beauty to the vegetable world" (*Rambler* 2, *Works*, 3: 11–12). The term "vitiated" is often used by Johnson to evoke a contaminating mental process. Contributing the obligatory moralist ending to Charlotte Lennox's *The Female Quixote* (1752), he exposes the heroine's "senseless fictions, which at once vitiate the mind, and pervert the understanding."[12] But in the Rambler's portrait of the original, "vitiated," in connection with the metaphor of the sun, evokes instead a quality of staggering ambivalence. Very likely this is an allusion to Cervantes' sun, blazing down on the stark ghostly landscapes of La Mancha, dazzling and toxic all at once. It fires the hero's heated striving, but cannot soberly be called innoxious.[13] Fantasy thus defies logical categories. It registers the mind as a maker of fictions, some morbid and pathogenic, to be sure, but others invigorating and helpful. No matter the consequences, Johnson ever affirms its bracing ascendancy: "The power of [fictional] example is so great, as to take possession of the memory by a kind of violence, and produce effects almost without the interventions of the will" (*Rambler* 4, *Works*, 3: 22). This psychodynamic view enables him in large to resist the philosophical conundrums set up by his age: judgment versus fancy; reason versus imagination; the intellect versus the emotions.[14] Loath to adopt such riddling inconsistencies, he seeks explanations that are scientifically intelligible. If, indeed, "deluded imagination" causes madness, the principal lesson of Cervantes, as well as of Battie and Locke, Johnson argues it is no condition fixed by polarities, but one which shifts, often imperceptibly, and in everyone: "Disorders of intellect . . . happen much more often than superficial observers will easily believe. Perhaps, if we speak with rigorous exactness, no human mind is in its right state. There is no man whose imagination does not sometimes predominate over his reason, who can regulate his attention wholly by his will, and whose ideas will come and go at his command" (*Rasselas*, *Works*, 16: 150). It is this cool penetration into the workings of the mind—flying in the face of prejudicial methods and systems—that informs his every critical judgment.[15]

Owing to the imperious role of imagination in works of art, Johnson readily educes their splendid quality of fabrication and distortion of the real world. In his well-known refutation of the dramatic unities, he detects the influence of irrational springs of belief, immune to fact and niggling materiality: "Delusion, if delusion be admitted, has no certain limitation; if the spectator can be once persuaded, . . . he is in a state of elevation above the reach of reason, or of truth, and from the heights of empyrean poetry, may despise the circumscriptions of terrestrial nature" ("Preface to Shakespeare," *Works*, 7: 76–77). At the same time, he distinguishes how acts of the imagination make possible an excitement arising from the release of tensions in the mind. Thus with impunity, we are allowed to trespass, as it were, on a hidden stockade of fears and wishes: "The reflection that strikes the heart is not, that the evils before us are real evils, but that they are evils to which we ourselves may be exposed. If there be any fallacy, it is not that we fancy the players, but that we fancy ourselves unhappy for a moment; but we rather lament the possibility than suppose the presence of misery, as a mother weeps over her babe, when she remembers that death may take it from her." The deliberate control of these feelings and the safe boundaries erected around them allow for certain pleasure: "The delight of tragedy proceeds from our consciousness of fiction; if we thought murders and treasons real, they would please no more" (*Works*, 7: 78).[16] What is more, this experience often denotes empathic identification, entering into the thoughts and feelings of another. The famous beginning of *Rambler* 60 on biography explains the instant access to a fellow human being through imaginative faculties: "All joy or sorrow for the happiness or calamities of others is produced by an act of the imagination, that realizes the event however fictitious, or approximates it however remote, by placing us, for a time, in the condition of him whose fortune we contemplate; so that we feel, while the deception lasts, whatever motions would be excited by the same good or evil happening to ourselves." Johnson's "motions" stress the wholly psychodynamic means by which he appreciates the compelling aspects of art: "Our passions are therefore more strongly moved, in propor-tion as we can more readily adopt the pains or pleasures proposed to our minds, by recognizing them as once our own, or considering them as naturally incident to our state of life" (*Works*, 3: 318–19). Thus the artist's representations trigger our own psychology of motivation.

No doubt the vast explanatory range of Johnson's literary criticism, as well as his purely creative writing, stems from his view of the mind. Alert to the intricate workings of a mental apparatus, he brings the focus of literary value from the author and the text to the reader. What will *shock* the mind and what will *please* the mind are his most basic conceptual gauges.[17] At every turn, Johnson catches the palpable transaction between reader and writer, which elicits a shared repository of ideas. Defining, for example, what constitutes Pope's genius, he names "Imagination, which strongly impresses on the writer's mind and enables him to convey to the reader the various forms of nature, incidents of life, and energies of passion" (*Lives*, 3: 247). Or take his famous pronouncement on Gray's *Elegy*: "The *Churchyard* abounds with images which find a mirror in every mind, and with sentiments to which every bosom returns an echo" (*Lives*, 3: 441). No wonder that his own works of fiction are so uncannily charged by the raw materials of psychical life. The omnipotence of thought, wish-fulfillment, the latent power to do harm or good, lend the fullest momentum to their fabulous designs. If we return now to the 1750s, the decade of Johnson's astonishing personal and intellectual growth, *Rasselas* emerges as the culminating product. The well-known state of affairs surrounding its composition—his mother's death, his guilt at not having visited her for twenty-two years, his ever-grinding poverty—is the very sort of life crisis that would reactivate familiar intrapsychic conflict. Conveyed throughout the tale are hidden currents of fantasy, awakened and transformed, no less Johnson's than our own.

* * *

Of all Johnson's works, *Rasselas* is perhaps the most amenable to a classical psychoanalytic reading, by virtue of its wealth of metaphor.[18] In the bizarre images of the "happy valley," the story teems with unconscious fantasy as well as vigorous presentations of mental events. Indeed, the conventions of the eighteenth-century philosophical tale, the literary genre most applicable to *Rasselas*, allowed Johnson much room to articulate recurrent intrapsychic themes.[19] If an illness may be precipitated when a real situation corresponds to an earlier traumatic experience, then the event of Johnson's mother's death must have caused him all but intolerable anxiety.[20] The desperate urgency of his letters home to Lichfield during the dreaded occasion bear only partial witness to his unspeakable suffering. Indeed, ten years earlier, he had anticipated the loss of his mother as "one of the few calamities on which I think with terrour."[21] Viewed for its deeper content, *Rasselas* explores such intense feelings, resonating with allusions to separation, death, escape, reunion, incarceration. The last figures prominently in Johnson's private mythos, rife with convictions of being persecuted and abused. It recalls, in effect, the original image of the child being beaten, as he has hitherto bent the world to his confining phobias. Dashing and irreverent, the escape from the happy valley represents his breaking the bars of his prison, no longer to bask in idle illusion but to seek out the provoking truth.

In the initial chapters of *Rasselas*, before the prince can grasp the full significance of the happy valley, a curious event takes place: it happens that inner fantasy takes over objective reality, and Rasselas momentarily loses the ability to differentiate between the two. This is the scene where he recreates a favorite fiction of virtue in distress, with himself in the role of rescuer:

> One day, as he was sitting on a bank, he feigned to himself an orphan virgin robbed of her little portion by a treacherous lover, and crying after him for restitution and redress. So strongly was the image impressed upon his mind, that he started up in the maid's defense, and ran forward to seize the plunderer, with all the eagerness of real persuit. Fear naturally quickens the flight of guilt. Rasselas could not catch the fugitive with his utmost efforts; but, resolving to weary, by perseverance, him whom he could not surpass in speed, he pressed on till the foot of the mountain stopped his course. (*Works*, 16: 18)

Clearly we see familiar elements of the fantasy of terror and oppression, but with some notable exceptions: this time we are meant to identify not with the victim but with the benefactor, not with a threat of unmerited loss but with a promise that evil will be rectified and the world set right at last. It is a new twist to an old story, as Rasselas appears in the fresh-created role of hero. What is more, he smiles at his own folly when he failed to distinguish between make-believe and real, and in this remarkable flash of insight, he is transformed. For the instant the prince grasps the difference between inner fantasy and objective reality, he also knows he is in a prison: "This . . . is the fatal obstacle that hinders at once the enjoyment of pleasure, and the exercise of virtue. How long is it that my hopes and wishes have flown beyond this boundary of my life, which yet I have never attempted to surmount!" (18). Rasselas's dawning awareness that the happy valley functions as a "boundary of my life," a "fatal obstacle" to the world beyond, is a key to its latent meaning. The valley is a fortress of fantasy, holding mysterious, buried secrets, and with a peculiarly sinister aspect, it represents a bondage to infantile, largely unconscious mental experience. It is a fixed private sphere, containing archaic remnants from the past and wielding ever-seductive illusory powers. Only when he senses its intrusive and destructive effects does Rasselas vow to flee.

A creation of Johnson's restless genius, the happy valley articulates old fantasies of punishment and retaliation through a narrative about captivity. Inherently splintered by contradiction, the valley stands, on the one hand, for omnipotent self-possession, on the other, for crushing defeat: it is at the same time a world of bliss and a wretched, stifling prison. Out of this ironic tension comes its essential meaning as a retreat from ancient battlegrounds here given up, beyond remedy and beyond hope. As the sages of Abyssinia recollect, the real world was overrun by "miseries," "calamity," and "discord," where "man preyed upon man" (11). These traumatizing experiences from a long-buried past now provide the psychical *raison d'être* for a place at once secure and threatening, sensual and hostile, guilt-relieving and guilt-inducing. In short, those finding the world intolerable turn away from it, though it is ever with them, to be embroidered in fantasy life. Johnson explores these heavily veiled tapestries through the metaphor of being imprisoned, a condition integrally related to the old theme of being beaten. Thus he reifies what has been experienced, dreaded, and longed for throughout psychical development.

As psychoanalysis reminds us, prisoners with mind-forged manacles are unconsciously real criminals, after all. Psychical imprisonment often represents such complete domination by libidinal and aggressive impulses that one actually holds the conviction, knowingly or not, of having violated any number of potent taboos through evil-minded, shameful acts. Based upon archaic wishes—cruel, sadistic, erotic, and so forth—such acts need to be punished and continually prevented anew: thus the prisoner is always serving time.[22] The condition of life in the happy valley conveys the sense of being vigilantly guarded and narrowly confined, of being incriminated, as it were, through a dark knowledge from a primitive, tainted past. The structure of the palace where Rasselas lives suggests a picture of the mind, as houses in dreams frequently do, in this case, tunneled with underground, labyrinthine spaces, vaguely primordial and oppressive:

> This house, which was so large as to be fully known to none but some ancient officers who successively inherited the secrets of the place, was built as if suspicion herself had dictated the plan. To every room there was an open and secret passage, every square had a communication with the rest, either from the upper stories by private galleries, or by subterranean passages from the lower apartments. Many of the columns had unsuspected cavities, in which a long race of monarchs had reposited their treasures. They then closed up the opening with marble, which was never to be removed but in the utmost exigencies of the kingdom; and recorded their accumulations in a book which was itself concealed in a tower not entered but by the emperour, attended by the prince who stood next in succession. (*Works*, 16: 10–11)

Secret, suspicion, private, subterranean, and *concealed* are words laden with the mystique of unconscious life by Johnson's lexicon, as we have seen. In this dim, foreboding atmosphere Rasselas is still more walled in by a landscape, which also appears to have portentous psychical dimensions. Its rude configuration calls up more of the same domination by persecutory authorities. With a looming facade, the valley turns into an uncanny stronghold, its access all but impregnable: "The mouth which opened into the valley was closed with gates of iron, forged by the artificers of ancient days, so massy that no man could, without the help of engines, open or shut them"; and its issues stealing into oblivion: "[The] lake discharged its superfluities by a stream which entered a dark cleft of the mountain on the northern side, and fell with dreadful noise from precipice to precipice till it was heard no more" (8).

Here is a place so dire and immuring that Rasselas almost loses hope of breaking its defenses: "The iron gate he despaired to open; for it was not only secured with all the power of art, but was always watched by successive sentinels, and was by its position exposed to the perpetual observation of all the inhabitants" (21). The conspiracy of others, who function dually as jailor-inmates, testifies to the self-perpetuating nature of a prison fantasy. Having forged the bars and chains from their own worst imaginings, psychical prisoners are most reluctant to give up the all-purpose rationale for failure and suffering. As Imlac says, inhabitants of the valley "are either corroded by malignant passions, or sit stupid in the gloom of perpetual vacancy. . . . The invitations, by which they allure others to a state which they feel to be wretched proceed from the natural malignity of hopeless misery. They are weary of themselves, and of each other, . . . and would gladly see all mankind imprisoned like themselves" (55). To such individuals, subjugation becomes a comfort as well as a bane.

Being imprisoned in the happy valley can also mean a splendid isolation and retreat into an onanistic solitude, a wish-fulfillment of grandiosity and blameless perfection. Such is the consolatory aspect of withdrawal from the cold, cruel world and its attributable guilt and sorrow. The other side of tyranny and punishment, this version of the prison fantasy celebrates a secret victory in finding a safe place to hide while savoring forbidden fruit. In this sense, the valley represents a delectable asylum, yielding every conceivable delight, exquisitely contrived: "All the diversities of the world were brought together, the blessings of nature were collected, and its evils extracted and excluded" (9). Under such conditions, confinement appears as narcissistic abandon, a regression to earliest stages of development, in which the self is the object of erotic pleasure. That "every desire was immediately granted," was the emperor's credo, and this haven of sensuality holds and protects an infantile grandiose self. The valley suggests a megalomanic triumph and its cocoon-like environment encourages a subjectivity so intense as to appear autoerotic: "Here the sons and daughters of Abyssinia lived only to know the soft vicissitudes of pleasure and repose, attended by all that were skillful to delight, and gratified with whatever the senses can enjoy. They wandered in gardens of fragrance, and slept in the fortresses of security. Every art was practiced to make them pleased with their own condition" (11).

Thus the illusion of self-sufficiency is maintained: removed from the dangers of the world, removed from the possibilities of want, misfortune, strife, error, Rasselas occupies an Olympian magical bubble, as it were, not giving or receiving impressions from the outside. The artificers of the happy valley, together with its royal patrons, promote a state of non-relatedness, devoid of real passion and real life. These would-be gods believe they are thoroughly autonomous, but this appearance of great power ironically belies extreme dependency. Rasselas finds that he greedily seeks the outside world, for all its trouble and conflict, since it gives him "something to desire." Ultimately, this desire challenges the mute custodianship, which anathematizes and quarantines fundamental human need. He now articulates his complaint, by analogy to other animal life, in the terms of rampant insatiability: "Every beast that strays beside me has the same corporeal necessities with myself. . . . I am, like him, pained with want, but am not, like him, satisfied with fulness. . . . I can discover within me no power of perception which is not glutted with its proper pleasure, yet I do not feel myself delighted. Man has surely some latent sense for which this place affords no gratification, or he has some desires distinct from sense which must be satisfied before he can be happy" (13). For all his weary indulgence, Rasselas clamors yet for something more. Thus Johnson starkly exposes man's instinctual nature as a wishing animal and commences his hero's "choice of life."

Johnson's original title for his narrative, "The Choice of Life," is a comprehensive index to his psychiatric theme. It suggests the hoped-for choice of sanity over insanity, as he shows how characters perversely construct the fortifications and battlements of their own peculiar happy valleys. Infantilized and self-absorbed, while garrisoned under dread authority, they act out the roles of wretched prisoners. They are the protagonists in any number of stories of adversity, gilded over by appearances of pleasure and satisfaction. From high to low to middle stations, they relate fanatical schemes which cover up buried tensions and unrelieved longing. Thus prison inmates lock up their most urgent emotions, just as Imlac, who reflects on his earlier self-exile: "Wearied at last with solicitation and repulses, I resolved to hide myself forever from the world, and depend no longer on the opinion or caprice of others. I waited for the time when the gate of the Happy Valley should open, that I might bid farewell to hope and fear" (54). Like many other characters—Rasselas, the hermit, the stoic and benevolist philosophers, various individuals in courts and private life, Nekayah, and the mad astronomer—Imlac gave himself up to an imaginary sphere, at once to avoid and maintain a helpless, hopeless condition. In tune with the horrors of this self-destructive fantasy beats the subversive heart of *Rasselas*, sounding its radical proclamation of happenings in the mind. Not through warped and wicked outside enemies but by their own appalling devices, human beings wreak the havoc of their lives. In the culminating chapters, the mad astronomer sits high within his observatory, a monument to complete surrender of self. His paranoid delusions of grandeur and persecution, as he regulates the weather, represent the final devastating effects of overpowering fantasy. He has sacrificed natural instinct and active participation in human affairs for a citadel of unreality, a fixed, frozen void. He is described as the most ravaged prisoner of all, having "drawn out his soul in endless calculations," his thoughts "long fixed upon a single point," with "some painful sentiment [which] pressed upon his mind" (142–43). Far more menacing than other characters' happy valleys, the astronomer's captivity exposes a shocking loss of personal identity and conscious volition.

In the brilliant chapter 44 of *Rasselas*, "The Dangerous Prevalence of Imagination," Johnson reviews the storyline of his unconscious life, once more in the light of a stunning objectivity. Much as he had set about in periodical essays and in the "Review" of Soame Jenyns only two years earlier, he unveils the grim specter of a projectively apprehended world. By deftly shifting his focus from the external to the internal, he exposes the purposeful distortion of reality and finds the "origin of evil," so-called, to come from within. He interprets the meaning of deeply entrenched suffering and its powerful share in human unhappiness. The terroristic lexicon is saliently intact—*tyrannise, force, dominion, fixes, reign, imperious, despotic, fasten*—through a sturdy analytic dispensation:

> No man will be found in whose mind airy notions do not sometimes tyrannise, and force him to hope or fear beyond the limits of sober probability. . . . Indulg[ing] the power of fiction, . . . [one] confers upon his pride unattainable dominion. . . . In time some particular train of ideas fixes the attention, all other intellectual gratifications are rejected, the mind, in weariness or leisure, recurs constantly to the favourite conception, and feasts on the luscious falsehood whenever she is offended with the bitterness of truth. By degrees the reign of fancy is confirmed; she grows first imperious, and in time despotic. Then fictions begin to operate as realities, false opinions fasten upon the mind, and life passes in dreams of rapture or of anguish. (150–52)

With more tensile images of constraining fetters and vicious tormentors, the astronomer himself describes his subjugation, now slowly dissipating by the glimmer of understanding: "If I am accidentally left alone for a few hours . . . my inveterate persuasion rushes upon my soul, and my thoughts are chained down by some irresistible violence . . . I am like a man habitually afraid of spectres, who is set at ease by a lamp and wonders at the dread which harrassed him in the dark, yet, if his lamp be extinguished, feels again the terrours which he knows that when it is light he shall feel no more." And he gives voice to the fiendish tribunal by which he stands ever accused: "I am sometimes afraid lest I indulge my quiet by criminal negligence, and voluntarily forget the great charge with which I am intrusted. If I favour myself in a known errour, or am determined by my own ease in a doubtful question of this importance, how dreadful is my crime!" (162). Thus Johnson assiduously follows the course of unremitting impulses and shows how they are converted into cruel and brutalizing forces within the mind. He reveals the mechanism through which they are projected onto external reality and thereby foretells the devastating scourge of the impaired superego: "No disease of the imagination . . . is so difficult of cure, as that which is complicated with the dread of guilt: fancy and conscience then act interchangeably upon us, and so often shift their places that the illusions of one are not distinguished from the dictates of the other" (162). By the terms of this boldly dynamic point of view, Johnson educes the fell operations of unconscious self-punishment.

With the case of the mad astronomer, Rasselas and company are shocked into confessing and recanting their own secret lives. But there is a sense in which we are never completely free of fantasy, nor would we want to be, given the inevitable lesson that "Human life is every where a state in which much is to be endured, and little to be enjoyed" (50). Thus Johnson allows everyone some measure of former protective custody, as it were, on the condition of realistic self-awareness: Pekuah dreams of ruling a convent, the princess a college, Rasselas a kingdom, and Imlac and the recuperating astronomer "were contented to be driven along the stream of life without directing their course to any particular port." But "of these wishes that they had formed they well knew that none could be obtained" (176). In the end, they resolve to return to Abyssinia, presumably the happy valley itself, to which there is no return, and perhaps essentially there was no escape. A creation implicitly identified with its creatures, the happy valley stands for psychical life, however we brave our way through it and make our choice. The inherent boundaries, the baleful barricades and forbidden moats, make it the undisputed master in its own house.

How, then, is the choice of life to be found? Johnson again is largely silent about moral and religious dicta. For all their dangerous illusions, the characters in *Rasselas* hardly suffer the common variety of pious, punishing, or invalidating correctives. By contrast to characters in satire and novels, they are never subjected to physical abuse or vicious reproach. Their problems seem, in fact, as unaffected by the stigma of sin and evil as one gets during this period.[23] Instead, Johnson concentrates on psychological ordeals, for him increasingly the single most absorbing dimension of his work. In the conclusion of *Rasselas*, "in which nothing is concluded," he taps mankind's most cherished goal of securing freedom from the grips of causality. And just as in earlier writings, where mining deepest layers of buried truth, he unearths a transforming intelligence. Out of the lowest part of mental life, he also finds powers of the highest authority. Utilizing the traditional Christian idiom, Nekayah gives utterance to the fear and hope—the primal perceptions of death and redemption—that constitute reverence. Eminently focused on human concerns, it is Johnson's psychological testament to the integrity of free will: "But the Being . . . whom I fear to name, the Being which made the soul, can destroy it. . . . To me . . . the choice of life is become less important; I hope hereafter to think only on the choice of eternity" (174–75).

*   *   *

The early and mid-1760s mark a none-too-pleasant interlude in Johnson's life, when he sought to forestall acute mental crisis by massive undertaking. He began work on the Shakespeare edition, assisted Robert Chambers in the Vinerian lectures on English law (1766–70) and Bishop Percy in the *Reliques of Ancient English Poetry* (1765), traveled a good deal, and he made brave efforts to enlarge his circle of acquaintance. Evidently, he also launched a formal self-analysis, some record of which remains in the *Annals, Prayers, and Meditations*.[24] The founding of the famous Club, the model for scores of such conversational groups, and the beginning of his momentous friendships with Boswell (1763) and the Thrales (1765) also took place at this time, as did the award of his annual pension (1762), assuring a measure of financial security. But for all the outward show of success, he appears at the same time to have been wrecked by it. As he piercingly analyzed the symptoms a few years earlier, he seems to have suffered from unallayed pangs of remorse and dejection, rooted deep in the psyche. At a time he might have exulted in well-deserved victory, he goes down to defeat. And if former writings explicitly detailed the problem, he now portrays it once again through the medium of fantasy.

In his only other piece of extended fiction, "The Fountains: A Fairy Tale" (1766), Johnson evokes the familiar features of waif-like prostration and implacable enmity. Through the rich imaginative resources of a tale of enchantment, written in the throes of protracted depression, he works through long-festering psychical wounds and advances his astonishing insight into self-inflicted grief. If *Rasselas* made cunning inroads to the dread fortress of self-delusion, "The Fountains" follows this remarkable tack, now assisted by a growing friendship with the Thrales. Their accepting Johnson, for all his incredibly imagined wickedness, need for punishment, and "disturbances of the mind very near to madness,"[25] must have helped to calm the terrifying apparitions he never could appease. To the extent that Mrs. Thrale's affection and approval must have reawakened childhood experience of a far different order, she becomes the object of his adoring gratitude.[26] "The Fountains" is a moving tribute to Mrs. Thrale's care for Johnson in his sickness. If Imlac was a fancied mentor who advises a befuddled prince, Floretta, the heroine of "The Fountains," is a picturesque play on the real Mrs. Thrale, who rescues a now barely subsistent creature, a broken songbird, crying out "in such a note as she had never observed before" (*Works*, 16: 231). Like a dream, the fairy tale, as the late Bruno Bettelheim and others have shown, offers important clues into the hidden secrets of the mind. Its submerged themes, representing painful inner conflicts, point the way to clarity and resolution.[27] So Johnson also explored this possibility by daring to engage the private innuendos and imagery of his fantasy life.

Probably more than anyone else, Mrs. Thrale witnessed the state of Johnson's mind in the mid-1760s, during one of his most serious bouts of mental depression:

> In the year 1766 his health, which he had always complained of, grew so exceedingly bad, that he could not stir out of his room in the courts he inhabited for many *weeks* together, I think *months*.
>
> Mr. Thrale's attentions and my own now became so acceptable to him, that he often lamented to us the horrible condition of his mind, which he said was nearly distracted; and though he charged *us* to make him odd solemn promises of secrecy on so strange a subject, yet when we waited on him one morning, and heard him, in the most pathetic terms, beg the prayers of Dr. Delap, who had left him, as we came in, I felt excessively affected with grief, and well remember my husband involuntarily lifted up one hand to shut his mouth, from provocation at hearing a man so wildly proclaim what he could at last persuade no one to believe; and what, if true, would have been so very unfit to reveal.[28]

It was soon afterward that the Thrales took him in, but before this, he had been dining with them about once a week, sometimes more frequently, during the winter of 1765–66. And during that winter, just before the onset of severe depression, Johnson composed "The Fountains," which first appeared in Anna Williams' *Miscellanies in Prose and Verse*.[29] Moreover, the strange little tale followed on the heels of the great "Preface to Shakespeare," written only a few months earlier, and containing some of his most discerning views on the powers of imagination and imaginative projection. Lending its own unique imprimatur to the uses of enchantment, "The Fountains" is likely the most personal thing Johnson ever published.

Simply put, "The Fountains" is the story of the young woman Floretta's generous deed, which redeems the fairy Lilinet, who is under a spell cast by the queen of the fairies. Changed into a goldfinch, a small songbird, for her disobedience, Lilinet must search the world for "some human being [who] shall shew thee kindness without any prospect of interest" (*Works*, 16: 234). After a long and arduous quest, she meets Floretta, who breaks the spell, and in token of thanks, Lilinet gives the girl magical powers. But the exercise of these powers can never equal the grace and bounty of the original loving act, and in the end, they both are resigned to the "course of nature."

With a strong personal interest, Mrs. Thrale provides some insight into more tantalizing meaning of "The Fountains," which relates her to Floretta. She recalls its composition, when Johnson needed more copy to fill Anna Williams's slim volume. He turned to her for a contribution, which she supplied, and then he said, "Come Mistress, now *I'll* write a Tale and your Character shall be in it."[30] It is clear from the story that the identities of the heroine Floretta and Mrs. Thrale almost wholly coincide: Floretta's generosity and tender-heartedness are a compliment to Johnson's hostess and express much of his gratitude and affection to her. Other details such as the setting of the tale near Plinlimmon in Wales, the country of Mrs. Thrale's birth and a source of great pride in her boasting an ancient and distinguished lineage; the rather unflattering characterization of Floretta's mother, who very likely represents Mrs. Thrale's mother, Mrs. Salusbury, with whom Johnson was initially on hostile terms; and the fact that Mrs. Thrale herself apparently identified strongly in real life with Floretta, in several references which appear in her own writings—all of these are strong arguments that Johnson's new friend was the model for the portrait of his heroine.[31]

As "The Fountains" begins, Floretta rescues a poor panic-struck songbird from the talons of a fierce hawk about to devour it. For protection, she "put him in her bosom" (*Works*, 16: 231), until the danger subsides; then, after some soothing and gentle attentions, she gives him back his freedom. A scene awash in allusion, it calls up the deepest yearnings of an ailing child to be reclaimed and made well by his mother's all-abounding love. If Mrs. Thrale is the model for Floretta, it is obvious that Johnson himself is much entangled in the character of the creature she restores. Mrs. Thrale provides another key to the latent meaning of "The Fountains" by explaining a collaboration she and Johnson undertook during the beginning of their friendship: "It was about the year 1765 when our Doctor told me that he would translate the Consolations of Philosophy, but said, I must do the Odes for him, and produce one every Thursday [the day on which he regularly came to dinner]: he was obeyed; and in commending some, and correcting others, about a dozen Thursdays passed away."[32] The project soon broke off, but it is significant in reference to the epigraph of "The Fountains," which is from *Book III, Metre 12* of Boethius, translated by Johnson: "Happy he whose eyes have view'd / The transparent Fount of good" (ll. 1–2, *Works*, 6: 260). This particular *Metre* tells the story of Orpheus' descent to the underworld to recover his dead wife, which he almost accomplishes through the magical power of his song. But just as he reaches daylight, he disobeys a hallowed command, looks back into the inferno, and he loses everything. The theme of irreparable loss opens a welter of associations to Johnson's habitual torments and longings. It stirs the memory of his most profound attachments, summoning images of former beloved women: his mother, his wife, Hill Boothby (the late lamented "Sweet Angel," whom he probably intended to marry after Tetty's death)[33]. Losing them, he has lost himself, blasted by his own fatal imperfection, just as Orpheus, who may as well have perished with Eurydice, in the world of the dead. As he translates it:

> Just emerging into Light
> Orpheus turn'd his eager sight,
> Fondly view'd his following bride,
> Viewing lost and losing died.

(ll. 49–52, *Works*, 6: 263)

Buried deep in "The Fountains" is a knowledge sprung from Johnson's intrapsychic life, a knowledge which touches on the breaking of sacred oaths and injunctions. Orpheus is destroyed for want of faith.

Though granted a special dispensation from the gods, he does not keep his bargain or his trust. The character of Orpheus traditionally represents the heavenly heights to which man aspires: his artistry is the very soul of sublime and liberating aims. As Johnson translates the full quatrain from Boethius:

> Happy he whose Eyes have view'd
> The transparent Fount of Good;
> Happy whose unfetterd mind
> Leaves the Load of Earth behind.
>
> (ll. 1–4, *Works*, 6: 260)

But betraying these lofty aims, Orpheus sinks back into the primitive deep, as it were, by the weight of his doubt and despair. In Johnson's story, the enchanted songbird was also punished for disobedience, being made to scour the lower depths of human nature. It is mortified and degraded, suffering and making others suffer all manner of mischiefs, until redeemed by Floretta. As a reward, the girl is shown two fountains, one of joy, the other of sorrow: to drink from the first will grant her wish, to drink from the second will revoke it. Thus she acquires and gives back, in turn, beauty, a lover, an aggressive personality, riches, longevity, but holds on to wit. She learns the corruptibility of every desire, even wit, which she nevertheless decides to keep. With Floretta's disillusionment, we are reminded once more of Johnson's rendering of the Orpheus myth:

> To you whose gen'rous wishes rise
> To court communion with the skies
>   To you the tale is told;
> When grasping bliss th' unsteady mind
> Looks back on what she left behind,
>   She faints and quits her hold.
>
> (ll. 53–58, *Works*, 6: 263)

In the end, it seems man's baser instincts prevail; like Orpheus, he wavers, timid and insecure, ridden by insoluble ambivalence.[34] But if Johnson envisions this dismal obliquity, he makes no unwonted leaps of faith. Out of the gracious act, mercifully bestowed, he discovers a dynamic integrative ideal that masters the archaic heritage and conciliates the gnashing hellish fury of the mind. "The Fountains" concludes much like *Rasselas*, in a mood of forbearance and peace. The final sad embrace between Floretta and her fairy-friend suggests a truce between the feuding factions of inner life, the restive wishes and the heart corroded by denial, which ever provoke the hawk's devouring rage. And it pledges a commitment, however tainted by frailty and error, to the free current of human enterprise: "Lady Lilinet dropped a tear, impressed upon her lips the final kiss, and resigned her, as she resigned herself, to the course of Nature" (*Works*, 16: 249).

*   *   *

It is no coincidence that the Vinerian lectures on law, to which Johnson contributed from 1766 to very likely 1770, echo themes of man's ethical and social development. Using implicit analogies between the individual and his culture, they attempt to show how want and fear are grounded in the childhood of humanity, how archaic mental processes recapitulate the course of events in the distant human past. While plagued by apprehensions of danger and disintegration, even struggling to preserve his sanity, Johnson came to assist his young friend Robert Chambers, Vinerian Professor of English Law at Oxford, in putting together the great encyclopedic series. Doubtless he influenced its radical vision that man's highest achievement evolved out of a barbaric history. Taken as a whole, the lectures make Johnson's tenacious argument for the inherent and ineradicable ambivalence of human life. Strife and contention were the original motives for developing a strong ruling authority. As our ancestors fought the original battle of irreconcilable emotions—love and hate, hope and fear, desire and destruction—they learned to channel these in legitimate ways. Johnson's passionate tones are heard to resonate through many sections of the lectures, as he also struggles to conquer the raging primitive underworld, to partake of what is highest, most civilized, and just. From Part II, Lecture I, "Of Criminal Law, and First of the General Nature of Punishments," his urgent voice is unmistakable:

> While mankind continued in the state of gross barbarity in which all were eager to do wrong and all unwilling to suffer, it is apparent that every man's fear would be greater than his hope, for an individual, thinking himself at liberty to act merely for his own interest, would consider every other individual as his enemy who acted only by the same principle. When they came to deliberate how they should escape what many had felt and all dreaded, they would soon find that safety was only to be obtained by setting interest on the side of innocence, by such a scheme of regulation as should give every man a

prospect of living more happily by forbearing than by usurping the property of another; and which should repress the passions of anger and revenge by making their gratification the cause of immediate misery. . . . Law is made for no other reason but that men may not do that which they desire.[35]

Perhaps Johnson's work on the ferocious dramatic origins of culture helped to break the spell of his crippling depression. For he first discovered the drama within himself. Some years later, when he took the tour with Boswell to the Hebrides, he went in search of a primordial inheritance, the starting point, so he intimates, for civilized life. And while the "savage virtues and barbarous grandeur" (*Works*, 9: 58) were no longer physically visible, he nonetheless found what he set out for. *A Journey to the Western Islands of Scotland* (1775) discovers a realm reconstituted by myth and reverie, as exotic in its own right as the fabulous voyages he relished in Homer, Defoe, and Cervantes. Unlike Boswell's *Tour to the Hebrides* (1785), which wings its way through the present and transparent itinerary, Johnson's narrative finds him ruminating on ancient ceremonials and archaic rituals. He imaginatively embellishes the map of his travel with folklore and superstition. At every juncture, he thrills to the deepest longings and horrors of mankind. Ghosts of archetypal legend, tossed by peril and adversity, ever haunt his landscape. The spirit of Macbeth: "We went forwards the same day to Fores, the town to which Macbeth was travelling, when he met the weird sisters in his way. This to an Englishman is classic ground. Our imaginations were heated, and our thoughts recalled to their old amusements" (25); and of Ulysses: "Without is the rough ocean and the rocky land, the beating billows and the howling storm: within is plenty and elegance, beauty and gaiety, the song and the dance. In Raasay, if I could have found an Ulysses, I had fancied a Phaeacia" (66).

So does the scene before him yield projections of a primitive mental domain, invested with ruthless abandon. The view of "an unknown and untravelled wilderness," where he sat lost in contemplation, inspired him to write the *Journey*, he explains: "Whether I spent the hour well I know not; for here I first conceived the thought of this narration" (40). And throwing his fantasies upon the rude mountain range, he gives himself over to vengeful Nature, the unconquerable enemy, rising up against him: "The phantoms which haunt a desert are want, and misery, and danger; the evils of dereliction rush upon the thoughts; man is made unwillingly acquainted with his own weakness, and meditation shews him only how little he can sustain, and how little he can perform." His mind turns upon instincts of life and death: "Whoever had been in the place where I sat, unprovided with provisions and ignorant of the country, might, at least before the roads were made, have wandered among the rocks, till he had perished with hardship, before he could have found either food or shelter." His angle of vision knows no limit: "Yet what are these hillocks to the ridges of Taurus, or these spots of wildness to the deserts of America?" (41). In the superstition of the "second sight," he likewise educes the extraordinary powers of imaginative projection. To buried mental content he ascribes, much like Freud, the manifestations of the uncanny.[36] He notes how mainly hostile and destructive impulses press upon consciousness: "Almost all remarkable events have evil for their basis; and are either miseries incurred, or miseries escaped. Our sense is so much stronger of what we suffer, than of what we enjoy, that the ideas of pain predominate in almost every mind. . . . The 'second sight' is only wonderful because it is rare, for, considered in itself, it involves no more difficulty than dreams" (108–09). In a diary entry of January 1759, shortly after the death of his mother, Johnson wrote, "The dream of my Brother I shall remember" (*Works*, 1: 67). And to Mrs. Thrale he confessed, "The first corruption that entered into my heart was communicated in a dream."[37] Invariably, he listened to these enigmatic messages, meaningfully disguised.

Throughout Johnson's famous travels, sumptuous fantasy imbued with passion ever accompanies him. He is never far from the mystique of early years when, as he loved to relate, the ghost scene from *Hamlet* so terrified him that he bolted from the room where he read it, frantic to break its spell.[38] At every opportunity, his thoughts give play to a fervent imagination. He puts himself in the place of the straggler, a familiar pose, who strays in the dead of night: "In travelling even thus almost without light thro' naked solitude, when there is a guide whose conduct may be trusted, a mind not naturally too much disposed to fear, may preserve some degree of cheerfulness; but what must be the solicitude of him who should be wandering, among the craggs and hollows, benighted, ignorant, and alone?" (*Works*, 9: 77). But happily he escapes disaster, much like his favorite heroes of old: "The fictions of the Gothick romances were not so remote from credibility as they are now thought. In the full prevalence of the feudal institution, when violence desolated the world, and every baron lived in a fortress, forests and castles were regularly succeeded by each other, and the adventurer might very suddenly pass from the gloom of woods, or the ruggedness of moors, to seats of plenty, gaiety, and magnificence." So does he participate in the fears of being forsaken and the joys of rescue: "Whatever is imagined in the wildest tale, if giants, dragons, and enchantment be excepted, would be felt by him, who, wandering in the mountains without a guide, or upon the sea without a pilot, should be carried amidst his terror and uncertainty to the hospitality and elegance of Raasay or Dunvegan" (77).

It is precisely this spirit of brave exploit which shapes Johnson's most compelling identity in the *Journey*. He dreams of owning a remote island and conquering another, as Boswell and company cheer him on. Boswell recounts:

> There is a beautiful little island in the Loch of Dunvegan, called *Isa*. M'Leod said, he would give it to Dr. Johnson, on condition of his residing on it three months in the year; nay one month. Dr. Johnson was highly amused with the fancy. . . . He talked a great deal of this island;—how he would build a house there,—how he would fortify it,—how he would have cannon,—how he would plant,—how he would sally out, and *take* the isle of Muck;—and then he laughed with uncommon glee, and could hardly leave off. . . . M'Leod encouraged the fancy of Dr. Johnson's becoming owner of an island; told him, that it was the practice in this country to name every man by his lands; and begged leave to drink to him in that mode: "*Island Isa*, your health!"— Ulinish, Talisker, Mr. M'Queen, and I, all joined in our different manners, while Dr. Johnson bowed to each, with much good humour.[39]

He plays at being a denizen of the isles: in a flash, Boswell marvels, he is transformed into a fierce warrior-chief: "One night, in Col, he strutted about the room with a broadsword and target, and made a formidable appearance." Or a bard of antiquity: "Another night, I took the liberty to put a large blue bonnet on his head. His age, his size, and his bushy grey wig, with this covering on it, presented the image of a venerable *Senachi*: and, however unfavourable to the Lowland Scots, he seemed much pleased to assume the appearance of an ancient Caledonian." Or a ferocious creature of the wild: "He laid hold of a little girl, Stuart Dallas, niece to Mrs. Riddoch [Boswell's cousin], and, representing himself as a giant, said, he would take her with him! telling her, in a hollow voice, that he lived in a cave, and had a bed in the rock, and she should have a little bed cut opposite to it."[40] Too much in the *Journey* Johnson protests about seeing things as they are, that is, the political and social problems of present-day Scotland, an altogether different theme, to be sure, of the narrative.[41] But his profoundest exploration here, and at every turn in his writing, surely discloses more than would meet the eye. The *terra incognita* he traverses holds for him wondrous and alluring caverns of meaning. And perhaps he pays greatest tribute to "the uses of enchantment" when he surveys the ancient

ruins at Iona. Struck with awe by these monuments to human enlightenment, which sprung from the shadows of discord and suffering, he fuels the
flame of his heart's desire. In this famous scene, he breathes the miraculous
freedom and majesty conferred by the powers of the mind:

> We were now treading that illustrious island, which was once the luminary of
> the Caledonian regions, whence savage clans and roving barbarians derived
> the benefits of knowledge, and the blessings of religion. To abstract the mind
> from all local emotion would be impossible, if it were endeavoured, and would
> be foolish, if it were possible. Whatever withdraws us from the power of our
> senses; whatever makes the past, the distant, or the future predominate over
> the present, advances us in the dignity of thinking beings. Far from me and
> from my friends, be such frigid philosophy as may conduct us indifferent and
> unmoved over any ground which has been dignified by wisdom, bravery, or
> virtue. (*Works*, 9: 148)

Notes

1. *Johnsonian Miscellanies*, 1: 156. See also Johnson's conversation with Lady
Rothes, as reported by Mr. John Longley:

> I remember Lady Rothes spoke of the advantage children now derived from
> the little books published purposely for their instruction. Johnson contro-
> verted, asserting that at an early age it was better to gratify curiosity with
> wonders than to attempt planting truth, before the mind was prepared to
> receive it, and therefore *Jack the Giant-Killer*, *Parsimus and Parismenus*, and *The
> Seven Champions of Christendom* were fitter for them than Mrs. Barbauld and
> Mrs. Trimmer. (*Life*, 4: 8, n. 3)

2. *Life*, 1: 49. Percy adds: "I have heard him attribute to these extravagant
fictions that unsettled turn of mind which prevented his ever fixing in any profession." Certainly Johnson at times reproved the "wild strain of imagination" in works
of fiction. See the famous discussion in *Rambler* 4, *Works*, 3: 19–25, and in book 9,
chapter 11, attributed to him, of Charlotte Lennox's *The Female Quixote* (1752; rpt.
(New York: Oxford University Press, 1973), pp. 368–82. But his real esteem and
honest appreciation more often overcome such doleful cautionary notes, as we shall
see.
3. *Letters*, 1: 206, no. 197 (14 March 1768).
4. Carey McIntosh, *The Choice of Life: Samuel Johnson and the World of Fiction*
(New Haven, Conn.: Yale University Press, 1973), p. ix.
5. "Annotations to Crousaz, *Commentary* on Pope's *Essay on Man*," *Oxford
Authors*, p. 92.
6. *Life*, 5: 13.
7. *Life*, 1: 67.

8. See Katherine Balderston, "Dr. Johnson and William Law," *PMLA* 75 (September 1960): 382–94.

9. See *Works*, 7: 3–6, 122–23, 160; and *Works*, 8: 752–55, 969–70.

10. For some of the most discerning views of Johnson on imagination and fancy, see the discussions in R. D. Havens, "Johnson's Distrust of the Imagination, *ELH* 10 (1943): 243–55; Hagstrum, *Literary Criticism*, pp. 89–96; Alkon, *Moral Discipline*, pp. 69–76.

11. "Was there ever yet any thing written by mere man that was wished longer by its readers, excepting Don Quixote, Robinson Crusoe, and the Pilgrim's Progress?" he exclaimed to Mrs. Thrale, and she confirms, "After Homer's Iliad, Mr. Johnson confessed that the work of Cervantes was the greatest in the world, speaking of it I mean as a book of entertainment" (*Johnsonian Miscellanies*, 1: 332–33).

12. *Female Quixote*, p. 374.

13. See "The Life of Butler," where Johnson summarizes his view of the Don's character:

Cervantes shews a man who, having by the incessant perusal of incredible tales subjected his understanding to his imagination, and familiarised his mind by pertinacious meditation to trains of incredible events and scenes of impossible existence, goes out in the pride of knighthood to redress wrongs and defend virgins, to rescue captive princesses, and tumble usurpers from their thrones, attended by a squire whose cunning, too low for the suspicion of a generous mind, enables him often to cheat his master. . . . Cervantes had so much kindness for Don Quixote that, however he embarrasses him with absurd distresses, he gives him so much sense and virtue as may preserve our esteem: wherever he is or whatever he does he is made by matchless dexterity commonly ridiculous, but never contemptible. (*Lives*, 1: 209–10)

14. Indeed, Johnson sometimes made fun of them. See, for example, his derisive comment in the "Life of Roscommon":

The observation, that his imagination would probably have been more fruitful and spritely if his judgement had been less severe, may be answered, by a remarker somewhat inclined to cavil, by a contrary supposition, that his judgement would probably have been less severe if his imagination had been more fruitful. It is ridiculous to oppose judgement to imagination; for it does not appear that men have necessarily less of one as they have more of the other. (*Lives*, 1: 235)

15. In the Introduction to *Modern Critical Views: Dr. Samuel Johnson and James Boswell*, ed. Harold Bloom (New York: Chelsea House, 1986), Harold Bloom calls Johnson "the strongest critic in the varied history of Western literary culture," largely on these grounds. "Johnson . . . show[s] us that memorable criticism is experiential criticism, that there is no method except oneself" (p. 2). Further, Bloom suggests that Johnson's view of Shakespeare is shaped by a psychological understanding: "To have created the modern representation of the mind was the

achievement neither of Montaigne nor (belatedly) of Freud, but of Shakespeare alone. What Johnson teaches us is that Shakespeare invented our psychology, to an astonishing degree" (p. 7).

16. So it often has been said that the poet can objectify, while at the same time gain access to deepest structures of the mind: "Psychotherapy and art both serve to place a distance between the individual and his unconscious conflicts, a distance from which he can contemplate with comfort derivatives of his unconscious fantasies" (David Beres and Jacob Arlow, "Fantasy and Identification in Empathy," *Psychoanalytic Quarterly* 63 [1975]: 46).

17. Clearly the best studies of Johnson's literary criticism take up his inquiries into what readers really feel, how meaning comes through psychological identification. Jean Hagstrum's pioneering study led the way for considering Johnson's psychological criteria of literary value, as he writes: "[Literature] was for Johnson a moral and psychological instrument of communication that pointed outside itself to the empirical reality which it 'imitated,' to the mind that had created it, or to the mind that was to enjoy it and be instructed by it" (*Samuel Johnson's Literary Criticism*, p. 37; see also pp. 76–96). Arguments along these lines include Paul Alkon, *Moral Discipline*, pp. 109–45; William Edinger, *Samuel Johnson and Poetical Style* (Chicago: University of Chicago Press, 1977), pp. 31–77; John B. Radner, "Samuel Johnson, The Deceptive Imagination, and Sympathy," *Studies in Burke and His Time* 16 (1974): 23–46; and Leopold Damorosch, Jr., in both *The Uses of Johnson's Criticism* (Charlottesville: University Press of Virginia, 1976), pp. 38–57; and "Samuel Johnson and Reader-Response Criticism," *The Eighteenth Century: Theory and Interpretation* 21 (1980): 91–108. See also Hagstrum's witty and shrewd assessment of contemporary literary theory vis-à-vis Johnson in "Johnson Among the Deconstructionists," rpt. in *Eros and Vision: The Restoration to Romanticism* (Evanston, Ill.: Northwestern University Press, 1989), pp. 139–51.

18. The critical studies of *Rasselas* are legion and some of the traditional views of its intellectual background are among the best, in particular, Gwin Kolb, "The Structure of *Rasselas*," *PMLA* 66 (Sept 1951): 698–717; Paul Fussell, *Samuel Johnson and the Life of Writing* (New York: Harcourt Brace Jovanovich, 1971), pp. 216–45; Howard Weinbrot, "The Reader, the General and the Particular," *ECS* 5 (1971): 80–96; Arieh Sachs, *Passionate Intelligence*, pp. 67–108; Eric Rothstein, *Systems of Order and Inquiry in Later Eighteenth-Century Fiction* (Berkeley and Los Angeles: University of California Press, 1975), pp. 23–61. For a survey from 1759 to 1986, complete with bibliography, see Edward Tomarken, *Johnson, Rasselas, and the Choice of Criticism* (Lexington: University of Kentucky Press, 1989), pp. 5–37, 194–202. Not unexpectedly, *Rasselas* has generated prolix and interminable arguments about its orthodox Christian, moral, and philosophical dimensions, with only a casual nod now and again at the psychological. Exceptions, which in fact stress the psychological, include: Richard B. Hovey, "Dr. Samuel Johnson, Psychiatrist," *Modern Language Quarterly* 15 (1954): 321–35; W.J. Bate, *The Achievement*, passim; Kathleen M. Grange, "Dr. Samuel Johnson's Account of a Schizophrenic Illness in *Rasselas*," *Medical History* 6 (April 1963): 162–69; Sheridan Baker, "*Rasselas*: Psychological Irony and Romance," *Philological Quarterly* 45 (1966): 249–61; Kenneth T. Reed, "This Tasteless Tranquility: A Freudian Note on Johnson's 'Rasselas,'" *Literature*

and Psychology 19 (1969): 61–62; John Wain, "A Death and a Journey in the Mind," in *Samuel Johnson*, pp. 206–15; W. B. Carnochan, *Confinement and Flight: An Essay on English Literature of the Eighteenth Century* (Berkeley: University of California Press, 1977), pp. 147–70; Frederick Keener, *The Chain of Becoming*, pp. 217–40; Alan Liu, "Toward a Theory of Common Sense: Beckford's *Vathek* and Johnson's *Rasselas*," *Texas Studies in Language and Literature* 26 (1984): 183–217; Gloria Sybil Gross, "Dr. Johnson's Practice: The Medical Context for *Rasselas*," *Studies in Eighteenth-Century Culture* 14 (1985): 275–88. Of these, Carnochan reaches the Foucauvian understanding: "[Johnson] believed that captivity was a natural condition and that life could be figured as life in chains. . . . We feel the powerfulness of Johnson walking like one in fetters, because Johnson makes us feel it in his life and work, as almost a natural joy. . . . His struggling gait was the mark, on him, of life's vital chain" (pp. 168–70).

19. See Keener, *The Chain of Becoming*, pp. 3–14, 217–40, for an astute reading of the philosophical tale in relation to modern psychological analysis:

> What I would assert about the philosophical tale . . is that . . . the sentiments and motives of tale characters are *not* generally far removed from those of readers, indeed constantly bring to mind realities of thought, feeling, and motivation. . . . Much more than the [eighteenth-century] novel, the philosophical tale is occupied with the theme of the main character's psychological self-assessment, at least his need for it, promoting such realism on his part as prerequisite to all other judgments. The tale sets realism of psychological self-assessment against the other forms of realism typical of the novel, English and French, just as Locke and many of his successors, in their campaign to establish and preserve sanity and ward off delusion, insisted that philosophy begin with scrutiny of the rational and irrational processes of the natural mind, the subordination for better or worse of persons to their ideas. (pp. 12–14)

20. Freud's discovery, which is now common knowledge, of the onset of a neurotic illness is summed up by the noted psychoanalyst, Jacob Arlow. He points to experiences of similarity between the past and the present: "The new experience contains in it elements that are unconsciously interpreted as a repetition of the original trauma. . . . The concept of how neurotic illness may be precipitated in adult life may be found in the consonance between the realistic situation, and the specific, unconscious fantasy which it reactivates." See "Unconscious Fantasy and Conscious Experience," *Psychoanalytic Quarterly* 38 (1969): 1–27.

21. *Letters*, I: 31 (no. 25).

22. Roy Schafer, the distinguished psychoanalyst and psychoanalytic theorist, explores the metaphoric meaning of imprisonment in *The Analytic Attitude*, (New York: Basic Books, 1983). See pp. 257–80, "The Imprisoned Analysand:

> The psychical prisoner insists on his or her helplessness, hopelessness, and apathy, meanwhile continuing unconsciously to construct beating fantasies and biting fantasies and soiling fantasies. More than construct these fantasies, the analysand constructs actual situations which, psychically, verify and justify imprisonment; this may be done by consistently provoking the domineering and brutalizing tendencies of others. (pp. 270–71)

23. G. B. Hill notes the difference in his famous comment about the deluded aeronaut: "Johnson is content with giving the artist a ducking. Voltaire would have crippled him for life at the very least; most likely would have killed him on the spot" (*Rasselas*, ed. G. B. Hill [Oxford: Clarendon Press, 1927], p. 165). And one can only speculate on the excruciation and mayhem that would be in store for him at the hands of, say, Pope, Swift, Fielding, or Smollett. These contemporary writers were sure to have their characters severely punished for their mental defects. In *Candide* (1759), Voltaire has the hero beaten, enslaved, and narrowly miss death many times, and the heroine see her parents butchered, while suffering herself all kinds of physical torture.

24. The dating of the manuscript, according to its editors, lies somewhere between 1765 and 1772, and it survives in fragments. See *Works*, 1: xv.

25. *Works*, 1: 264, from a diary entry of 30 March 1777: "When I survey my past life, I discover nothing but a barren waste of time with some disorders of body, and disturbances of the mind very near to madness."

26. Irwin's discussion of this complex relationship in *A Personality in Conflict*, pp. 125–43, is, if overstated, still one that hits the mark:

> Finding Mrs. Thrale a sweet creature with a temper the most delightful of any woman he knew, he opened his heart to her and poured forth not only the unfulfilled longings of his childhood, but also the repressed resentment of a child. And finding in Mrs. Thrale the acceptance he craved, he found in her a mother-substitute under whose care he was able to relive and finally escape the traumatic experiences of his childhood. The transference relationship which Johnson had unconsciously sought but failed to establish with his wife and also with Hill Boothby was at last to be realized and completely fulfilled. (p. 128)

27. In his masterly study, *The Uses of Enchantment: The Meaning and Importance of Fairy Tales* (1975; New York: Vintage Books, 1977), Bruno Bettelheim explains how stories imbrued with myth and the supernatural work to uncover the dark side of personality, but how they also can be used to encourage healthy emotional development:

> The fairy tale is therapeutic because the patient finds his *own* solutions, through contemplating what the story seems to imply about him and his inner conflicts at this moment in his life. . . . The figures and events of fairy tales . . . personify and illustrate inner conflicts, but they suggest ever so subtly how these conflicts may be solved, and what the next steps in the development toward a higher humanity might be. . . . The fairy tale reassures, gives hope for the future, and holds out the promise of a happy ending. (pp. 25–26)

28. *Johnsonian Miscellanies*, 1: 234.

29. Interestingly, "The Fountains" enjoyed a greater popularity than is generally acknowledged today: as part of Anna William's volume, it was favorably reviewed in several publications, and between 1766 and 1791, it was reprinted in eight popular periodicals (Robert D. Mayo, *The English Novel in the Magazines 1740–1815* [Evanston, Ill.: Northwestern University Press, 1962], p. 497).

30. From the Mainwaring Piozziana, as quoted in Clifford, *Hester Lynch Piozzi*, p. 61.

31. For an elegantly detailed analysis of Mrs. Thrale's identity and persistent interest in "The Fountains," see Gwin J. Kolb, "Mrs. (Thrale) Piozzi and Dr. Johnson's *The Fountains: A Fairy Tale*," *Novel* 13 (1979): 68–81.

32. Mrs. Piozzi, *Letters to and from the late Samuel Johnson* (London, 1788), 1: vi.

33. See Bate, *Samuel Johnson*, pp. 319–21, 327.

34. Johnson's old friend, Elizabeth Carter, for one, found the conclusion of "The Fountains" to be "so unsatisfactory and melancholy, that it left only a gloomy impression on my mind," *A Series of Letters . . . Carter . . . Talbot*, ed. M. Pennington (1809), 3: 135, as quoted in Bate, *Samuel Johnson*, p. 411.

35. Sir Robert Chambers (composed in association with Samuel Johnson), *A Course of Lectures on the English Law, Delivered at the University of Oxford 1767–1773*, ed. Thomas M. Curley (Madison: University of Wisconsin Press, 1986), 1: 308, 311. See also related passages from this section:

> The experience of many ages has taught every civilized nation that as in the physical disposition of the universe every planet is detained in its orbit by an exact equipoise of contrary tendencies, so in the economy of the moral world contrary passions debilitate each other. Every man desires to retain his own in proportion as he desires to seize what is another's, and no man can be allowed to rob, where none are willing to be robbed; we therefore mutually agree to protect and be protected, and every invader of property is opposed by the whole community, at least by all that part of it which has any thing to lose. . . . If the evil of penalty could not exceed the advantage of wickedness, the mind, so far as it is influenced merely by the laws of man, could never pass beyond an equipoise of passion, and the nearer good would generally outweigh the remoter evil. But such is the frame of man that the dread of evil may be always made more powerful than the appetite of good. He that possessing a hundred sheep shall steal a hundred more, will by no means gain such a degree of happiness as he will lose if his own hundred be taken away. Even the *lex talionis* [law of retaliation: "an eye for an eye, a tooth for a tooth"] has upon this principle a very powerful operation, for no man can have as much pleasure in pulling out the eyes of another as he will suffer pain from the pulling out of his own. (1: 306, 309)

36. See Freud's essay, "The 'Uncanny'" (1919):

> An uncanny effect is often and easily produced by effacing the distinction between imagination and reality, such as when something that we have hitherto regarded as imaginary appears before us in reality, or when a symbol takes over the full functions and significance of the thing it symbolizes, and so on. . . . The infantile element in this, which also holds sway in the minds of neurotics, is the over-accentuation of psychical reality in comparison with physical reality—a feature closely allied to the belief in the omnipotence of

thoughts. . . . The uncanny is nothing else than a hidden, familiar thing that has undergone repression and then emerged from it." (*Standard Edition*, 17: 244–45)

37. *Johnsonian Miscellanies*, 1: 159.

38. *Johnsonian Miscellanies*, 1: 158; *Life*, 1: 70. See also Johnson's comment in the *Observations on Macbeth* (1745): "He that peruses Shakespeare, looks round alarmed, and starts to find himself alone" (*Works*, 7: 20).

39. *Journal of a Tour to the Hebrides, with Samuel Johnson, LL.D.* (1786) ed. R. W. Chapman (London: Oxford University Press, 1970), p. 327.

40. *Journal of a Tour to the Hebrides*, pp. 379, 215.

41. For this perspective, see John B. Radner, "The Significance of Johnson's Changing Views of the Hebrides," in *The Unknown Samuel Johnson*, ed. John J. Burke, Jr. and Donald Kay (Madison: University of Wisconsin Press, 1983), pp. 131–49. Also see Thomas M. Curley's study of Johnson's passion for travel in *Samuel Johnson and the Age of Travel* (Athens: University of Georgia Press, 1976), pp. 183–219 and passim.

7. Character and Culture

HAVING WEARILY CONCLUDED THE REVISION OF THE *Dictionary* for a fourth edition in late 1772, Johnson drew from feelings of bruising unrest and self-doubt to write a very private poem. Its title, transliterated from the Greek as *Gnothi Seauton*, meaning "Know Thyself," comes from the famous exhortation written over Apollo's Temple at Delphi, a city of dizzying steep slopes, with forbidding cliffs above it and a gulf beneath. If perhaps he envisioned this treacherous terrain, the seat of the oracle who spoke in riddles and dread secrets, Johnson was moved to explore the buried content of his own uneasiness and guilt. "Know Thyself" (written in Latin but here presented through John Wain's splendid translation) opens to a staggering malediction:

> Scaliger, when with scant sense of achievement he had scrawled
> his lexicon's last page, after prolonged toil, loathing
> the mindless menial grind, the small problems piled into mountains,
> in hate groaning, he gave his thought to guide grave judges
> that the penal system should prescribe for all hard prisoners
> found guilty of devilment, the drudgery of making a dictionary—
> one punishment, for the most impenitent, all punishments
>   compounding![1]

(ll. 1–7)

Following the bitter condemnation with more regret and disdain, Johnson comes to the main point when he looks into a state of mind pervaded by unsatisfied longing. He tells of being stricken by desires unacknowledged, save in harried dreams, which entangle him in crippling convictions of blame and defeat. More drastically is he held in check by prohibitions against voracious appetite. More furiously is he driven, in the terms of *Rasselas*, by "that hunger of imagination which preys incessantly upon life, and must be always appeased by some employment" (*Works*, 16: 118). Despite vast stores of effort and accomplishment,

. . . I find myself still fettered to myself:
the dull doom of doing nothing, harsher than any drudgery,
stays for me, and the staleness of slow stagnation.
Cares beget cares, and a clamouring crowd of troubles
vex me, and vile dreams, the sour sleep of an empty mind.

(ll. 25–29)

He describes the suppression of tempestuous need, which continues to
fester persistently and elusively to seek its desperate utterance. In effect, he
regresses to an archaic style of thinking:

Trembling, I trudge everywhere, peering, prying, into everything,
    trying
passionate to know if somewhere, anyhow, a path leads up to a
    more perfect pasture,

(ll. 33–34)

He is depleted and robbed of the very spirit he hoped would sustain him:

but glooming over grand schemes I never find my growing-point,
and am always forced finally to face myself, to own frankly
that my heart is illiterate, and my mind's strength an illusion
I labour to keep alive. . . .
. . . .
Every endeavour, every avenue, ends in frustration always.

(ll. 35–38, 41)

Its desires thus deprived and obstructed, the mind retaliates in ghastly,
primeval representations of negation and terror:

Turning to survey its territory, that night-shadowed tundra,
the mind is full of fear—of ghosts, of the fleeting glimmer
of the thin shadows of nothing, the absence of shapes, the shimmer.

(ll. 50–52)

Even so, he will not give over the struggle, let the deviltry do its worst.
Perhaps his ruminations on the ancient world, wrought of pregnant mystery, led him to ponder the myth of Sisyphus.[2] As punishment in Hades for
an unspecified impious act, the legendary hero had to spend eternity in

futile attempts to push an enormous boulder to the top of a steep hill, where it was fated always to roll down again. For twentieth-century existentialists, Sisyphus was a symbol of the absurd hero, passionate, tortured, yet superior to his fate.[3] So like the gritty self-portrait of Johnson, who ends his meditation on a note of profoundest irony. The pathetic quest for human happiness and its preordained failure generate an astonishing point of view: that which constitutes his suffering at the same time crowns his victory:

> What then am I to do? Let my declining years go down to the dark?
> Or get myself together, gather the last of my gall,
> and hurl myself at some task huge enough for a hero?
> And if that's too much, perhaps my friends might find me
> some dull, decent job, undemanding: like making a dictionary . . .
>
> (ll. 53–57)

While the last line's jest may soften the scorn and defiance, still the Sisyphean rage at insoluble predicament looms large as ever. In the realm of the mind, desire, to use the Freudian parlance, is ever doomed to extinction. And this vision of the contending forces of mental life, laden with paradox and rankling inconsistency, determines the radical bent of Johnson's last major work, *The Lives of the Poets*.

Announcing to Boswell that he was hired to write "little Lives, and little Prefaces, to a little edition of the English Poets,"[4] Johnson might have been playing with the wish to refrain from old anxieties and harassments in his "declining years," just as he finally mocked his unsubdued passion in "Know Thyself." But far from "some dull, decent job, undemanding," the work ran to fifty-six octavo volumes, his prefaces to be published in ten. "I have been led beyond my intention, I hope, by the honest desire of giving useful pleasure" (*Lives*, 1: xxvi), he states in the Advertisement to *Prefaces Biographical and Critical to the Works of the English Poets* (as they were originally entitled), the first four volumes appearing in 1779, the last six in 1781. Indeed, the work was more like a heroic endeavor, staking out wide horizons and waxing formidable through its brave disclosures and daring interpretations of character. Johnson had decided views on the art of biography, his favorite and arguably most accomplished literary genre. Boswell recounts his minimal regard for his predecessors in English literary biography,[5] and Edmond Malone recalls how he resolved to write no "honeysuckle" life of Milton (*Lives*, 1: 84), intent as he was on a far different strain in this, the most notorious of the *Lives*. His own words attest to a determined purpose to present a documentary of real life, as he heartily defends his portrait of Addison:

> If nothing but the bright side of characters should be shewn, we should sit down in despondency, and think it utterly impossible to imitate them in *any thing*. The sacred writers . . . related the vicious as well as the virtuous actions of men; which had this moral effect, that it kept mankind from *despair*, into which otherwise they would naturally fall, were they not supported by the recollection that others had offended like themselves.[6]

In earnest hopes that he too might inspire this sympathetic kinship, Johnson utilizes a fundamental model of psychological identification. He had, as we have seen, studied the aesthetic dimensions of intense, elemental relation of one person to another, and this idea continues unabated through his works. Almost three decades earlier, he proposed it, also in reference to the art of biography:

> There is such an uniformity in the state of man, considered apart from adventitious and separable decorations and disguises, that there is scarce any possibility of good or ill, but is common to human kind. . . . The eye is not very heedful or quick, which cannot discover the same causes still terminating their influence in the same effects, though sometimes accelerated, sometimes retarded, or perplexed by multiplied combinations. We are all prompted by the same motives, all deceived by the same fallacies, all animated by hope, obstructed by danger, entangled by desire, and seduced by pleasure. (*Rambler* 60, *Works*, 3: 320)

It is a stirring affirmation of each individual's abundant links to a common psychical heritage.[7]

To furnish the materials for writing biography, Johnson sought, in his own tantalizing phrase, the "domestick privacies," which, in turn, piqued a curiosity for the surreptitious side of life. "No man so acutely discerned the reason of every fact, the motive of every action, the end of every design,"[8] marveled Mrs. Thrale, who also recalls how he once corrected her for making the popular, but all too facile, assumption that Richardson's Clarissa was a "perfect character," open and infallibly honest. "On the contrary (said he), you may observe there is always something which she prefers to truth."[9] With this brilliant *aperçu*, he ventures a look at more puzzling and unsavory aspects of human behavior. In effect, he strikes to the very core of disturbance in the novel, to the repressed sexuality and ironic complicity of motives in the heroine's tragic plight.[10] On the deeper level, Johnson understands, and more, he strives to engage, the mental underworld. Here essentially is the target of his uncompromising surveillance, penetrating beneath the squeamish and pious professions of his age. In the unseemly, in the irrational, he finds potent stores of meaning, often at variance with the usual modes of panegyric and the "dignity" of man, so touted by his contemporaries.[11] For he first turned the sights of his surveillance on himself.

Not long after he wrote the Latin poem, "Know Thyself," Johnson composed a letter in French to Mrs. Thrale in which he lays open the tangled roots of terrifying fantasy, acting out the relentless drama of his intrapsychic life. In this remarkable record, which doubtless bears the stamp of his intrepid self-analysis, he assumes the old role of the child being beaten, at once dreading and craving the punishment which has fastened on his mind. He reverts to the rage and indignation of his childhood relation to his parents in that house of bickering complaint, but now more insightfully than ever. The letter suggests that he recognizes in himself the need for subjugation, but what is paradoxical, the need also to control his subjugator. He wishes to be treated as a naughty child, having committed any number of unspecified crimes, but he presumes to dictate the terms of his chastisement. The letter is a tissue of contradiction, where he creates the temptation to "forbidden" acts (*"que m'est interdit"*), which must then be reproached by authority. Yet all of this is under his full direction. Cunningly the tone shifts by turns, now profusely submissive, now dictatorial. It is an extraordinary exercise in passive manipulation: "If it seems better to you that I should remain in one defined place, I beg of you to spare me the necessity of confining myself, by making it impossible for me to leave the place in which you think it best for me to remain. That will cost you no more trouble than the turning of a key in the door, twice every day. You must act wholly as Mistress, if your judgment and your vigilance are to come to the rescue of my weakness."[12] And more, in embellishing the fantasy of abject obedience, his taskmaster is hardly severe or exacting but gentle and beneficent: *"des soins et de la protection d'une âme si aimable par sa douceur"* (of the care and protection of a soul so amiable in its gentleness). Vaguely we are reminded of Floretta in "The Fountains," the image of his kind *Maitresse*, who saved the distraught songbird from imminent disaster. She is even remiss, so *he* rebukes *her*, by not keeping her pledges to discipline him:

Is it too much to ask of a spirit like yours, that, holding sway over others, it should hold sway over itself, and triumph over that inconstancy which has so often caused it to neglect the execution of its own decrees, and forgotten so many promises, and condemned me to so many repeated pleadings, of which the remembrance fills me with horror? One must give, or refuse; and one must remember what one has given. I hope, my lady, that your authority over me will always make itself felt, and that you will keep me in that bondage which you know so well how to make into a happiness.

What parades as humiliation and self-abasement can be amazingly its reverse. *"Il faut ou accorder, ou refuser; il faut se souvenir de ce qu'on accorde,"* and in these words Johnson claims his share of respect and approval. The child being beaten, as Freud has demonstrated, originates in the child being loved. In both, the principal idea springs from the very nucleus of unconscious life.[13] Johnson also approaches this extraordinary enigma, tunneling layer after layer into the ghastly chasms of his passive beating fantasies. Being punished also stands for his fondest wish to be valued and accepted. As he delves into archaic springs of meaning, *"que la resouvenance me fait horreur,"* he makes terrifying discovery after discovery.[14] All of this, and more, marks the audacity of his approach to the *Lives of the Poets*.

*   *   *

While the "moral" incentive of Johnson's biographies is well documented, his practice often belies what might be expected by conventional eighteenth-century standards.[15] As we have seen, the "Life of Savage," prominently displayed in the *Lives of the Poets*, explores the characterological symptoms of a severely impaired personality: "An irregular and dissipated manner of life had made him the slave of every passion that happened to be excited by the presence of its object, and that slavery to his passions reciprocally produced a life irregular and dissipated. He was not master of his own motions, nor could promise any thing for the next day" (*Lives*, 2: 431). In this typically conceptual passage which occurs near the end, Johnson enjoins us to be affected by Savage's uncontrollable compulsions.[16] Throughout the "Life" and as he concludes the riveting character analysis, he enlists the spirit of a common psychical endowment, and he expressly avoids condemning the person, while he may condemn the rueful waste and despoilment. Indeed, he clearly intended a starker finale, unembellished by the moralistic advice, which appears in the printed version. Here is the way Johnson wished the "Life of Savage" to end, reeling with the shock of recognition: "Those are no proper judges of his conduct who have slumbered away their time on the down of plenty, nor will any wise man presume to say, 'Had I been in Savage's condition, I should have lived or written better than Savage'" (*Lives*, 2: 433).[17] In a *Rambler* article deploring capital punishment, Johnson also ascertains a shared heritage of dark and iniquitous secrets: "The learned, the judicious, the pious Boerhaave relates, that he never saw a criminal dragged to execution without asking himself, 'Who knows whether this man is not less culpable than me?' On the days when the prisons of this city are emptied into the grave, let every spectator of the dreadful procession put the same question to his own heart" (*Rambler* 114, *Works*, 4: 242).[18]

For Johnson, that which divides the criminal from the law-abiding rest is the ability to master those ill-begotten, deviant instincts he smokes out from the psychical deep. The struggle for control takes the form of renunciation and sacrifice, which, in itself, creates morality. In exploring the origins of culture, he commonly educes the idea that mankind must be subdued by institutions: "The end of all civil regulations is to secure private happiness from private malignity; to keep individuals from the power of one another" (*Idler* 22, *Works*, 2: 70). Thus do his views so fundamentally coincide with the seventeenth- and eighteenth-century tradition of Hobbes and Mandeville, linking up to the early twentieth-century Freudian dispensation, reiterated in the somber cadences of *Civilization and Its Discontents* (1930).[19] Like Freud, Johnson proposes a theory of culture which closely engages his theory of character, arguing that the wider stage of social and political unrest mirrors a resistless demand on the part of the individual: "The world is full of fraud and corruption, rapine and malignity; interest is the ruling motive of mankind, and every one is endeavouring to increase his own stores of happiness by perpetual accumulation, without reflecting upon the numbers whom his superfluity condemns to want. . . . Mankind are universally corrupt, but corrupt in different degrees" (*Adventurer* 137, *Works*, 2: 488–89). The last is a prophetic opening to Johnson's biographies, where the relative stages of his subjects' personal and social development become a vital conceptual gauge. The *Lives* present a panoramic picture of civilized humanity, where individuals must rein in their passions and define legitimate modes of expression for their love, hate, envy, fear, and other provocations to irrationality. As Frances Reynolds often heard him remark: "'Man's chief merit consists in resisting the impulses of his nature.' . . . 'Nay, nay,' he would say (to a person who thought that Nature, Reason, and Virtue were indivisable [sic] in the mind of man, as inherent characteristic principles) "If man is by nature prompted to act virtuously and right, all the divine precepts of the Gospel, all its denunciations, all the laws enacted by man to restrain man from evil had been needless.'"[20] To Johnson's analytic thinking, this view of man's vicious propulsions is the implicit concern of his last and most ambitious encyclopedic project. He works from the basic premise of man's insatiable need, and he finds how, to greater and lesser extents, it is precariously held in check. He seeks the grand antagonism of primitive instinct mobilizing in the cultural sphere, with the same urgency and tactics, as in man's unconscious. A milestone in the evolution of biographic literature, *The Lives of the Poets* is no less brilliant than it is radical.

The most personally challenging of his subjects, Milton becomes for Johnson a figure of sullen, brutish irascibility, but not without a certain pathos. By way of a startling and prescient anecdote, he launches into an account of Milton's early life when, at Cambridge, "The unkindness with which he was treated was not merely negative: I am ashamed to relate what I fear is true, that Milton was one of the last students in either university that suffered the publick indignity of corporeal correction" (*Lives*, 1: 88). At some length, he dwells on Milton's "punishment" and "exile," which left him "alienated either by the injudicious severity of his governors, or his own captious perverseness" (89–90). Doubtless the story calls up Johnson's own foul trials of humiliation and reprisal, and the identification provides him with his most penetrating insights into Milton's virulent, driven character. "The thoughts of obedience, whether canonical or civil, raised his indignation" (91). Milton's uniqueness, his fierce wrestling for integrity, was couched in lawlessness and the deliberate violation of authority. According to Johnson, he defied nearly every institution: the academy, the church, the state, the family, even, to an extent, the conventions of art. Much like his own Satan, flung down from the heavens of his imaginary omnipotence, he raged at the treatment accorded him. So his vigilant biographer catches the sense of baleful resistance and fiendish bent for retaliation when he remarks of the poet, ever embroiled in controversy, "Such is his malignity *that hell grows darker at his frown*" (104). From *Paradise Lost* (II, 719), the allusion is to Satan's murderous wrath as he braces himself for combat. In this manner, Milton's struggle with his political adversary, Salmasius—in a dispute which Johnson presents as the lurid spectacle of two mad senseless demons wreaking their mutual hate— left one dead and the other blind: "As Salmasius reproached Milton with losing his eyes in the quarrel, Milton delighted himself with the belief that he had shortened Salmasius's life; and both perhaps with more malignity than reason. Salmasius died at the Spa, Sept. 3, 1653; and, as controvertists are commonly said to be killed by their last dispute, Milton was flattered with the credit of destroying him" (115).

At every turn Johnson finds his subject "peevish" (90), "savage" (102), "angry" (105), "offensive" (104), "acrimonious and surley" (156), "severe and arbitrary" (157), a man who wantonly "gratified his malevolence" (125), who willfully instigated a private and public regime of hectoring abuse. Evidently straining his neutrality to the breaking point, Johnson is exasperated when he looks at the famous invocation of *Paradise Lost*, book 7, and he bristles: "Of 'evil tongues' for Milton to complain required impudence at least equal to his other powers—Milton, whose warmest advocates must allow that he never spared any asperity of reproach or brutality of insolence" (140). Milton's drastic fury incites him to violent breaches of the established order, and Johnson shrewdly exploits the insight that the individual's fomenting aggression is repeated on a grander scale. Milton's chosen arena was politics and art. On the subject of his purely polemical offices, Johnson can be philosophical and more than commonly sparing. As he well knew, a pamphleteer's temptation to half-wild rhetoric, at times demagoguery, comes from honest persuasions, pardonable by the fact that many held the same:

> While he contented himself to write, he perhaps did only what his conscience dictated; and if he did not very vigilantly watch the influence of his own passions, and the gradual prevalence of opinions, first willingly admitted and then habitually indulged, if objections by being overlooked were forgotten, and desire superinduced conviction, he yet shared only the common weakness of mankind, and might be no less sincere than his opponents. (110)

But when it comes to analyzing Milton's fanaticism and his role in the bloody rebellion, Johnson explodes the subterfuge of political faction and party. Through him, we mark the ineradicable traces of the child being beaten, the deep festering wounds of mortification and loathing. From the depths of his own bitter contempt, he spews out Milton's rage. The famous passage, while carrying full vehemence, is trenchant and deliberate:

> Milton's republicanism was, I am afraid, founded in an envious hatred of greatness, and a sullen desire of independence; in petulance impatient of control, and pride disdainful of superiority. He hated monarchs in the state and prelates in the church; for he hated all whom he was required to obey. It is to be suspected that his predominant desire was to destroy rather than estab-

lish, and that he felt not so much the love of liberty as repugnance to authority. (157)[21]

If Milton's politics were infested by a poisonous contempt for those in power, his poetry is flawed by an appalling inability to rouse the gentler affections or excite fellow-feeling.[22] According to Johnson, the English poems contain a "repulsive harshness" (162) and *Lycidas* "is not to be considered as the effusion of real passion." It invokes no "tenderness" over loss and in fact the "remote allusions and obscure opinions" are offensive. More than anything a self-flattering college exercise, "its inherent improbability always forces dissatisfaction on the mind" (163). *Comus* is likewise bereft of human warmth, resembling a starchy ethical oration, "tediously instructive," which Johnson finds tasteless and uncompelling. Its characters "have not the spriteliness of a dialogue animated by reciprocal contention, but seem rather declamations deliberately composed and formally repeated on a moral question. The auditor therefore listens as to a lecture, without passion, without anxiety" (168). *Sampson Agonistes* elicits more accusations of detachment and emotional obliquity, from which Milton's defects in dramatic writing are inferred: "He knew human nature only in the gross, and had never studied the shades of character, nor the combinations of concurring or the perplexity of contending passions." Though amply book-learned, he "had mingled little in the world, and was deficient in the knowledge which experience must confer" (189). As for *Paradise Lost*, Johnson's notorious pronouncement sounds the hollowness and the anguished solitude of Milton's life: "It comprises neither human actions nor human manners. The man and woman who act and suffer are in state which no other man or woman can ever know. The reader finds no transaction in which he can be engaged, beholds no condition in which he can by any effort of imagination place himself; he has, therefore, little natural curiosity or sympathy" (181). Devoid of that essential link to common humanity, the poem takes its laborious way through an occlusive world of thought: "The want of human interest is always felt. . . . None ever wished it longer than it is. Its perusal is a duty rather than a pleasure. We read Milton for instruction, retire harassed and overburdened, and look elsewhere for recreation; we desert our master, and seek for companions" (183–84).

In the end, however, Johnson cannot but pay tribute to Milton's uncapitulating struggle. In the annals of "heroes," "he was born for whatever is arduous" (194). As Johnson readily adduces, Milton's towering fantasies redound to the credit of his works. His mighty achievement stands unquestioned, invested though it is with the chilling occurrences in his mind. He possesses the cold virtues of "sublimity," "gigantick loftiness," the ability to "astonish" and "the power of displaying the vast, illuminating the splendid, enforcing the awful, darkening the gloomy, and aggravating the dreadful" (177). But the very tenor of Johnson's praise, rife with frightening presentiment, would indicate more than casual reservations. It is no real compliment that he envisions the flinty specter of Milton, "the defender of the regicides," meeting the reception of *Paradise Lost* in 1667 with icy reserve and self-righteous disdain: "I cannot but conceive him calm and confident, little disappointed, not at all dejected, relying on his own merit with steady consciousness, and waiting without impatience the vicissitudes of opinion and the impartiality of a future generation" (144).[23] No matter his achievement, Milton's character imparts a menacing threat of disintegration, a troubling fissure in the edifice of culture. The poet's ferocious insurrection upsets the balance, all the more tottering, between raging impulse and its constraint. Evidently this brinkmanship is inherent in his greatness, with a hard-bitten vehemence that strains the tensile objectivity of the "Life." If, for Milton, such vehemence constitutes genius, in the case of Swift, Johnson finds little to make amends.

Johnson's "Swift" is a portrait of nasty, snide antagonism, which is found to be embedded in all aspects of the subject's life. His approach frequently termed hopelessly biased,[24] Johnson selects any number of unflattering episodes, marked by acrimony and perverseness, from which he wholly recoils. With an unusual vengeance, he heaps upon Swift the features of a blackguard, who has gorged himself on vicious pleasures. Swift's writing, at least the poetry, is divided into "gross" and "trifling" (*Lives*, 3: 66), and with that, the literary appraisal is virtually over. Certainly in the character of "Swift," we sense an affinity to the picture of Milton's odious effrontery and, what is more, to Johnson's own reproachful pride. But he evidently finds the creative transformation of Swift *agonistes* so intolerable as to call up feelings of a deeper aversion. If Milton's vehement fantasies were played out on lofty plains, Swift's degenerate into something crude and repugnant. Underscoring his subject's obsession with noxious themes, he puzzles near the end of the "Life": "The greatest difficulty that occurs, in analysing his character, is to discover by what depravity of intellect he took delight in revolving ideas from which almost every other mind shrinks with disgust. The ideas of pleasure, even when criminal, may solicit the imagination; but what has disease, deformity, and filth upon which the thoughts can be allured to dwell?" (62). But he has already answered the question.

   Throughout the "Life," Johnson interprets a covert sadistic cruelty, which he educes from his subject's quaint preoccupations and odd engagements. As he sees it, Swift's peculiar compulsion was an all but lascivious desire to control. Amply documented are his manifold ceremonies and rituals. His zany regimen of jogging and bathing: "He thought exercise of great necessity and used to run half a mile up and down a hill every two hours. . . . He had a kind of muddy complexion, which, though he washed himself with oriental scrupulosity, did not look clear" (5, 55). His stern prosecution in affairs of money: "He required that the day of promised payment [of debt] should be exactly kept. A severe and punctilious temper is ill qualified for transactions with the poor; Swift had made no provision of patience or pity. He ordered his debtors to be sued" (45).[25] His exacting demands of inferiors (related incidentally to his writings): "To his domesticks he was naturally rough; and a man of a rigorous temper, with that vigilance of minute attention which his works discover, must have been a master that few could bear." So he glowers with "tyrannick peevishness," and does not spare the servants of others: "Once, when he dined alone with the Earl of Orrey, he said, of one that waited in the room, 'That man has, since we sat to the table, committed fifteen faults'" (56). His coerced attentions and arrogated superiority over friends: "He indulged his disposition to petulance and sarcasm, and thought himself injured if the licentiousness of his raillery, the freedom of his censures, or the petulance of his frolicks were resented or repressed. He predominated over his companions with very high ascendancy, and probably would bear none over whom he could not predominate" (59). And most unnerving for Johnson—who knew the buried fantasies of sexual domination—his peremptory sway over "the unfortunate Stella." Transfixed by this alleged horror, Johnson reverts to the style of earlier works—*London*, *Irene*, the "Life of Savage"—when imagining scenes of florid abuse, and he waxes histrionic: "From the time of her arrival in Ireland he seems resolved to keep her in his power, and therefore hindered a match sufficiently advantageous by accumulating unreasonable demands and prescribing conditions that could not be performed. While she was at her own disposal he did not consider his possession as secure; resentment, ambition, or caprice might separate them." Quoting Macbeth's murderous oath to hold *his* power, Johnson divines the virulence of Swift's claims: "He was therefore resolved to make 'assurance double sure,' and to appropriate her by a private marriage, to which he had annexed the expectation of all the pleasures of perfect friendship, without the uneasiness of conjugal restraint. . . . When he offered to acknowledge her, . . . 'it was too late.' She then gave up herself to sorrowful resentment, and died under the tyranny of him by whom she was in the highest degree loved and honoured" (41–42).

The last is a certain key to this relentless disciplinarian, and Johnson's observation bears the same stamp of modern conjectures on Swift, which draw from Freud's research into the anal-erotic character.[26] In effect, Johnson captures the primitive coupling of malicious and loving aims, as he analyzes "this excentrick tenderness, by which the laws of nature were violated to retain her" (42). He shows that Swift's possessiveness was governed by a tormenting ambivalence and was echoed in his relations with the woman he adored, with all of his objects. That which he sought to protect was loved and hated by him simultaneously. In this vein, Johnson reports the striking anecdote concerning Archbishop Boulter, an unimpeachable Irish patriot, to whom he boasted in the fray of the Drapier cause: "If I had lifted up my finger, they would have torn you to pieces" (37). For Johnson, Swift's energies were exerted through the twisted roots of irreconcilable emotion. Not unfounded was his "dread of hypocrisy," which is explained at some length. With shrewd penetration, Johnson exposes the queer pleasure in *appearing* wicked; thus could Swift evade what must have been disquieting feelings of "goodness" by exaggerated professions of the opposite: "Instead of wishing to seem better, he delighted in seeming worse than he was." When in London, he slipped out to early prayers, so as not to be seen, and to his servants, he read prayers with "such dexterous secrecy," even to elude the notice of longstanding guests. "He was only careful to hide the good which he did, but willingly incurred the suspicion of evil which he did not" (54–55).

It is this spectacular transformation of right into wrong which colors Johnson's view of Swift's turbulent life and hints at his unmerciful denunciation. "Disease, deformity, and filth" are the residues of human impulse gone awry. Swift's unpalatable inconsistencies reach to the very core of human experience, but with an impact so staggering that even Johnson reels with alarm. For all his consorting with mental demons, he apparently regards Swift's vision as too demoralizing. He tampered too brazenly with the delicate balance of ethical values. He bent too liberally the rules by which primitive instinct is restrained in the service of the community. He depicted mankind as driven solely by brute appetite and its frenzied effects, so haplessly revealed in his character. And if exploring that character, Johnson casts up the old compulsions to grueling unrest and despair, it is a knowledge finely calibrated and disclosed. Taking the Dean's measure, he fixes upon the unavailing wrath and how it pervasively spoils Swift's every design: "He seems to have wasted his life in discontent, by the rage of neglected pride and the languishment of unsatisfied desire. He is querulous and fastidious, arrogant and malignant; he scarcely speaks of himself but with indignant lamentations, or of others but with insolent superiority when he is gay, and with angry contempt when he is gloomy." He sums up how Swift's vile misanthropy pollutes the very ideals he hoped to inspire: "From the letters that pass between him and Pope it might be inferred that they, with Arbothnot and Gay, had engrossed all the understanding and virtue of mankind, that their merits filled the world; or that there was no hope of more. They shew the age involved in darkness, and shade the picture with sullen emulation" (61–62).[27]

By contrast to the blind, bursting fury of "Swift," Johnson's "Pope" is a vastly more sympathetic personality. The last written of the *Lives*,[28] it shows the biographer's undiminished zeal in grappling with oblique and secret riddles of the mind. Pope was a baffling subject, owing largely to all the rancor and bitterness he harbored, despite his sturdy "self-confidence," "genius," and more than sufficient worldly success. Simply to draw a correlation between his mental and physical distress was the obvious tack for Pope's biographers, but evidently Johnson rejects such a tidy solution.[29] Instead, he entertains clues to Pope's character by searching out, as usual, motives and their objects, through the hidden passageways of inner life. Relying on stark factual data, he relates Pope's infirmity: his delicate constitution, his deformity, and the necessary dependence upon others to assist him. And if his illness could not but affect his spirits, Johnson finds in that a more pregnant opening to the complex state of mind. In a key section about two-thirds into the "Life," he emphatically sums up his observations on Pope's child-like fragility. He distinguishes an inconsolable sense of injury, yet drastic need to be cared for, in effect, a potent admixture which converts weakness into ascendancy:

> The indulgence and accommodation which his sickness required had taught him all the unpleasing and unsocial qualities of a valetudinary man. He expected that every thing should give way to his ease or humour, as a child whose parents will not hear her cry has an unresisted dominion in the nursery:
> > 'C'est que l'enfant toujours est homme,
> > C'est que l' homme est toujours enfant.'
> (*Lives*, 3: 198)

Like a suffering child, Pope craved a magical restitution, which he himself supplied, in part through art and learning, in part through ingenious ploys for attention. With this awareness, Johnson explores a pattern of hurt and compensation, revolving around the subjective depths of Pope's invalidism. He underscores a frantic need to be satisfied, an unappeasable craving. From the age of adolescence, "he was indefatigably diligent, and insatiably curious; wanting health for violent, and money for expensive pleasures, . . . but he read only to store his mind with facts and images, seizing all that his authors presented with undistinguishing voracity, and with an appetite for knowledge too eager to be nice" (94). Much the same, his need to be glutted with food takes the tone of a compensatory act: "He had another fault, easily incident to those who suffering much pain think themselves entitled to whatever pleasure they can snatch. He was too indulgent to his appetite: he loved meat highly seasoned and of strong taste, and, at the intervals of the table, amused himself with biscuits and dry conserves." Pope at table becomes the sorry farcical spectacle of one who gorges himself into oblivion, compelled to eat and eat until he could eat no more: "If he sat down to a variety of dishes he would oppress his stomach with repletion, and though he seemed angry when a dram was offered him, did not forbear to drink it. . . . The death of Pope was imputed by some of his friends to a silver saucepan, in which it was his delight to heat potted lampreys" (199–200). And the account of the famous grotto likewise elicits the pathos of starving deprivation, masked by "frivolous and childish" self-indulgence. While it was a place aglow with lavish amusement, Johnson deduces the more covert meaning of his subject's onerous indemnity: "Pope's excavation was requisite as an entrance to his garden, and, as some men try to be proud of their defects, he extracted an ornament from an inconvenience" (135).[30]

Pope's attitude toward his work often betrays an over-solicitude, as if to heal that which is ever ailing. He incessantly toils at repairing his compositions, an act which his biographer understands and much piques his interest. Like a hovering mother, Pope tends his poetry; so Johnson captures the private drift of fretful concern and apprehension: "To make verses was his first labour, and to mend them was his last. . . . He examined lines and words with minute and punctilious observation, and retouched every part with indefatigable diligence, till he had left nothing to be forgiven." If he pretends to quit caring for his poems after publication, Johnson believes this was not so: "His parental attention never abandoned them" (218–21).[31] Johnson had earlier introduced this revealing section on Pope's obsessive duties with a cogent definition of his genius. Both analyses are stirred by the drama of harried enterprise, the poet ever straining his faculties, as Johnson draws the vaulting spirit in implicit contrast to the stunted, enfeebled body: "Pope had . . . a mind active, ambitious, and adventurous, always investigating, always aspiring; in its widest searches still longing to go forward, in its highest flights still wishing to be higher; always imagining something greater than it knows, always endeavouring more than it can do" (217). And while his passions soared, he was also quite at risk, for reasons, likewise intimated, of his utter physical defenselessness: "He pleased himself with being important and formidable, and gratified sometimes his pride, and sometimes his resentment; till at last he began to think he should be more safe if he were less busy" (181).[32]

If his cherished work helped to defray his losses, Johnson also shows how Pope turned others to his profit. With sly dexterity, he maneuvered friends and foes alike into serving his needs. An acute and eternal sense of affliction must have been thus somewhat eased by his cleverly veiled applications. Johnson persistently unmasks the sheer felicity in Pope's scheming: "In all his intercourse with mankind he had great delight in artifice, and endeavoured to attain all his purposes by indirect and unsuspected methods. 'He hardly drank tea without a stratagem'" (200). The ridiculous "posthumous offence," in which Bolingbroke, after Pope's death, discovers that his dear friend secretly printed a complete edition of *The Patriot King*, is attributed by Johnson to that same daffy delight in guile and deceit: "His unjustifiable impression of *The Patriot King*, as it can be imputed to no particular motive, must have proceeded from his general habit of secrecy and cunning: he caught an opportunity of a sly trick, and pleased himself with the thought of outwitting Bolingbroke" (200–01).[33] To his friends, he petted and sulked only to be mollified and condoled:

> If at the house of his friends he wanted any accommodation he was not willing to ask for it in plain terms, but would mention it remotely as something convenient; though, when it was procured, he soon made it appear for whose sake it had been recommended. Thus he teized Lord Orrery till he obtained a screen. He practiced his arts on such small occasions that Lady Bolingbroke used to say, in a French phrase, that "he plaid the politician about cabbages and turnips." . . . He was fretful and easily displeased, and allowed himself to be capriciously resentful. He would sometimes leave Lord Oxford silently, no one could tell why, and was to be courted back by more letters and messages than the footmen were willing to carry. (200–02)

But those same intrigues and fits of pique seemed to have largely backfired when he tried them on his enemies.

Pope's infamous literary tantrums are analyzed by Johnson with a keen appreciation of their origins in grief and disappointment. At first, his triumph and belligerence in the mad fray with the Dunces quite plausibly conceal the anguish that lurks beneath: "For a while his natural sensibility was suspended, and he read reproaches and invectives without emotion, considering them only as the necessary effects of that pain which he rejoiced in having given" (150). But this eccentric jubilation arouses Johnson's suspicions, and he gathers quite another story, that Pope's vicious assaults on his adversaries betray in fact his own piercing mortification: "Pope confessed his own pain by his anger; but he gave no pain to those who provoked him. He was able to hurt none but himself." Quoting a Mr. Richardson's rather harrowing account of seeing Pope at the height of his asperity, Johnson arrives at his real feelings: "I have heard Mr. Richardson relate that he attended his father the painter on a visit, when one of Cibber's pamphlets came into the hands of Pope, who said, 'These things are my diversion.' They sat by him while he perused it, and saw his features writhen with anguish" (187–88). Like one hoisted by his own petard, Pope feels his "shafts of malice" more than any of his intended victims. No matter that he tries to hide it, he ever lives on the margins of explosive tension, as Johnson clarifies: "He pretends insensibility to censure and criticism, though it was observed by all who knew him that every pamphlet disturbed his quiet, and that his extreme irritability laid him open to perpetual vexation" (209).

So habitual is Pope's deception that, flaunting his grievances and punishing (so he alleges) mankind, he threatens to abandon his career, only that others might beseech him not to. Much as he fretted and fussed at the homes of his friends, even quit the premises in affected high dudgeon, he expected to be placated and caressed. Thus could he wallow in importance, as he secretly wallowed in anger and pain. Johnson makes it apparent that here is merely the raving of a self-undermining poseur, who shores up his fragile psyche by extorting preposterous tributes. And he uncovers, for all the provocative suffering, a blindly self-ruinous hoax. Intermingled with Pope's grandiosity is the certain flirtation with exposure, if not disaster. Johnson's analogy to one developmentally arrested is caustic and telling: "I have heard of an idiot who used to revenge his vexations by lying all night upon the bridge." As Hill's note explains, Johnson revised the sentence, which originally read, "an idiot who used to enforce his demands by threatening to beat his head against the wall" (153, n. 5). Obviously the original was too crude a picture of rampant infantile aggression, and Johnson tones it down, but not to diminish the ludicrous and pathetic transparency: "Pope had been flattered till he thought himself one of the moving powers in the system of life. When he talked of laying down his pen, those who sat round him intreated and implored, and self-love did not suffer him to suspect that they went away and laughed" (153–54). Even more ludicrous and pathetic is the episode of leaving his own house so as not to appear to wish the Queen's visit. But certainly he wished it, just as fiercely as he spurned it, fearing the distinction was not forthcoming. To be sure, the visit was no settled thing, perhaps even Caroline's "careless effusion, thought on no more." But alarmed by the tumult of his conflicting emotions, Pope fled. So very deftly and subtly Johnson conveys the profound struggle of his avid desire and shame: "Pope, pretending to decline what was not yet offered, left his house for a time, not, I suppose, for any other reason than lest he should be thought to stay at home in expectation of an honour which would not be conferred." What is more, he was forced to suffer this tormenting ambivalence in silence: "He was, therefore, angry at Swift, who represents him as 'refusing the visits of a Queen,' because he knew that what had never been offered had never been refused" (171).

Johnson's "Pope" aches with unsatisfied longing. Rarely indeed can he take what is *truly* offered—eminence, wealth, affection—without an elaborate arsenal of defenses, which shield a deplorable injury unredressed. Uncannily, Johnson penetrates the smoke screen of imposture, idiosyncrasy, and brittle self-conceit in order to glimpse the features of Pope's real struggle. Here entangled are the strands of his sympathetic attachment, which fill the "Life of Pope," in Boswell's phrase, *con amore*.[34] Clearly Johnson's poetical appraisal is not limited to his requisite third section, often regarded as somewhat careless and prompted by others. But hardly so, for his fresh appraisal of the courageous poet is rooted psychologically in the life history. He never loses touch with the relentless outrage that drives the brilliant imagination.[35] Through exhaustive accounts of "the incessant and unappeasable malignity of Pope" (185), he understands how the bellicose obsessions make restitution for that which has been ruefully defaced. Thus bringing Pope's motives to light, he ultimately justifies the vindictive fury of the satire, holding that "it rectifies error and improves judgement: he that refines the publick taste is a publick benefactor" (242). More than an ethical pronouncement, the terms recall Pope's painstaking refinement, which made poetry "the business of his life" (217). Johnson never loses sight of this passion for purity, as he fondly lingers on the unexceptionable novelty of *The Rape of the Lock*, the burnished elegance of the *Epistle of Eloise to Abelard*, the "exquisitely beautiful" passages in the *Characters of Men*. Pope's achievement reaches to the spiritual foundations of a culture: "If Pope be not a poet, where is poetry to be found?" (251). Despite the hectic internal commotion and fractious self-display, Johnson unriddles an ineffable beauty, which haunts his narrative, even as it once was so poignantly evinced in the "remarkable gentleness and sweetness of disposition"; the image of the "little Nightingale" (83); "He is said to have been beautiful in his infancy" (196). Like the broken songbird of "The Fountains," Johnson's own blasted self-image, he suffered a foul and wicked indignity. If in this the two are secret sharers, Johnson conveys his deepest understanding of the poet's piercing vulnerability in a passage which aches with his own secret longing. By the perfect devotion to his parents, Pope's ferocious armature falls away, and at last he is granted his magical restitution. It is Johnson's own unique smuggled version of a family romance:36

> The filial piety of Pope was in the highest degree amiable and exemplary; his parents had the happiness of living till he was at the summit of poetical reputation, till he was at ease in this fortune, and without a rival in his fame, and found no diminution of his respect or tenderness. Whatever was his pride, to them he was obedient; and whatever was his irritability, to them he was gentle. Life has, among its soothing and quiet comforts, few things better to give than such a son. (154)

*   *   *

Reading and writing biography entails a willingness to identify with the subject, as Johnson doubtless knew. His arguments on a shared psychological heritage often specify the desideratum of a vital transaction between individuals: "The high and low, as they have the same faculties and the same senses, have no less similitude in their pains and pleasures. The sensations are the same in all. . . . Men thus equal in themselves will appear equal in honest and impartial biography; and those whom fortune or nature place at the greatest distance may afford instruction to each other" (*Idler* 84, *Works*, 2: 263). The appeal of personal history is thus vigorous and elemental: "No species of writing seems more worthy of cultivation than biography, . . . none can more certainly enchain the heart by irresistible interest" (*Rambler* 60, *Works*, 3: 319). Composing the *Lives*, Johnson identified readily with his subjects. This willingness to partake imaginatively in the fortunes of others lent him special powers of discernment, not ordinarily adduced in the biographic and historical writings of his day. Channeling his emotions into Savage's story becomes the intellectual and artistic frame of reference for his narrative and similarly, in "Milton," "Swift," and "Pope," he ignites those unsavory impulses and appalling passions which smolder in every individual, necessarily linking one life to another. If these are cases bristling with adversity, "Dryden" offers Johnson a more congenial figure, possibly one he would have liked to emulate. "When I was a young fellow . . . I wanted to write the *Life of Dryden*," he confides to Boswell and describes early efforts to interview those still alive who had known him.[37] But this emulation is slyly inwrought and restive and more complicated than meets the eye.[38]

While he protests an aversion to Dryden's theatrical career, even scoffs at "tracing the meanders of his mind through the whole series of his dramatick performances," (*Lives*, 1: 336) Johnson nonetheless provides a startling donnée for the "Life" when reviewing *The Conquest of Granada*. Though he tries to slight, he cannot but admire its sweeping grandeur, and reluctantly, he falls under the spell of Dryden's hero. Taken by surprise, he is fascinated by the idea of raw, unfettered passion, of "a theatrical meteor of incredible love and impossible valour":

> All the rays of romantick heat, whether amorous or warlike, glow in Almanzor by a kind of concentration. He is above all laws; he is exempt from all restraints; he ranges the world at will, and governs wherever he appears. He fights without enquiring the cause, and loves in spite of the obligations of justice, of rejection by his mistress, and of prohibition from the dead. Yet the scenes are, for the most part, delightful; they exhibit a kind of illustrious depravity and majestick madness." (349)

Johnson is not usually enamored of the delirious or the chaotic, and his remarks are tantalizing clues to the deeper revelations of his "Dryden." For here he fashions an idol who can flout the stern injunctions to comply and obey. The poet's genius, like that of his dramatic offspring, summons up the image of a conquistador. Imagining Dryden, Johnson revels in the glorious escapades he once described in the *Rambler*: "It is the proper ambition of the heroes in literature to enlarge the boundaries of knowledge by discovering and conquering new regions of the intellectual world" (*Rambler* 137, *Works*, 4: 362). In Dryden, Johnson hails a pugnacious intellect, whose style is pure reckless courage. His powers lay in "ratiocination" (*Lives*, 1: 459), by which he routs the passions and forges his world out of magisterial thought. The melting moods and soothing gestures of common life never cross the torrid exercise of his mind. The milder emotions scarcely move him, as Johnson quotes a ranting speech from *Tyrranic Love*, that "may contribute to the explanation of [Dryden's] character." Like the fiery rhymed couplets of the heroic drama, he is tempestuous and incendiary: "Dryden's was not one of the 'gentle bosoms' . . . He hardly conceived [of Love] but in its turbulent effervescence with some other desires: when it was inflamed by rivalry or obstructed by difficulties; when it invigorated ambition or exasperated revenge" (458).

If this were not enough, Johnson raves on, transported beyond the pale of ordinary happenings by Dryden's superheroic deeds. Disclaiming "natural sentiments," Dryden fixes his audience by the sheer excitement of polemic: "When once he had engaged himself in disputation, thoughts flowed in on either side: he was now no longer at a loss; he had always objections and solutions at command" (459). So are his resources inexhaustible and his bold poetical leaps bordering on the extraterrestrial: "Next to argument, his delight was in wild and daring sallies of sentiment, in the irregular and excentrick violence of wit. He delighted to tread upon the brink of meaning, where light and darkness begin to mingle; to approach the precipice of absurdity, and hover over the abyss of unideal vacancy" (460). Dryden's brinkmanship may have ended sometimes in poetical disaster, in that outré phrase, "the abyss of unideal vacancy"; on the other hand, "There is surely reason to suspect that he pleased himself as well as his audience; and these [works], like the harlots of other men, had his love, though not his approbation" (462). So Johnson draws the terms of his imperial prerogative. With resounding accolades, rarely found elsewhere in the *Lives*, Johnson extols the virtues of Dryden's high and mighty spirit: the dashing genius, fearless curiosity, the vast intellectual munitions. Boasting these and more, his was a mind "to which every understanding was proud to be associated, and of which every one solicited the regard by an ambitious display of himself" (417). But strangely coexisting with this boisterous adulation is a series of quieter, often disconcerting contradictions, as if to ask what this "Dryden" is all about.

At various junctures in the "Life," Johnson admits some less than complimentary knowledge of his all but deific hero. For one, he notes a quality of pallid indifference toward his work. He is lax and casual, rushing through it the nearest and least difficult way: "To write *con amore*, with fondness for the employment, with perpetual touches and retouches, with unwillingness to take leave of his own idea, and an unwearied pursuit of unattainable perfection, was, I think, no part of his character" (413). And again: "Dryden was no rigid judge of his own pages; he seldom struggled after supreme excellence, but snatched in haste what was within his reach. . . . While there was no name above his own [he] was willing to enjoy fame on the easiest terms" (464–65). Even if awarded the laurels for "genius" in the "Life of Pope," Dryden's professional integrity is another matter. By contrast to Pope's "parental attention" to his work, Dryden's attitude is cursory and brusque: "He spent no time in struggles to rouse latent powers; he never attempted to make that better which was already good, nor often to mend what he must have known to be faulty. He wrote, as he tells us, with very little consideration; and, when once it had passed the press, ejected it from his mind." And what is worse, he wrote for sheer financial gain: "When he had no pecuniary interest, he had no further solicitude" (*Lives*, 3: 220–21).

It is no accident that these facts about Dryden's languid and mercenary disposition, not to mention the squandering of his great talent, never impair nor do they leave hardly a blemish on Johnson's graven image of the "father of English criticism" (*Lives*, 1: 410). If he worships at the feet of this idol, he also realizes, but oddly refuses to concede, their tincture of clay. And there is more. Of Dryden's "bashfulness," he once again makes excuses where doubtless he knows better. From an indisputable vantage point, he had long ago exposed the tainted roots of fear and guilt and wreckage from within that bedevil the successful man. But at present, he willfully denies his own hard-won findings. Dryden's annoying diffidence is conveniently explained away by his lordly self-importance, and that is all. While modest and "slow to advance," he was also proud, having set "a very high value on his own powers and performances": "He probably did not offer his conversation, because he expected it to be solicited; and he retired from a cold reception, not submissive but indignant, with such reverence of his own greatness as made him unwilling to expose it to neglect or violation" (395). Uncharacteristically, Johnson backs away from this troubling inconsistency, just as he avoids taking a stand on Dryden's baffling "saturnine" temper, and offers instead the unedifying, rather palavering view that basically some men are just more comfortable in private than in public.[39]

Johnson is more severe about Dryden's relation to his public, which alternates between bitterness, ingratiation, and whining complaint. He dwells on the histrionics of self-pity, where the poet regularly issues his jeremiads that "he has few thanks to pay his stars that he was born among Englishmen" (400). He amply lists the episodes of "indignation" and "malignant impatience" (342), "brutal fury" (343), "venting his malice" (345), "rage with little provocation and terrour with little danger" (346), and "frequent bursts of resentment" (370). He dutifully records Dryden's puzzling financial difficulties (331–32, 365), as the poet puts it, his "suffering

under a publick infliction" (384). Perhaps he is hardest on Dryden's ob-
sequiousness, rehearsed at some length. But the intent is scarcely to detect
underlying habits of mind, but to rebuke the lofty intelligence that could
stoop so low. Indeed, Johnson seems quite embarrassed by the "strain
of flattery which disgraces genius, and which it was wonderful that any
man that knew the meaning of his own words could use without self-
detestation" (359). In a long passage which reviews the history of sycophancy and Dryden's inexhaustible fund egregious dedications to the
great, we come no closer to understanding this amazing exercise in abject
servility. While in the end Johnson names the conscious sway of self-interest
as a plausible motive,[40] he drops the matter there, as if to preclude his
customary inquiry into less manifest causes. The interpretation is oblique
and equivocal and far from Johnson's normally direct mark: "It is indeed
not certain that on these occasions his judgement much rebelled against his
interest. There are minds which easily sink into submission, that look on
grandeur with undistinguishing reverence, and discover no defect where
there is elevation of rank and affluence of riches" (400).

Thus is Dryden largely exempt from the analytic searchlights which
play so intensely over characters in the other major *Lives*. Johnson may
allege, "Of the great poet whose life I am about to delineate, the curiosity
which his reputation must excite will require a display more ample than can
now be given. His contemporaries, however they reverenced his genius, left
his life unwritten; and nothing therefore can be known beyond what casual
mention and uncertain tradition have supplied" (331).[41] But this seems
more like special pleading, in view of the abundant evidence already sifted
on Dryden's contentiousness, disdainful pride, negligence, self-pity, arrant
sycophancy, and so on. What grist for the mill of Johnson's mighty analytic
census. How skillfully could he take apart this vexing problem of ill-
assorted wishes and disguised truth. But he declines to dismantle his hero,
thus turning the focus from his subject to himself.

Can it be, as was first suggested, that the venerable figure represents all
he hoped to emulate, a genius more acceptable than, say, Milton, Swift, or
Pope? He knew how, like the machinations of a spiteful child, their goals
were mayhem, both on the individual and the larger collective scale. By
contrast, Dryden is "the father of English criticism," a progenitor of culture, invested as he is with awesome paternity. If here indeed is the object of
Johnson's most profound emulation, the image takes on hues of regal
splendor, which he famously evokes: "What was said of Rome, adorned by
Augustus, may be applied by an easy metaphor to English poetry embel-

lished by Dryden, 'lateritiam invenit marmoream reliquit,' he found it
brick, and he left it marble" (469). In Johnson's mind the poet's patriarchal
image glistens, as opulent as it is unrivalled. And in the shadows of such a
father, what of the real one, Michael Johnson, who is mentioned as a
witness to Dryden's resplendent reign.[42] We remember the famous scene of
penance at Uttoxeter, occurring near the time that Johnson wrote the *Lives*
and laying open the excruciating ambivalence of his love and hate, his grief
and contempt.[43] Is the broken, tormented old book-seller somehow entangled in his son's fantasies of a blameless, all-conquering hero? Is this one
more magical restitution, another figment of Johnson's family romance?[44]
Does the portrait of Dryden at last expiate the unconscious rage and guilt
by offering an undefiled paternal substitute?

So it would seem, as Johnson pays rare homage to one man's unchallenged authority: "He has been described as magisterially presiding
over the younger writers, and assuming the distribution of poetical fame;
but he who excels has a right to teach, and he whose judgment is incontest-
able may, without usurpation, examine and decide" (396). It is a ravishing
dream of a father who emerges inviolate and undefeated, whose excellence
derives from the urgent displacement of the original. Johnson has effec-
tively sabotaged any prying intrusion, and thus his "Dryden" holds sway in
solitary grandeur. Scarcely is he depicted in ordinary transactions, by Johnson's own standards, the "domestick privacies," which divulge a real existence, even as we glimpse Milton and his wives and daughters; Swift and
Stella; Pope and his parents; Addison and Steele.[45] For Johnson, Dryden
stands alone, great and mysterious.

*   *   *

"A parson in a tye-wig" (*Lives*, 2: 123) was Mandeville's character of
Addison, which Johnson embellishes with a good deal more luster, along
with some surprising twists to this high-minded, staunchly principled
personality. From Milton to Swift, Pope, Dryden, and Addison, as we have
undertaken this discussion of the *Lives*, from the least to the most amicable
of men, Johnson's survey covers a wide psychological continuum. And in it
we perceive the rudiments of an even larger, more sweeping design. Not
unlike former inquiries into the nucleus of character and culture, he seeks
how the individual's struggle lies at the foundation of civilization itself,
how his development is often replicated in the development of a society.[46]
Here is Johnson's implicit concern, from Milton's sustained campaign of

demolition, to Swift and Pope's fomenting rage, to Addison, the standard-bearer, as it were, of decency and tempered grace. His achievement was to domesticate the wilder sallies of instinct and emotion, as they appear in everyday life. Before Addison, "England had no masters of common life. No writers had yet undertaken to reform either the savageness of neglect or the impertinence of civility; to shew when to speak, or to be silent; how to refuse, or how to comply" (93). An "*arbiter elegantiarum*," Addison promotes a higher prerogative through "intellectual elegance," much to the advancement, Johnson avers, of manners and morals and the public good. But this knight of chaste decorum guards his demesne with considerable sacrifice.

If Johnson praises Addison for his just and honorable beliefs, instilled by a pious upbringing (79), he also notes a strained, volatile tension that occasionally erupts in perplexing acts. From the beginning, the son of the dean of Lichfield was not the "Angel" of his lofty inventions.[47] At school he led his classmates in the mischief of "barring-out," where "growing petulant at the approach of liberty, some days before the time of regular recess, [they] took possession of the school, of which they barred the doors, and bade their master defiance from the windows" (80). That Johnson cites this harmless school-boy's prank is a measure of his arch curiosity about Addison's repeated infractions. The next one follows closely, and now with serious repercussions, in the disgraceful treatment of Steele, as everyone knew, a lifelong intimate friend. Apparently Addison took some mean amusement in mocking his good-hearted but somewhat shiftless ally with jests that were never reciprocated. To him these were the tokens of his haughty superiority. What is more, the practice of jeering put-down, what Johnson calls "the sneer of jocularity," seems to have grown into full-blown persecution. After having lent one hundred pounds to Steele, who is represented with some of the roguery sans the danger of a Richard Savage, he files a legal execution to get the money back. This heartless and altogether unwarranted assault on a down-on-his-luck scamp is on Addison's part all the more indefensible: "Steele felt with great sensibility the obduracy of his creditor; but with emotions of sorrow rather than of anger" (81–82). And later, in the vehement dispute over the Peerage Bill, in which the two friends were at bitter odds, Johnson quotes the nasty epithet aimed anonymously at "little *Dicky*, whose trade it was to write pamphlets," and he observes, "Dicky, however, did not lose his settled veneration for his friend, but contented himself with quoting some lines of *Cato*, which were at once detection and reproof" (115).

Another of Addison's regrettable transgressions was to draw others into foolishness, a trick which seems to have tickled the queer fancies of Swift and Stella: "One slight lineament of his character Swift has preserved. It was his practice when he found any man invincibly wrong to flatter his opinions by acquiescence, and sink him yet deeper in absurdity. This artifice of mischief was admired by Stella; and Swift seems to approve her admiration" (124). If not quite idiot-baiting, which Johnson might conclude a favorite pastime of Swift's, the custom must have been unnerving enough to those who endured it: "He was a man in whose presence nothing reprehensible was out of danger: quick in discerning whatever was wrong or ridiculous, and not unwilling to expose it. 'There are,' says Steele, 'in his writings many oblique strokes upon some of the wittiest men of the age'" (124). But naturally, Johnson is not writing on Swift, and he is quick to tone down his remarks: "His delight was more to excite merriment than detestation, and he detects follies rather than crimes" (125). And further, he insists that Addison uses the barbs of wit mainly in the service of virtue, thus reinstating the moral rectitude of his subject's knightly crusade. Addison marshals the passions and forges the paths to mankind's finest goals: "No greater felicity can genius attain than that of having purified intellectual pleasure, separated mirth from indecency, and wit from licentiousness; of having taught a succession of writers to bring elegance and gaiety to the aid of goodness; and, if I may use expressions yet more awful, of having 'turned many to righteousness'" (126). But if he waxes biblical in his admiration, Johnson is hardly blind to the portentous question of such a man's personal ordeal.

According to Johnson, Addison's life was passed amid a "storm of faction" (125), not only from the outside—social and political unrest—but from within. While he tread softly on the thin ice of Dryden's provoking discomfiture, he now plunges boldly to the depths of Addison's private hell. Heeding the frightful experience of his own wreckage, he understands how Addison was buffeted by conflict, which subverted his most ardent wishes. He knows how the aggressive striving for wealth, fame, and social position belies pressures just as powerful in the opposite direction, ones brimming with reproach and self-loathing. Addison's repeated ugly outbursts catch the drift of a certain unmeasured hostility, which injures his own reputation, Johnson infers, as much as he injures that of others.[48] Even more detrimental are the episodes of paralyzing inhibition, also owing to furious internal strife. In the office of secretary to the regency, Addison froze when he had to deliver news of the Queen's death: "To do this would not have been difficult to any man but Addison, who was so overwhelmed with the greatness of the event and so distracted by choice of expression that the lords, who could not wait for the niceties of criticism, called Mr. Southwell, a clerk in the house, and ordered him to dispatch the message" (109). As secretary of state, he was similarly rendered mute: "For this employment he might be justly supposed qualified by long practice of business and by his regular ascent through other offices; but expectation is often disappointed: it is universally confessed that he was unequal to the duties of his place. In the house of commons he could not speak" (111). This truly astonishing paradox is not evaded by Johnson, though others might offer their plausible explanations: "Of his habits, or external manners, nothing is so often mentioned as that timorous or sullen taciturnity, which his friends called modesty by too mild a name" (118). Unconvinced by these and other surmises, Johnson offers an adroit and knowing analysis. By sharp contrast to the obliquity and the camouflage of "Dryden," he penetrates to the heart of Addison's tormenting inner conflict:

> This modesty was by no means inconsistent with a very high opinion of his own merit. He demanded to be the first name in modern wit; and with Steele to echo him, used to depreciate Dryden, whom Pope and Congreve defended against them. There is no reason to doubt that he suffered too much pain from the prevalence of Pope's poetical reputation; nor is it without strong reason suspected that by some disingenuous acts he endeavoured to obstruct it: Pope was not the only man whom he insidiously injured, though the only man of whom he could be afraid. (120)

Thus Johnson argues how Addison is goaded by a dastardly, virulent antagonism, breaking through the surfaces of his noble and upright demeanor. The principal battle of his life is in managing the fury which his needs create in him. His bouts of drinking are attributed largely to a desperate pitch for freedom. However beleaguered by mental demons, he could dispel them, but, as Johnson knew only too well, at considerable hazard.[49] The addiction to alcohol, far from liberating or a panacea for pain, was one more chain of Habit, driving its victim to harder captivity:[50]

> From the coffee-house he went again to a tavern, where he often sat late and drank too much wine. In the bottle discontent seeks for comfort, cowardice for courage, and bashfulness for confidence. It is not unlikely that Addison was first seduced to excess by the manumission which he obtained from the servile timidity of his sober hours. He that feels oppression from the presence of those to whom he knows himself superior will desire to set loose his powers of conversation; and who that ever asked succour from Bacchus was able to preserve himself from being enslaved by his auxiliary? (123)

Addison's "restless and unappeasable solicitude" (101) over his writings; his unhappy marriage, contracted of "ambitious love" (111); the certain pangs of chagrin and remorse he suffered from the peculiarly struck bargain, at once to overreach and grovel at the feet of his betters—these familiar spectacles of being wrecked by success were the incurable bane of his existence. Still Addison was a worthy man, as Johnson ever reminds us. He won the trust and high approval of his countrymen, friend and foe alike.[51] And his well-balanced, temperate approach to morality and religion evokes celestial models: "All the enchantment of fancy and all the cogency of argument are employed to recommend to the reader his real interest, the care of pleasing the Author of his being" (149). But all of the fruits of his labor could not release him from the grinding compulsions of mental life.

*   *   *

To define the imperfect crusader would have sufficed for a single essay, but Johnson infuses the *Lives of the Poets* with this fascinating theme.[52] Once and for all, he poses the riddle he had set for himself long ago on the fundamental ambivalence of mental life: that love and hate, desire and destruction, coexist in every character, as they do in culture itself. Such is the paradox of man's destiny, and in the secular realm, one can pass no further. But the knowledge is enough to unsettle the foundations of an antiquated world view, and doubtless for this reason, Johnson abandons his timeworn stake in the theory of poetic justice.[53] Now willing to sacrifice that last bastion of moral-didactic presumption, wrought of old rationalism, he asks us to confront what he has observed all along. Now with an absolute avowal of the chaotic energies that issue from the hidden recesses of the mind, he asks us also to brave that profound irrationality. Not the "just distribution of good or evil,"[54] but good and evil, simultaneously, lie at the foundation of man's every effort and accomplishment. In the lowest as well as in the most elevated of human acts, they are soldered together, one with the other. It comes as no surprise that in the "Life of Addison" Johnson out and out dismisses John Dennis's abstruse moralistic aesthetics as merely "wishes." Thus we may unconditionally allow that "wickedness often prospers in real life," that a view of the world unshrouded by the scrims of sophistry "ought to shew us sometimes what we are to expect" (*Lives*, 2: 135). If the character of "Addison" salutes the best of mankind, Johnson does not hesitate to expose those sources of ferocity it shares with the worst. Here and in other Lives, he lays open a common endowment of vicious motives, thoughts, and actions, by others reticently cloaked. The tangled and intricate web of subterfuge never eludes him. The most rigid postures in fact arouse his strongest suspicions. At every turn, his keenest powers of penetration are in play. He had initially targeted his sights in the "Life of Cowley": "So differently are things seen and so differently are they shown; but actions are visible, though motives are secret" (*Works*, 1: 15).[55] From this analytic perspective, there is hardly a pretext that escapes his vigilant eye.

Some two years before his death, Johnson summed up his radical explorations of human nature with the cogent remark, "As I know more of mankind I expect less of them, and am ready to call a man *a good man*, upon easier terms than I was formerly."[56] This is the Johnson who had quaked with outrage and bellowed his way to hell and perdition when he first launched his fortunes in London over forty years ago. Now staunchly in possession of a epoch-making new world view, he reflects on the frightful and precipitous landscapes he traversed. More than catechistic pieties or tendentious moralizing could ever explain, he knows that the archaic inheritance—grasping, cruel, mendacious—is ineradicably printed in mental experience. The eloquent drama of *The Lives of the Poets* may hint at Johnson's private gloom, but it also shows an astonishing tolerance for those dark and unpalatable residues never wholly to be erased. As for *a good man*, Johnson's terms are also written in the palimpsest of mental life. In one of the most famous passages in all his work, he pays respect to Gilbert Walmsley, his old mentor of half a century past. With simple grace, he lingers on a happy scene from those distant formative years: "He was one of the first friends that literature procured me, and I hope that at least my gratitude made me worthy of his notice. He was of an advanced age, and I was only not a boy; yet he never received my notions with contempt. . . . Such was his amplitude of learning and such his copiousness of communication that it may be doubted whether a day now passes in which I have not some advantage from his friendship" (*Lives*, 2: 20–21). The affection born of these indelible impressions leads him to think on other old friends, now recently lost: Robert James, some three years previous; and David Garrick, who died unexpectedly in 1779, just as Johnson was finishing this first major installment of the *Lives*, in which the Walmsley testimonial appears. The sudden aspect of death fetches the mournful sigh, "But what are the hopes of man!" These words do bring us back to Johnson's elegy on Dr. Levet, with his exquisite imagining of "Hope's delusive mine." Amidst the ghostly etchings, he labors in treacherous caverns to find meaning in the empty center and bottom of life. Mrs. Thrale aptly reminds us that Johnson thought "the vacuity of Life the source of all ye Passions," and more, "the general Tenor of his reasonings commonly ended in that [theme]."[57] We can now better understand why Johnson was an inveterate finder of ambivalence, for he ultimately imposes meaning by the turbulent, often irrational play of human emotion. Hardly a messianic vision or a transcendent morality, his wisdom echoes with the secrets, persistent and timeless, of the psyche.

Notes

1. John Wain, *Johnson on Johnson: A Selection of the Personal and Autobiographical Writings of Samuel Johnson (1709–1784)* (London: J.M. Dent, 1976), pp. 182–84. The original Latin poem appears in *Works*, 6: 271–74.

2. Doubtless Johnson understood the vehicles of Greek myth to embody powerful emotions, such as the unavailing rage of Sisyphus. We know that his translations from the classics were made, sometimes for amusement, other times to help stave off physical and mental distress. With two very useful references, G. B. Hill annotates Boswell's information that Johnson translated many epigrams from the Greek *Anthologia*. From a letter written 19 April 1784 to Mrs. Thrale: "When I lay sleepless, I used to drive the night along, by turning Greek epigrams into Latin. I know not if I have not turned a hundred" (*Letters*, 3: 157, no. 954); and from the "Life of Boerhaave" written forty-five years earlier, describing how the great Dutch physician, "when he lay whole days and nights without sleep, he found no method of diverting his thoughts so effectual as meditation upon his studies, and that he often relieved and mitigated the sense of his torments by the recollection of what he had read, and by reviewing those stores of knowledge which he had reposited in his memory" (*Oxford Authors*, p. 64). See also *Works*, 6: xvii, 315–16.

3. Albert Camus, *The Myth of Sisyphus and Other Essays* (New York: Knopf, 1955), pp. 119–23. In *Printing Technology, Letters & Samuel Johnson* (Princeton, N.J.: Princeton University Press, 1987), Alvin Kernan also speculates on the "existential Johnson":

> The enormous amounts of writing that both men did [Johnson and Boswell] was, by their own admission, another and a primary defense against anomie, and in the character of Johnson that Boswell constructed in the *Life*, the life of writing became an integral part of a continuing psychological as well as social struggle against chaos, meaninglessness, even nothingness. It seems likely that this psychomachia reflects at least something of Boswell's own existential uneasiness, probably something of Johnson's as well. But the image transcended these personal concerns to become a culture hero, a generally accepted definition of the writer in the age of print, a struggler with words against emptiness, a maker of meaning in language in the face of a threatening meaninglessness. (p. 129)

4. *Letters*, 2: 170 (no. 515).

5. "Talking of Biography, he said, he did not think that the life of any literary man in England had been well written. Beside the common incidents of life, it should tell us his studies, his mode of living, the means by which he attained to excellence, and his opinions of his own works" (*Journal of a Tour to the Hebrides*, p. 320).

6. As related to Edmond Malone in *Life*, 4: 53.

7. See also *Idler* 84, *Works*, 2: 263:

> The high and low, as they have the same faculties and the same senses, have no less similitude in their pains and pleasures. The sensations are the same in all, tho' produced by very different occasions. The prince feels the same pain when an invader seizes a province, as the farmer when a thief drives away his cow.

And *Idler* 51, *Works*, 2: 159:

> Such is the constitution of the world, that much of life must be spent in the same manner by the wise and the ignorant, the exalted and the low. Men, however, distinguished by external accidents or intrinsick qualities, have all the same wants, the same pains, and, as far as the senses are consulted, the same pleasures.

8. *Johnsonian Miscellanies*, 1: 308.

9. *Johnsonian Miscellanies*, 1: 297.

10. Ian Watt, in his classic *The Rise of the Novel: Studies in Defoe, Richardson and Fielding* (1957; rpt. Berkeley: University of California Press, 1971), pp. 228–29, was one of the first to call attention to Johnson's modern psychological view of *Clarissa*.

11. For the background of this prevalent laudatory style, see the accounts in Robert Folkenflik, *Samuel Johnson, Biographer* (Ithaca, N.Y.: Cornell University Press, 1978), pp. 19–55; and John A. Vance, *Samuel Johnson and the Sense of History* (Athens: University of Georgia Press, 1984), pp. 5–30.

12. *Letters*, 1: 323–24 (no. 307.1). The English translation is John Wain's from *Johnson on Johnson*, pp. 187–88.

13. "In the male phantasy . . . the being beaten stands for being loved. . . . So the original form of the unconscious male phantasy was not the provisional one that we have hitherto given: 'I am being beaten by my father,' but rather: *I am loved by my father*" (*Standard Edition*, 17: 200).

14. Was Mrs. Thrale Johnson's dominatrix, real or imagined? The speculations are best left to biographers. See Balderston's original keen surmises in "Johnson's Vile Melancholy." See also Bate, *Samuel Johnson*, pp. 384–89, 439–41; and Wain, *Samuel Johnson: A Biography*, pp. 286–92. The "hard" and "soft" schools of thought on this matter are divided almost equally.

15. Most studies of Johnson's *Lives* underscore, if not at length, at least in passim, its moral design. See for example, Robert Folkenflik's two chapters, "Interpretation" and "Precedents and Form," in *Samuel Johnson, Biographer*, pp. 71–117;

Lawrence Lipking, *The Ordering of the Arts in Eighteenth-Century England* (Princeton, N.J.: Princeton University Press, 1970), pp. 405–62; Leopold Damrosch, Jr., *The Uses of Johnson's Criticism* (Charlottesville: University Press of Virginia, 1976), pp. 123–66; William McCarthy, "The Moral Art of Johnson's *Lives*," *Studies in English Literature* 17 (1977): 502–17; Mark W. Booth, "Johnson's Critical Judgments in the *Lives of the Poets*," *Studies in English Literature* 16 (1976): 505–16.

16. See Martin Maner, *The Philosophical Biographer: Doubt and Dialectic in Johnson's Lives of the Poets* (Athens: University of Georgia Press, 1988), pp. 57–73, which clearly shows how Johnson uses emotional conflict to shape the reader's responses to Savage.

17. Here, of course, is the way the printed version ends, as Donald Greene suggests, perhaps on Cave's advice, "concerned for sales and anxious not to antagonize the right-thinking" ("Samuel Johnson's *The Life of Richard Savage*," in *The Biographer's Art: New Essays*, ed. Jeffrey Meyers [London: Macmillan Press, 1989], p. 30):

> This relation will not be wholly without its use if those who languish under any part of his sufferings shall be enabled to fortify their patience by reflecting that they feel only those afflictions from which the abilities of Savage did not exempt him; or those who, in confidence of superior capacities or attainments, disregard the common maxims of life, shall be reminded that nothing will supply the want of prudence, and that negligence and irregularity long continued will make knowledge useless, wit ridiculous, and genius contemptible. (*Lives*, 2: 434)

Clarence Tracy points to Johnson's marginal manuscript note, "Added," to this paragraph in a copy of the "Life" preserved in the University of Glasgow Library (Samuel Johnson, *An Account of the Life of Savage*, ed. Clarence Tracy [Oxford: Oxford University Press, 1970], p. 140, and n. 103).

18. See also the "Life of Boerhaave" (*Oxford Authors*, p. 70) for the original.

19. The chief lesson of Freud's *Civilization and Its Discontents*, firmly anchored in the tradition of Hobbes, Locke, and Mandeville, is that culture arose as a defense against aggressive instincts: "It is impossible to overlook the extent to which civilization is built up upon a renunciation of instinct, how much it presupposes precisely the non-satisfaction (by suppression, repression or some other means?) of powerful instincts. This 'cultural frustration' dominates the large field of social relationships between human beings" (*Standard Edition*, 21: 98).

20. *Johnsonian Miscellanies*, 2: 285.

21. See also the "Life of Akenside," where he similarly shreds the outward dressing of social activism:

> He certainly retained an unnecessary and outrageous zeal for what he called and thought liberty—a zeal which sometimes disguises from the world, and not rarely from the mind which it possesses, an envious desire of plundering wealth or degrading greatness; and of which the immediate tendency is innovation and anarchy, an impetuous eagerness to subvert and confound, with very little care what shall be established. (*Works*, 3: 411–12)

22. For a detailed study of how Johnson connects Milton's life and art, see Stephen Fix, "Distant Genius: Johnson and the Art of Milton's Life," *Modern Philology* 81 (1984): 244–64. It is not the purpose here, nor in the discussion of other Lives, to treat Johnson's literary criticism, except in so far as he interprets a writer's work, drawing on inferences from his analysis of a writer's character. This very point about life/art connections and distinctions has become a bone of contention in the criticism of Johnson's literary biographies, especially "Milton," in Lipking, *The Ordering of the Arts*, pp. 434–42 and Damrosch, *The Uses of Johnson's Criticism*, pp. 137–41. See also the arguments applied to the entire *Lives* in Folkenflik, *Samuel Johnson, Biographer*, pp. 118–73. While Johnson sometimes warned against relating a poet's art to his life (*Rambler* 14, *Works*, 3: 74–80; the "Life of Thompson," *Lives*, 3: 297–98; the "Life of Akenside," *Lives*, 3: 417), there is ample evidence to suggest that he in fact made exceptions when focusing on psychological themes.

23. See also Johnson's cutting enough remark, "It appears in all his writings that he had the usual concomitant of great abilities, a lofty and steady confidence in himself, perhaps not without some contempt of others; for scarcely any man ever wrote so much and praised so few" (*Lives*, 1: 94).

24. From the beginning, intimations of Johnson's personal dislike for Swift prompted Boswell to inquire: "He seemed to me to have an unaccountable prejudice against Swift; for I once took the liberty to ask him, if Swift had personally offended him, and he told me, he had not" (*Life*, 5: 44). More discerning views of Johnson's prejudice point to temperamental affinities from which he apparently cringed. See, for example, W. B. C. Watkins, *Perilous Balance*, pp. 25–48; Jeffrey Meyers, "Autobiographical Reflections in Johnson's *Life of Swift*," *Discourse* 8 (1968): 37–48. For the intellectual and factual bases of Johnson's opinion, see Paul J. Korshin, "Johnson and Swift: A Study in the Genesis of Literary Opinion," *Philological Quarterly* 48 (1969): 464–78. Korshin finds "an unaccustomed insight into Johnson's ethical balance, which was severely disturbed by the satire of Part IV [of *Gulliver's Travels*]," p. 474. Also, Frederick W. Hilles, "Dr. Johnson on Swift's Last Years: Some Misconceptions and Distortions," *Philological Quarterly* 54 (1975): 370–79, considers Johnson's interpretation of Swift's illness.

25. Johnson later adds: "His beneficence was not graced with tenderness or civility; he relieved without pity, and assisted without kindness, so that those who were fed by him could hardly love him" (*Lives*, 3: 57–58).

26. In his notorious chapter, "The Excremental Vision," in *Life Against Death: The Psychoanalytic Meaning of History* (Middletown, Conn.: Wesleyan University Press, 1959), pp. 179–201, Norman O. Brown presents the standard analytic approach. See also Phyllis Greenacre, *Swift and Carroll: A Psychoanalytic Study of Two Lives* (New York: International University Press, 1955), pp. 88–115; John Middleton Murry, *Jonathan Swift: A Critical Biography* (New York: Farrar, Strauss & Giroux, 1955), pp. 432–48.

27. See also in the "Life of Pope,": "In the letters both of Swift and Pope there appears such narrowness of mind as makes them insensible of any excellence that has not some affinity with their own, and confines their esteem and approbation to so small a number, that whoever should form his opinion of the age from their

representation would suppose them to have lived amidst ignorance and barbarity, unable to find among their contemporaries either virtue or intelligence, and persecuted by those that could not understand them" (*Lives*, 3: 212).

28. *Lives*, 3: 82, n. 1. But see F.W. Hilles, "The Making of *The Life of Pope*," in *New Light on Dr. Johnson* (New Haven, Conn.: Yale University Press, 1959), pp. 258–60, for correction of the dating.

29. Perhaps no other Life has been so thoroughly studied by critics, with such mixed verdicts. On the one side are the claims that Johnson merely leafed through previous versions of Pope's life to write his own, for example, Benjamin Boyce, "Samuel Johnson's Criticism of Pope in the *Life of Pope*," *Review of English Studies*, n.s. 5 (January 1954): 37–46; and F. W. Hilles, "The Making of *The Life of Pope*," in *New Light on Dr. Johnson*, pp. 257–84. But on the other side, see the arguments about Johnson's vigorous rhetorical effects, in Lawrence Lipking, *The Ordering of the Arts*, pp. 448–52; Martin Maner, *The Philosophical Biographer*, pp. 121–42; Edward Tomarkin, *Johnson, Rasselas, and the Choice of Criticism* (Lexington: University of Kentucky Press, 1989), pp. 165–78. The latter would make it clear that Johnson was as deeply engaged in this project as any other. Lipking puts it succinctly, when steering us away from the over-emphasis on Johnson's method of literary biography: "Where Johnson excels all other biographers is not in method but in his profound analysis of behavior, an analysis which unites the virtues of the novelist and the moralist" (p. 452). And clearly the highest commendation is by George Sherburn, who stresses Johnson's excellent appraisal of Pope's personality: "One feels that on the whole Johnson understood Pope both man and artist better than any one can ever understand him now that he has been dead nearly two centuries" (*The Early Career of Alexander Pope* [Oxford: Oxford University Press, 1934], p. 15).

30. Maynard Mack also singles out this passage for its revelation of Pope's character: "Much in Pope's career, I think we must agree, *was* determined by an effort to extract ornament from inconvenience of a rather painful kind—to find, or make, some ground for pride in all too visible defects" (*The Garden and the City: Retirement and Politics in the Later Poetry of Pope* [Toronto: University of Toronto Press, 1969], p. 61).

31. See also in this long section about Pope's nervous, unabating ministrations to his work:

> He considered poetry as the business of his life, and, however he might seem to lament his occupation, he followed it with constancy. . . . From his attention to poetry he was never diverted. If conversation offered anything that could be improved he committed it to paper; if a thought, or perhaps an expression more happy than was common, rose to his mind, he was careful to write it; an independent distich was preserved for an opportunity of insertion, and some little fragments have been found containing lines, or parts of lines, to be wrought upon at some other time. He was one of those few whose labour is their pleasure; he was never elevated to negligence, nor wearied to impatience; he never passed a fault unamended by indifference, nor quitted it by despair. . . . He is said to have sent nothing to the press till it had lain two years

under his inspection: it is at least certain that he ventured nothing without nice examination. (*Lives*, 3: 217–20)

32. G.B. Hill takes the hint by quoting Horace Walpole: "When one of Pope's last satires was published a gentleman, in the presence of Lord Chesterfield, said he wondered nobody beat Pope for his abusiveness" (*Lives*, 3: 181, n. 5). The special context of this statement about Pope's safety is the arrest of Dodsley the publisher for an alleged seditious tract, but, as Johnson says, the whole business was a charade, probably meant to intimidate Pope, who was at the time lampooning political figures.

33. Johnson again adduces the virtuosity of Pope's guile when he publishes his own letters: "It seems that Pope, being desirous of printing his letters, and not knowing how to do, without imputation of vanity, what has in this country been done very rarely, contrived an appearance of compulsion: that when he could complain that his letters were surreptitiously published, he might decently and defensively publish them himself" (*Lives*, 3: 157).

34. *Life*, 4: 46.

35. For a trenchant reading of "Pope and outrage," exploring the many psychological and literary historical dimensions inherent in this theme, see G. S. Rousseau, "Pope and the tradition in modern humanistic education: '. . . in the pale of Words till death,'" in *The Enduring Legacy: Alexander Pope Tercentenary Essays*, ed. G. S. Rousseau and Pat Rogers (Cambridge: Cambridge University Press, 1988), pp. 199–239.

36. In his famous essay, Freud explains how imaginative stories of family relationship are used to correct actual painful ones, usually by replacing real parents with others of lofty rank. Moreover, the fantasy is remarkably flexible: "If there are any other particular interests at work they can direct the course to be taken by the family romance; for its many-sidedness and its great range of applicability enable it to meet every sort of requirement" (*Standard Edition*, 9: 240). Johnson's urgent need to replace his own parents for a family of all-bountiful love no doubt helped to shape this exalted representation of Pope's "filial piety." The fantasy is all the more poignant in view of his imminent loss of the Thrales, Mr. Thrale's illness and death happening almost concurrently with the writing of the "Life of Pope." Another variant of Johnson's family romance is represented in the "Life of Dryden," where in fact it is deeply embedded in the narrative (see above).

37. *Life*, 3: 71–72. And although Mrs. Thrale finds some of Johnson's criticism of Dryden in the "Life" severe, she grants he is a writer "whom he praises not only with Liberality but Fondness, not only with Esteem but Veneration" (*Thraliana*, 2: 622–23).

38. Boswell strangely believes that Johnson found in common with Dryden a so-called inability to engage the passions in his writings (*Life*, 4: 45). Others point to the obvious similarities of their composing hastily, laboring under the burden of financial necessity and whims of the public, and feeling guilty for a powerful genius not fully employed. But perhaps the most intriguing questions about Johnson and his "Dryden" pertain to the way he fanatically worships the image he creates while perfectly aware that it is deeply flawed. Many critics simply avoid this quandary by

insisting that Johnson admires the poet over the man, or by invoking a moral imperative to justify the inconsistencies of praise and blame. See, for example, Lipking, *The Ordering of the Arts*, pp. 442–48, and more elaborately, Damrosch, *The Uses of Johnson's Criticism*, pp. 166–91. However plausible, these arguments do not engage the more purely psychological issue of Johnson's customary identification with his subject, his formulation of a dynamic mental image of another, which often lends the finest edge to his insights. Here is an altogether different approach to this most enigmatic of the Lives.

39. "There are men whose powers operate at leisure and in retirement, and whose intellectual vigour deserts them in conversation; whom merriment confuses, and objection disconcerts; whose bashfulness restrains their exertion, and suffers them not to speak till the time of speaking is past; or whose attention to their own character makes them unwilling to utter at hazard what has not been considered, and cannot be recalled" (*Lives*, 1: 397).

40. For a penetrating view of this theme operating in the "Life," as well as Johnson's sage insights into the literary history of the Restoration, see Maximillian E. Novak, "Johnson, Dryden, and the Wild Vicissitudes of Taste," in *The Unknown Samuel Johnson*, ed. John J. Burke, Jr. and Donald Kay (Madison: University of Wisconsin Press, 1983), pp. 54–75.

41. Also see pp. 408–10, where Johnson again protests the "slight" and "scanty" information available to him on Dryden. Folkenflik, *Samuel Johnson, Biographer*, pp. 47, 91, believes this to be a special theme in the "Life."

42. *Lives*, 1: 373. Also see the "Life of Sprat," where Johnson remembers "my father, an old man, who had been no careless observer of the passages of those times" (*Lives*, 2: 37).

43. See chapter 5. Also see Clifford, *Young Sam Johnson*, p. 339, n. 17, which suggests the date of the penance as the autumn of 1781, citing the gloomy mood of two letters from Lichfield to Mrs. Thrale (*Letters*, 2: 444–46 (nos. 745, 746). The letters have to do with the loss of old friends: "To those whom I love here I can give no help, and from those that love me, none can I receive" (445).

44. See note 36.

45. If Johnson reprints the letter Dryden wrote to his sons, he never uses it in his narrative. See James M. Osborn, *John Dryden: Some Biographical Facts and Problems* (New York: Columbia University Press, 1940), pp. 37–38, who keenly observes that we get more of Dryden's personality here than in the whole rest of the "Life."

46. This was one of Johnson's principal arguments in the *Vinerian Lectures on English Law*, as we have seen. Defending his "diminutive observations" in the *Journal to the Western Islands of Scotland*, he therefore suggests: "The true state of every nation is the state of common life. . . . They whose aggregate constitutes the people, are found in the streets, and the villages, in the shops and farms; and from them collectively considered must the measure of general prosperity be taken" (*Works*, 9: 22).

47. The allusion is from Addison's early poem, *The Campaign* (1705), where Johnson contradicts the *Tatler*'s commendation of it as "one of the noblest thoughts that ever entered into the heart of man" (*Lives*, 2: 129).

48. In the "Life of Pope" he adduces more examples of Addison's vicious side: his unseemly "jealousy" of the budding poet (*Lives*, 3: 103), as well as his instigation of the famous dispute between Ambrose Phillips and Pope over the merits of their respective *Pastorals*. Seeing through the ruse of Pope's authorship of a Scriblerian-type essay of demolition, Addison "had malice enough to conceal his discovery, and to permit a publication which, by making his friend Philips ridiculous, made him for ever an enemy to Pope" (107).

49. For references to Johnson's fondness for drinking and later enforced abstinence, see Bate, *Samuel Johnson*, pp. 135–36, 358, 409. Boswell reports his surprise one time at finding Johnson resolved not to carouse as usual:

> At night I supped with him at the Mitre tavern, that we might renew our social intimacy at the original place of meeting. But there was now a considerable difference in his way of living. Having had an illness, in which he was advised to leave off wine, he had, from that period, continued to abstain from it, and drank only water, or lemonade. (*Life*, 2: 8)

50. See Roy Porter, ed. Thomas Trotter, *An Essay, Medical, Philosophical, and Chemical, on Drunkenness and its Effects on the Human Body* (1894; rpt. London: Tavistock Reprint Series in the History of Psychiatry, 1988). The introductory essay richly illustrates the tradition of Johnson's insight that drunkenness was a disease of the mind.

51. "Of his virtue it is a sufficient testimony that the resentment of party has transmitted no charge of any crime. He was not one of those who are praised only after death; for his merit was so generally acknowledged that Swift, having observed that his election passed without a contest, adds, that if he had proposed himself for king, he would hardly have been refused" (*Lives*, 2: 118).

52. Indeed, Johnson seems preoccupied many times in the *Lives* with this inherent contradiction in character. He stubbornly insists, for example, on Savage's principled quest for moral rectitude: "In cases indifferent he was zealous for virtue, truth, and justice: he knew very well the necessity of goodness to the present and future happiness of mankind; nor is there perhaps any writer who has less endeavoured to please by flattering the appetites or perverting the judgement" (*Lives*, 2: 432). In the "Life of Collins," he explains at some length how the poet's wisdom survived his misfortunes:

> His morals were pure, and his opinions pious; in a long continuance of poverty and long habits of dissipation it cannot be expected that any character should be exactly uniform. There is a degree of want by which the freedom of agency is almost destroyed; and long association with fortuitous companions will at last relax the strictness of truth, and abate the fervour of sincerity. That this man, wise and virtuous as he was, passed always unentangled through the snares of life, it would be prejudice and temerity to affirm; but it may be said that at least he preserved the source of action unpolluted, that his principles were never shaken, that his distinctions of right and wrong were never confounded, and that his faults had nothing of malignity or design, but proceeded from some unexpected pressure, or casual temptation. (*Lives*, 3: 338)

And in the "Life of Prior," he grants to the incorrigible bon vivant, somewhat grudgingly: "His opinions, so far as the means of judging are left us, seem to have been right; but his life was, it seems, irregular, negligent, and sensual" (*Lives*, 2: 200).

53. Johnson's statements in support of poetic justice are legion. In *Rambler* 4 on the new realistic novel, he presents his views at length and summarizes:

> In narratives, where historical veracity has no place, I cannot discover why there should not be exhibited the most perfect idea of virtue; of virtue not angelical, nor above probability, for what we cannot credit we shall never imitate, but the highest and purest that humanity can reach, which, exercised in such trials as the various revolutions of things shall bring upon it, may, by conquering some calamities, and enduring others, teach us what we may hope, and what we can perform. Vice, for vice is necessary to be shewn, should always disgust; nor should the graces of gaiety, or the dignity of courage, be so united with it, as to reconcile it to the mind. Wherever it appears, it should raise hatred by the malignity of its practices, and contempt by the meanness of its stratagems; for while it is supported by either parts or spirit, it will be seldom heartily abhorred. (*Works*, 3: 24)

Unfortunately, Shakespeare sometimes falls foul of this standard, and in the "Preface," he is reproved:

> His first defect is that to which may be imputed most of the evil in books or in men. He sacrifices virtue to convenience, and is so much more careful to please than to instruct, that he seems to write without any moral purpose. From his writings indeed a system of social duty may be selected, for he that thinks reasonably must think morally; but his precepts and axioms drop casually from him; he makes no just distribution of good or evil, nor is always careful to shew in the virtuous a disapprobation of the wicked. (*Works*, 7: 71)

And in the Endnote to *King Lear* Johnson naturally regrets the death of Cordelia:

> A play in which the wicked prosper, and the virtuous miscarry, may doubtless be good, because it is a just representation of the common events of human life: but since all reasonable beings naturally love justice, I cannot easily be persuaded, that the observation of justice makes a play worse; or, that if other excellencies are equal, the audience will not always rise better pleased from the final triumph of persecuted virtue. (*Works*, 7: 704)

For a lucid discussion of Johnson's complex view of poetic justice, see Edinger, *Samuel Johnson and Poetic Style*, pp. 179–92.

54. "Preface to Shakespeare," *Works*, 7: 71.

55. Also capturing the skeptical quality of this analytic search for truth, see the comments in his review of the *Account of the Conduct of the Duchess of Marlborough*: "Distrust is a necessary qualification of a student of history. Distrust quickens his discernment of different degrees of probability, animates his search

after evidence, and perhaps heightens his pleasure at the discovery of truth; for truth, though not always obvious, is generally discoverable" (1742), *Oxford Authors*, p. 114.

56. *Life*, 4: 239.
57. *Thraliana*, 1: 254, 179.

Conclusion

DURING JOHNSON'S LIFETIME, mental disorder, with its manifold faces of melancholy, delusion, frenzy, depression, and troubled spirits, was not the traditional preserve of any one profession. Philosophers, theologians, physicians, and poets alike dispensed their wisdom on psychiatric topics and, with few exceptions, they extolled the polemics of an intransigent rationalism. Where it was believed that the rules of self-command and the duties of that great catchall of abstractions, Reason, could safeguard mental health, there could be little incentive to launch a formal inquiry into the inward life. To some extent, Dr. Battie's new formulations on the nature of insanity helped to breach these hidebound attitudes. Using Lockean views of "deluded imagination" and endorsing observation and personal attention to individual patients, he stormed the ballasts of parochial authoritarianism. But even he would not, nor did Locke, choose to delve very far into the mysterious and treacherous depths of pure subjectivity. It remained for others to probe the secret springs of instinct and emotion. Theirs was the brave discovery of the dynamic unconscious, fired by a subversive and potent scientific empiricism.[1]

I have argued that Johnson was a pioneer in scientific empiricism as it would be espoused by Freud and his followers in a new scientific theory of the mind. Johnson's deep and abiding interest in medical science, complemented by a passionate concern with spiritual values, gave him a unique edge for ordering ideas of the psyche. It was the stimulating view of W. K. Wimsatt over forty years ago that the *Ramblers* "exhibit perhaps the most concentrated use in English literature of mechanical imagery turned inward to the analysis of the soul."[2] Evidently, this astonishing work was forged from Johnson's own radical and daring self-analysis. What is more, Johnson brought his grand erudition to bear on his research into the mental apparatus. His account of preparing to write the *Dictionary* is tantamount to his preparation in medical psychology: "I . . . extracted from philosophers principles of science; from historians remarkable facts; from chemists complete processes; from divines striking exhortations; and from poets beautiful descriptions."³ The conveyor of a redoubtable intellectual tradition, Johnson developed—as only a few individuals have—a fully humanistic, scientifically rigorous theory of human psychology.

Some, to be sure, have argued that the notion of Johnson's "vile melancholy," no better than Boswell's skewed portrait of the Great Cham huffing and puffing along his ponderous way, detracts our attention from Johnson's writings. In this respect, one grotesque personality merely replaces another: the modern neurotic sufferer for the boorish old bigot.⁴ But if Johnson's writings bear the traces of his life, clearly an informed and attentive reconstruction of that life history opens many tantalizing vistas which would be virtually inaccessible through traditional scholarly and historical routes, however edifying in their own right. In the shackling "Habits" of "The Vision of Theodore," the "invisible riot of the mind" of the periodical essays, the bizarre configurations of the "happy valley," the vast expanses of desert of the Western Islands of Scotland; in the pregnant accounts of Savage's rage, Milton's beating, and Pope's child-like fragility—in these more than literary tropes or Christian exhortations or biographical tidbits, we find the deepest sources of psychical meaning. That Johnson intended them is unmistakable, by virtue of his penetrating and unceasing preoccupation with the hidden order of the mind. He in fact may be the best advocate of all for a psychoanalytic dispensation, when he states, "The only end of writing is to enable the readers better to enjoy life, or better to endure it."

Throughout this study, I have maintained Johnson's distinct affinities with a movement and method of aggressive radicalism, which culminated in the late nineteenth century with the theories of Freud. The gain in such a reading is surely in its justice to the profoundly subversive quality of Johnson's thought. Thus he opposed his age's fashionable theodicies, gushing with pretentious enthusiasm. He rejected the current vogue of all too subtle presuppositions about human nature and drew his observations from the raw potency of mental events. He claimed the mastery that every man can attain for himself through hard won struggles over primitive instinct. And he spurned the safe encampments of fatuous utopianism to raid those awesome citadels which it shunned. To Johnson, vice and sin, long dreaded, were not the fell negations of Reason, to be darkly suppressed and confined. He had voyaged too familiarly in the underworld of the mind to concede such cruel and heartless reprobation. The intrepid explorer of forbidden wishes and unpalatable acts, he upheld the tenets of a devout, altogether militant humanism. Too readily is it assumed that his religious temperament, taken with the conservative nature of his political theory, would preclude any actively dissident stand. As we have plainly seen, Johnson, read in the terms of his psychological theory, was as much a child of the Enlightenment as Hume, Voltaire, Rousseau, or any other exponent of radical skepticism and reform.[5]

Doubtless, Johnson has much to say to contemporary readers, and today is surely a time when we can use him most. Neither the cheerful shallow optimism of those who trip giddily toward the next century nor the pallid lucubrations and massive denial peddled by many present academic theorists claims much of a stake in the inward life. With such dubious guides, we rarely approach the essential battlegrounds, the combustible motives, thoughts, and feelings behind human affairs. But for Johnson the inward life is the galling challenge to complacency and the key to under-standing—and to mastering—a world increasingly ridden by conflict and discontent. No self-satisfied or effete posturing, no pat or abstruse solutions, can quell the tensions which issue from the deepest recesses of the psyche. To expose our fondest illusions and make men and women see themselves more truthfully than before was his utmost goal. He expresses it unequivocally in the translation from book 2, metre 2 of Boethius's *Consolation of Philosophy*:

> Though countless as the grains of sand
> That roll at Eurus' loud command;
> Though countless as the lamps of night
> That glad us with vicarious light;
> Fair plenty gracious Queen shou'd pour
> The blessings of a golden show'r
> Not all the gifts of fate combin'd
> Would ease the hunger of the mind,
> But swallowing all the mighty store,
> Rapacity would call for more;
> For still where wishes most abound
> Unquench'd the thirst of gain is found;
> In vain the shining gifts are sent,
> For none are rich without content.

(*Works*, 6: 257–58)

Thus Johnson excavates the archaic machinery of human need and human wishes, running its relentless cycle to the last. Rooted out are the canting professions and evasions and dreams of transcendent prosperity. By this reckoning, hope is no more than a myth begotten of the random elements of desire. There is a brooding uneasiness about Johnson's vision of man's imagination of meaning grafted upon the meaningless whole he has evinced. And it is precisely this uneasiness, pleading for ideological certainty, which has led many back to the protective embraces of the Christian moralist. But Johnson contains other lessons too, by his task of ordering chaos. If we are, as he says, "Condemned to hope's delusive mine," he knows and proclaims its conditions, and he holds the possibility for a freedom of negotiation. He had this to inure himself to the inescapable suffering of human life. And it is this consciousness that ever links us to him.

Notes

1. In *Freud for Historians* (New York: Oxford University Press, 1985), as well as in the masterly biography, *Freud: A Life for Our Time* (New York: W. W. Norton, 1988), Peter Gay stresses the great scientific empirical tradition, springing from the eighteenth-century Enlightenment, to which Freud was heir. While some fine studies of the historical origins of psychoanalysis exist, such as Launcelot Law Whyte, *The Unconscious Before Freud* (London: Tavistock Publications, 1960) and Henri F. Ellenberger, *The Discovery of the Unconscious: The History and Evolution of Dynamic Psychiatry* (New York: Basic Books, 1971), they do not treat the eighteenth century in any detail. Compounding this situation, many revisionist historians who are the acolytes of Foucault have found it in their interest to debunk Freud and the integrity of psychoanalysis, thereby to forestall this much-needed inquiry. Such blinkered views should be weighed against the authority of Gay, whose compelling and eloquent arguments link the Enlightenment ultimately to the Freudian dispensation.

2. *Philosophic Words: A Study of Style and Meaning in the Rambler and Dictionary of Samuel Johnson* (New Haven, Conn.: Yale University Press, 1948), p. 104.

3. *Oxford Authors*, p. 318.

4. See John Middendorf's review-essay (of Bate, *Samuel Johnson*), which takes this position, albeit tolerantly, in "Johnson on the Couch," *Review* 1 (1979): 1–12.

5. See Mark J. Temmer, *Samuel Johnson and Three Infidels: Rousseau, Voltaire, Diderot* (Athens: University of Georgia Press, 1988) which speculates on Johnson's relation to the Enlightenment philosophes. Also see Martin Maner, *The Philosophical Biographer* for the background of Johnson's skeptical way of proceeding in the *Lives of the Poets*. Alvin Kernan well sums up the view of a subversive Johnson, more than was imagined up to the mid-twentieth century: "The last two generations of Johnsonian scholars, re-examining the evidence, have gradually replaced the author-

itarian Johnson with a much more complex Johnson, skeptical, deeply troubled in mind, mad at times, neurotic nearly always, radically doubtful of himself and of the social values he at the same time so stoutly defended. . . . This is a modern Johnson who accords with the needs of our own time, and may be somewhat suspect for this reason, but he has always been there . . ." (*Printing Technology, Letters & Samuel Johnson*), p. 117.

Bibliography

Alexander, Franz G. *Fundamentals of Psychoanalysis*. 1948. 2nd ed. New York: W.W. Norton, 1963.

Alexander, Franz G. and Sheldon T. Selesnick. *The History of Psychiatry*. New York: Harper & Row, 1966.

Alkon, Paul K. *Samuel Johnson and Moral Discipline*. Chicago: Northwestern University Press, 1967.

————. "The Intention and Reception of Johnson's *Life of Savage*." *Modern Philology* 72 (1974): 139–50.

Anderson, Robert. *The Life of Samuel Johnson, with critical observations on his works*. London: J. and A. Arch, 1795.

Arlow, Jacob A. "Unconscious Fantasy and Conscious Experience." *Psychoanalytic Quarterly* 38 (1969): 1–27.

Arnold, Thomas. *Observations on the Nature, Kinds, Causes and Prevention of Insanity*. 1782. 2nd ed. London: R. Phillips, 1806.

Baker, Sheridan. "*Rasselas*: Psychological Irony and Romance." *Philological Quarterly* 45 (1966): 249–61.

Balderston, Katharine C. "Johnson's Vile Melancholy." In *The Age of Johnson: Essays Presented to Chauncey B. Tinker*. Ed. F.W. Hilles. New Haven, Conn.: Yale University Press, 1949. 3–14.

————. "Dr. Johnson and William Law." *PMLA* 75 (1960): 382–94.

Bate, Walter Jackson. *The Achievement of Samuel Johnson*. New York: Oxford University Press, 1955.

————. *Samuel Johnson*. New York: Harcourt Brace Jovanovich, 1975.

Battie, William. *A Treatise on Madness*. London: J. Whiston, 1758.

Bender, John. *Imagining the Penitentiary: Fiction and the Architecture of Mind in Eighteenth-Century England*. Chicago: University of Chicago Press, 1987.

Beres, David and Jacob Arlow. "Fantasy and Identification in Empathy." *Psychoanalytic Quarterly* 63 (1975): 39–57.

Bergler, Edmund. "Samuel Johnson's 'Life of the Poet Richard Savage'—A Paradigm for a Type." *American Imago* 4 (December 1947): 42–63.

Bettelheim, Bruno. *The Uses of Enchantment: The Meaning and Importance of Fairy Tales*. 1975. New York: Vintage Books, 1977.

Blair, Patrick. *Some observations on the cure of mad persons by the fall of water*. 1725. Rpt. (in part) in *Three Hundred Years of Psychiatry*. 325–29.

Bloom, Harold. *Modern Critical Views: Dr. Samuel Johnson and James Boswell*. Ed. Harold Bloom. New York: Chelsea House Publishers, 1986. Introduction.

Bond, R.P., ed. *Studies in the Early English Periodical*. Chapel Hill: University of North Carolina Press, 1957.

Booth, Mark. "Johnson's Critical Judgments in the *Lives of the Poets*." *Studies in English Literature* 16 (1976): 505–16.

Boswell, James. *Journal of a Tour to the Hebrides, with Samuel Johnson, LL.D.* 1786. Ed. R.W. Chapman. 1924. London: Oxford University Press, 1970.

——. *Life of Samuel Johnson.* 1791. Ed. George Birkbeck Hill. Rev. L.F. Powell. 6 vols. Oxford: Clarendon Press, 1934–50.

Boulton, James T., ed. *Johnson: The Critical Heritage.* New York: Barnes & Noble, 1971.

Boyce, Benjamin. "Samuel Johnson's Criticism of Pope in the *Life of Pope*," *Review of English Studies* n.s. 5 (January 1954): 37–46.

——. "Johnson's *Life of Savage* and Its Literary Background." *Studies in Philology* 53 (October 1956): 576–98.

Brack, O M, Jr. *Samuel Johnson's Early Biographers.* Iowa City: University of Iowa Press, 1971.

Brack, O M, Jr. and Thomas Kaminski. "Dr. Johnson, Robert James, and the *Medicinal Dictionary*." *Modern Philology* 81 (1984): 378–400.

Brack, O M, Jr. and Robert E. Kelley, eds. *The Early Biographies of Samuel Johnson.* Iowa City: University of Iowa Press, 1974.

Brady, Frank. *James Boswell: The Later Years 1769–1795.* New York: McGraw-Hill, 1984.

Brain, W. Russell. "A Post-Mortem on Dr. Johnson." *London Hospital Gazette* 37, 5/6 (1934): 225–30, 288–89.

——. "Authors and Psychopaths." *British Medical Journal* 2 (24 Dec. 1949): 1427–32.

Brissenden, R.F. *Virtue in Distress: Studies in the Novel of Sentiment from Richardson to Sade.* New York: Macmillan, 1974.

——. "Authority, Guilt, and *The Theory of Moral Sentiments*." *Texas Studies in Language and Literature* 11 (1969): 945–62.

Bronson, Bertrand H. "Johnson Agonistes." In *Johnson Agonistes & Other Essays.* 1944. Rpt. Berkeley and Los Angeles: University of California Press, 1965. 1–52.

——. "Johnson's 'Irene': Variations on a Tragic Theme." In *Johnson Agonistes & Other Essays.*

Brown, Norman O. *Life Against Death: The Psychoanalytic Meaning of History.* Middletown, Conn.: Wesleyan University Press, 1959.

Burke, John J., Jr., and Donald Kay, eds. *The Unknown Samuel Johnson.* Madison: University of Wisconsin Press, 1983.

Burney, Frances. *Diary and Letters of Madame D'Arblay.* Ed. Austin Dobson. 6 vols. London: Macmillan, 1904–05.

Byrd, Max. *Tristram Shandy.* Boston: George Allen & Unwin, 1985.

——. *Visits to Bedlam.* Columbia: University of South Carolina Press, 1974.

Camus, Albert. *The Myth of Sisyphus and Other Essays.* New York: Knopf, 1955.

Carnochan, W.B. *Confinement and Flight: An Essay on English Literature of the Eighteenth Century.* Berkeley and Los Angeles: University of California Press, 1977.

Carter, Elizabeth, trans. *The Moral Discourses of Epictetus.* 1758. London: Everyman's Library, 1910.

Cash, Arthur. "The Birth of Tristram Shandy: Sterne and Dr. Burton." In *Studies in the Eighteenth Century*. Ed. R.F. Brissenden. Canberra: A.N.U. Press, 1968.

Cassirer, Ernst. *The Philosophy of the Enlightenment*. Trans. Fritz C.A. Koelln and James P. Pettegrove. Princeton, N.J.: Princeton University Press, 1951.

Chadwick, Owen. "The Religion of Samuel Johnson." *Yale University Library Gazette* 60 (April 1986): 119–36.

Chambers, Sir Robert, composed in association with Samuel Johnson. *A Course of Lectures on the English Law, Delivered at the University of Oxford 1767–1773*. Ed. Thomas M. Curley. 2 vols. Madison: University of Wisconsin Press, 1986.

Chapin, Chester. "Johnson and Pascal." In *English Writers of the Eighteenth Century*. Ed. John Middendorf et al. 3–16.

———. *The Religious Thought of Samuel Johnson*. Ann Arbor: University of Michigan Press, 1968.

Clifford, James. *Hester Lynch Piozzi (Mrs. Thrale)*. 1941. 2nd ed. Oxford: Clarendon Press, 1952.

———. *Dictionary Johnson: Samuel Johnson's Middle Years*. New York: McGraw-Hill, 1979.

———. *Young Sam Johnson*. New York: McGraw-Hill, 1955.

Clifford, James and Donald Greene. *Samuel Johnson: A Survey and Bibliography of Critical Studies*. Minneapolis: University of Minnesota Press, 1970.

Curley, Thomas M. *Samuel Johnson and the Age of Travel*. Athens: University of Georgia Press, 1976.

Damrosch, Leopold, Jr. "On Misreading Eighteenth-Century Literature: A Defense." *Eighteenth-Century Studies* 8 (1974–75): 202–06.

———. "Samuel Johnson and Reader-Response Criticism." *The Eighteenth Century: Theory and Interpretation* 21 (1980): 91–108.

———. *Samuel Johnson and the Tragic Sense*. Princeton, N.J.: Princeton University Press, 1972.

———. *The Uses of Johnson's Criticism*. Charlottesville: University Press of Virginia, 1976.

DePorte, Michael. *Nightmares and Hobbyhorses: Swift, Sterne, and Augustan Ideas of Madness*. San Marino, Calif.: Huntington Library, 1974.

Devlin, Christopher. *Poor Kit Smart*. London: Rupert Hart-Davis, 1961.

Dewhurst, Kenneth. *John Locke (1632–1704), Physician and Philosopher*. London: Wellcome Institute for the History of Medicine, 1963.

Doerner, Klaus. *Madness and the Bourgeoisie*. Trans. J. Neugroschel and J. Steinberg. Oxford: Basil Blackwell, 1981.

Dussinger, John A. *The Discourse of the Mind in Eighteenth-Century Fiction*. The Hague: Mouton, 1974.

Edinger, William, *Samuel Johnson and Poetic Style*. Chicago: University of Chicago Press, 1977.

Einbond, Bernard L. *Samuel Johnson's Allegory*. The Hague: Mouton, 1971.

Eliot, T.S., ed. Introduction to *London: A Poem and The Vanity of Human Wishes*. London: Etchells and Macdonald, 1930.

Ellenberger, Henri F. *The Discovery of the Unconscious: The History and Evolution of Dynamic Psychiatry*. New York: Basic Books, 1971.

Engell, James. *The Creative Imagination: Enlightenment to Romanticism.* Cambridge, Mass.: Harvard University Press, 1981.

⸻, ed. *Johnson and His Age.* Harvard English Studies 12. Cambridge, Mass., Harvard University Press, 1984.

Feder, Lillian. *Madness in Literature.* Princeton, N.J.: Princeton University Press, 1980.

Fitzgerald, Thomas. "Bedlam." In *Poems on several occasions.* London: Watts, 1733. Rpt. in *Three Hundred Years of Psychiatry.* 355–57.

Fix, Stephen. "Distant Genius: Johnson and the Art of Milton's Life." *Modern Philology* 81 (1984): 244–64.

Fleeman, J.D. *Early Biographical Writings of Dr. Johnson.* Westmead: Gregg, 1973.

⸻. "Johnson and the Truth." In *Johnsonian Studies.* Ed. Magdi Wahba.

⸻. "Some Notes on Johnson's Prayers and Meditations," *Review of English Studies* n.s. 19 (May 1968): 172–77.

Folkenflik, Robert. *Samuel Johnson, Biographer.* Ithaca, N.Y.: Cornell University Press, 1978.

Foucault, Michel. *Madness and Civilization, A History of Insanity in the Age of Reason.* Trans. Richard Howard. New York: Random House, 1965.

Fox, Christopher. *Locke and the Scriblerians: Identity and Consciousness in Early Eighteenth-Century Britain.* Berkeley and Los Angeles: University of California Press, 1988.

⸻, ed. *Psychology and Literature in the Eighteenth Century.* New York: AMS Press, 1987.

Freud, Sigmund. *The Standard Edition of the Complete Psychological Works of Sigmund Freud.* Ed. James Strachey. 24 vols. London: Hogarth Press, 1953–74.

Fussell, Paul. *Samuel Johnson and the Life of Writing.* New York: Harcourt, Brace, 1971.

Gay, Peter. *The Enlightenment: An Interpretation, The Rise of Modern Paganisim.* New York: Alfred A. Knopf, 1966–69.

⸻. *Freud: A Life for Our Time.* New York: W.W. Norton, 1988.

⸻. *Freud for Historians.* New York: Oxford University Press, 1985.

⸻. *A Godless Jew: Freud, Atheism, and the Making of Psychoanalysis.* New Haven, Conn.: Yale University Press, 1987.

Grange, Kathleen. "Dr. Johnson's Account of a Schizophrenic Illness in *Rasselas* (1759)." *Medical History* 6 (April 1963): 162–69.

⸻. "Samuel Johnson's Account of Certain Psychoanalytic Concepts." *Journal of Nervous and Mental Diseases* 135 (August 1962): 93–98. Rpt. in *Twentieth Century Views.* Ed. Donald J. Greene.

Gray, James. *Johnson's Sermons: A Study.* Oxford: Clarendon Press, 1972.

Greenacre, Phyllis. *Swift and Carroll: A Psychoanalytic Study of Two Lives.* New York: International University Press, 1955.

Greene, Donald J. *The Age of Exuberance: Backgrounds to Eighteenth-Century English Literature.* New York: Random House, 1970.

⸻. "Augustinianism and Empiricism: A Note on Eighteenth-Century Intellectual History." *Eighteenth-Century Studies* 1 (1967–68): 33–68.

⸻. "Johnson's 'Late Conversion': A Reconsideration." In *Johnsonian Studies.* Ed. Magdi Wahba. 61–92.

———. "Johnson, Stoicism, and the Good Life." In *The Unknown Samuel Johnson*. Ed. John J. Burke and Donald Kay. 17–38.

———. "On Misreading Eighteenth-Century Literature: A Rejoinder." *Eighteenth-Century Studies* 9 (1975): 108–18.

———. *The Politics of Samuel Johnson*. New Haven, Conn.: Yale University Press, 1960.

———, ed. *Samuel Johnson: A Collection of Critical Essays. Twentieth Century Views*. Englewood Cliffs, N.J.: Prentice-Hall, 1965.

———. *Samuel Johnson's Library: An Annotated Guide*. ELS Monograph Series 1. English Literary Studies. University of Victoria, 1975.

———. "Samuel Johnson's *The Life of Richard Savage*." In *The Biographer's Art: New Essays*. Ed. Jeffrey Meyers. London: Macmillan, 1989. 11–30.

———. Review of *Samuel Johnson and the Tragic Sense. Modern Philology* 71 (1974): 443–49.

———. "The Uses of Autobiography." In *Essays in Eighteenth-Century Biography*. Ed. Philip B. Daghlian. Bloomington: Indiana University Press, 1968. 67–95.

Greene, Donald J. and John A. Vance. *A Bibliography of Johnsonian Studies, 1970–1985*. English Literary Studies. University of Victoria, 1987.

Gross, Gloria Sybil. "Dr. Johnson's Practice: The Medical Context for *Rasselas*." *Studies in Eighteenth-Century Culture* 14 (1985): 275–88.

Grundy, Isobel. *Samuel Johnson and the Scale of Greatness*. Leicester: Leicester University Press, 1986.

Hagstrum, Jean H. "Dr. Johnson's Fear of Death." *ELH* 14 (Dec. 1947): 308–19.

———. "Johnson Among the Deconstructionists." In *Eros and Vision: The Restoration to Romanticism*. Ed. Jean Hagstrum. Evanston, Ill.: Northwestern University Press, 1989. 139–51.

———. *Samuel Johnson's Literary Criticism*. Minneapolis: University of Minnesota Press, 1952.

———. "Towards a Profile of the Word *Conscious* in Eighteenth-Century Literature." In *Psychology and Literature in the Eighteenth-Century*. Ed. Fox. 23–50.

Haslam, John. *Observations on Madness and Melancholy*. London: J. Callow, 1809.

Havens, R.D. "Johnson's Distrust of the Imagination." *ELH* 10 (1943): 243–55.

Hawkins, Sir John. *The Life of Samuel Johnson*. 1787. Ed. Bertram H. Davis. London: Jonathan Cape, 1962.

Hill, George Birkbeck, ed. *Johnsonian Miscellanies*. 2 vols. Oxford: Clarendon Press, 1897.

Hilles, Fredrick W. "Dr. Johnson on Swift's Last Years: Some Misconceptions and Distortions." *Philological Quarterly* 54 (1975): 370–79.

———. "The Making of *The Life of Pope*." In *New Light on Dr. Johnson*. Ed. F.W. Hilles. 257–84.

———, ed. *New Light on Dr. Johnson*. New Haven, Conn.: Yale University Press, 1959.

Hinnant, Charles H. *Samuel Johnson: An Analysis*. London: Macmillan Press, 1988.

Hitschmann, Edward. "Samuel Johnson's Character: A Psychoanalytic Interpretation." *Psychoanalytic Review* 32 (1945): 207–18.

Hovey, Richard B. "Dr. Samuel Johnson, Psychiatrist." *Modern Language Quarterly* 15 (1954): 321–35.

Hudson, Nicholas. *Samuel Johnson and Eighteenth-Century Thought*. Oxford: Clarendon Press, 1988.

Hunter, Richard, and Ida Macalpine, eds. *Three Hundred Years of Psychiatry 1535–1860*. London: Oxford University Press, 1963.

Irwin, George. *Samuel Johnson: A Personality in Conflict*. Auckland: Auckland University Press, 1971.

Jack, Ian. *Augustan Satire*. Oxford: Clarendon Press, 1952.

Jenyns, Soame. *A Free Inquiry into the Nature and Origin of Evil*. London: R. and J. Dodsley, 1757.

Johnson, Claudia L. "Samuel Johnson's Moral Psychology and Locke's 'Of Power.'" *Studies in English Literature* 24 (1984): 563–82.

Johnson, Samuel. *The Letters of Samuel Johnson*. Ed. R.W. Chapman. 3 vols. Oxford: Clarendon Press, 1952.

———. *Life of Savage*. Ed. Clarence Tracy. Oxford: Clarendon Press, 1971.

———. *Lives of the English Poets*. Ed. George Birkbeck Hill. 3 vols. Oxford: Clarendon Press, 1905.

———. *The Oxford Authors Series: Samuel Johnson*. Ed. Donald J. Greene. New York: Oxford University Press, 1984.

———. *Rasselas*. Ed. G.B. Hill. Oxford: Clarendon Press, 1887.

———. *The Works of Samuel Johnson, LL.D.* 9 vols. London: William Pickering; Oxford: Talboys and Wheeler, 1825.

———. *The Yale Edition of the Works of Samuel Johnson*. Ed. Allen T. Hazen and John Middendorf, et al. 16 vols. to date. New Haven, Conn.: Yale University Press, 1958–.

Keener, Frederick M. *The Chain of Becoming: The Philosophical Tale, the Novel, and a Neglected Realism of the Enlightenment: Swift, Montesquieu, Voltaire, Johnson, and Austen*. New York: Columbia University Press, 1983.

Kaminski, Thomas. *The Early Career of Samuel Johnson*. New York: Oxford University Press, 1987.

Kernan, Alvin. *Printing Technologies, Letters & Samuel Johnson*. Princeton, N.J.: Princeton University Press, 1987.

Kolb, Gwin J. "Mrs. (Thrale) Piozzi and Dr. Johnson's *The Fountains: A Fairy Tale*." *Novel* 13 (1979): 68–81.

———. The Structure of *Rasselas*." *PMLA* 66 (Sept 1951): 698–717.

———. "*The Vision of Theodore*: Genre, Context, Early Reception." In *Johnson and His Age*. Ed. James Engell.

Korshin, Paul J. "The Johnson-Chesterfield Relationship: A New Hypothesis." *PMLA* 85 (1970): 247–59.

———. "Johnson and Swift: A Study in the Genesis of Literary Opinion." *Philological Quarterly* 48 (1969): 464–78.

———. "Johnson's Last Days: Some Facts and Problems." In *Johnson After Two Hundred Years*. Ed. Paul J. Korshin.

———, ed. *The Age of Johnson*. Vol. 2. New York; AMS Press, 1989.

———, ed. *Johnson After Two Hundred Years*. Philadelphia: University of Pennsylvania Press, 1986.

Korshin, Paul J. and Robert R. Allen, eds. *Greene Centennial Studies: Essays Presented to Donald Greene*. Charlottesville: University Press of Virginia, 1989.

Krutch, Joseph Wood. *Samuel Johnson*. New York: Henry Holt and Company, 1944.

Ladell, R. Macdonald. "The Neurosis of Dr. Samuel Johnson." *British Journal of Medical Psychology* 9 (1929): 314–23.

Lennox, Charlotte. *The Female Quixote*. 1752. New York: Oxford University Press, 1973.

Liebert, Herman W. "Reflections on Samuel Johnson: Two Recent Books and Where They Lead." *Journal of English and Germanic Philology* 47.1 (1948): 80–88. Rpt. in *Samuel Johnson: A Collection of Critical Essays*. Ed. Greene. 15–21.

Lipking, Lawrence. "Learning to Read Johnson: *The Vision of Theodore* and *The Vanity of Human Wishes*." *ELH* 43 (1976): 517–37.

———. *The Ordering of the Arts in Eighteenth-Century England*. Princeton, N.J.: Princeton University Press, 1970.

Liu, Alan. "Toward a Theory of Common Sense: Beckford's *Vathek* and Johnson's *Rasselas*." *Texas Studies in Language and Literature* 26 (1984): 183–217.

Locke, John. *An Essay Concerning Human Understanding*. Ed. Peter H. Nidditch. Oxford: Clarendon Press, 1975.

MacDonald. Michael. *Mystical Bedlam: Madness, Anxiety, and Healing in Sevententh Century England*. Cambridge: Cambridge University Press, 1981.

Mack, Maynard. *The Garden and the City: Retirement and Politics in the Later Poetry of Pope*. Toronto: University of Toronto Press, 1969.

MacLaurin, Charles. *Mere Mortals: Medico-Historical Essays*. New York: George H. Doran Company, 1925. 17–39.

Maner, Martin. *The Philosopical Biographer: Doubt and Dialect in Johnson's "Lives of the Poets"*. Athens: University of Georgia Press, 1988.

Mayo, Robert D. *The English Novel in the Magazines 1740–1815*. Evanston, Ill.: Northwestern University Press, 1962.

McCarthy, William. "The Moral Art of Johnson's *Lives*." *Studies in English Literature* 16 (1976): 505–16.

McHenry, Lawrence C., Jr. "Samuel Johnson's Tics and Gesticulations." *Journal of the History of Medicine and Allied Sciences* 22 (1967): 152–68.

McIntosh, Carey. *The Choice of Life: Samuel Johnson and the World of Fiction*. New Haven, Conn.: Yale University Press, 1973.

McKenzie, Alan T. "The Systematic Scrutiny of Passion in Johnson's *Rambler*." *Eighteenth-Century Studies* 20 (1986/87): 129–52.

Mead, Richard. *Medical precepts and cautions . . . Translated from the Latin, under the author's inspection, by Thomas Stack, M.D., F.R.S.* London: Brindley, 1751. Rpt. (in part) in *Three Hundred Years of Psychiatry*. Ed. Hunter and Macalpine. 385–88.

Meyer, Bernard C. "Dr. Johnson's Secret Padlock." New York Psychoanalytic Society, New York. 26 Feb. 1980. Abstract in *Psychoanalytic Quarterly* 50 (1981): 469–70.

———. "Notes on Flying and Dying." *Psychoanalytic Quarterly* 52 (1983): 327–52.

———. "On the Application of Psychoanalysis in W. Jackson Bate's Life of Samuel Johnson." *Journal of the Philadelphia Association for Psychoanalysis* 6 (1979): 153–61.

———. "Some Observations on the Rescue of Fallen Women." *Psychoanalytic Quarterly* 53 (1984): 208–39.

Meyers, Jeffrey. "Autobiographical Reflections in Johnson's *Life of Swift.*" *Discourse* 8 (1968): 37–48.

————, ed. *The Biographer's Art: New Essays.* New York: New Amsterdam Books, 1989.

Middendorf, John, "Ideas vs. Words: Johnson, Locke, and the Edition of Shakespeare." In *English Writers of the Eighteenth Century.* 249–72.

————. "Johnson on the Couch." *Review* 1 (1979): 1–12.

————, ed. *English Writers of the Eighteenth Century.* New York: Columbia University Press, 1971.

Miller, Perry. *Errand into the Wilderness.* New York: Harper, 1954.

Monro, John. *Remarks on Dr. Battie's Treatise on Madness.* London: Clarke, 1758.

Murry, John Middleton. *Jonathan Swift: A Critical Biography* New York: Farrar, Strauss & Giroux, 1955.

Nath, Prem, ed. *Fresh Reflections on Samuel Johnson: Essays in Criticism.* New York: Whitston, 1987.

Newton, Peter. "Samuel Johnson's Breakdown and Recovery in Middle-Age: A Life Span Developmental Approach to Mental Illness and Its Cure." *International Review of Psychoanalysis* 11 (1984): 93–118.

Novak, Maximillian E. "Johnson, Dryden, and the Wild Vicissitudes of Taste." In *The Unknown Samuel Johnson.* Ed. Burke and Kay. 54–75.

Ober, William B. *Bottoms Up: A Pathologist's Essays on Medicine and the Humanities.* Carbondale: Southern Illinois University Press, 1987.

————. "Eighteenth-Century Spleen." In *Psychology and Literature in the Eighteenth Century.* Ed. Fox. 225–58.

Osborn, James M. *John Dryden: Some Biographical Facts and Problems.* New York: Columbia University Press, 1940.

Perfect, William. *Annals of Insanity, Comprising a selection of Curious and Interesting Cases.* 1787. 5th ed. London: Chalmers, 1800.

Pierce, Charles E., Jr. *The Religious Life of Samuel Johnson.* Hamden, Conn.: Archon Books, 1983.

Piozzi, Hester Thrale. *Letters to and from the late Samuel Johnson.* 3 vols. London, 1788.

————. *Thraliana: The Diary of Mrs. Hester Lynch Thrale (Later Mrs. Piozzi) 1776–1809.* Ed. Katharine Balderston. 2 vols. Oxford: Clarendon Press, 1942.

Pope, Alexander. *The Twickenham Edition of the Poems of Alexander Pope.* Ed. John Butt, et al. 11 vols. London: Methuen, 1938–68.

Porter, Roy. "'The Hunger of Imagination': Approaching Samuel Johnson's Melancholy." In *The Anatomy of Madness: Essays in the History of Psychiatry.* 2 vols. Ed. W.F. Bynum, Roy Porter, and Michael Shepherd. London: Tavistock Publications, 1985. 63–102.

————. *Mind-Forg'd Manacles: A History of Madness in England from the Restoration to the Regency.* Cambridge, Mass.: Harvard University Press, 1987.

Pottle, Frederick A. "The Dark Hints of Sir John Hawkins and Boswell." In *New Light on Dr. Johnson.* Ed. Hilles. 153–62.

Quinlan, Maurice. *Samuel Johnson: A Layman's Religion.* Madison: University of Wisconsin Press, 1964.

Radner, John B. "Samuel Johnson, the Deceptive Imagination, and Sympathy." *Studies in Burke and His Time* 16 (1974): 23–46.

———. "Samuel Johnson and the Vanity of Human Resolutions." *Enlightenment Essays* 4 (Fall–Winter 1973): 9–14.

———. "The Significance of Johnson's Changing Views of the Hebrides." In *The Unknown Samuel Johnson*. Ed. Burke and Kay. 131–49.

Randolph, Mary Claire. "The Medical Concept in English Renaissance Satiric Theory." *Studies in Philology* 38 (April 1941): 125–57. Rpt. in *Satire: Modern Essays in Criticism*. Ed. Ronald Paulson. Englewood Cliffs, N.J.: Prentice-Hall, 1971. 135–70.

Reade, Aleyn Lyell, ed. *Johnsonian Gleanings*. 11 pts. in 10 vols. Privately printed, 1909–52. Rpt. New York: Octagon Books, 1967.

Reed, Kenneth, T. "This Tasteless Tranquility: A Freudian Note on Johnson's 'Rasselas.'" *Literature and Psychology* 19 (1969): 61–62.

Robinson, Nicholas. *A New System of the Spleen, vapours, and hypochondriack melancholy*. London: A. Bettesworth, 1729. Rpt. (in part) in *Three Hundred Years of Psychiatry*. 342–47.

Rosen, George. "Irrationality and Madness in Seventeenth- and Eighteenth-Century Europe." In *Madness in Society: Chapters in the Historical Sociology of Mental Illness*. Chicago: University of Chicago Press, 1968. 151–71.

Rothstein, Eric. *Systems of Order and Inquiry in Later Eighteenth-Century Fiction*. Berkeley and Los Angeles: University of California Press, 1975.

Rousseau, George S., ed. *The Languages of the Psyche: Mind and Body in Enlightenment Thought*. Berkeley and Los Angeles: University of California Press, 1990.

———. "Pope and the Tradition in Modern Humanistic Education: 'In the pale of Words till death.'" In *The Enduring Legacy: Alexander Pope Tercentenary Essays*. Ed. G.S. Rousseau and Pat Rogers. Cambridge: Cambridge University Press, 1988. 199–239.

———. "Psychology." In *The Ferment of Knowledge: Studies in the Historiography of Eighteenth-Century Science*. Ed. G.S. Rousseau and Roy Porter. Cambridge: Cambridge University Press, 1980. 143–210.

———. *Tobias Smollett: Essays of Two Decades*. Edinburgh: T. & T. Clark, 1982.

Sachs, Arieh. *Passionate Intelligence: Imagination and Reason in the Work of Samuel Johnson*. Baltimore: Johns Hopkins University Press, 1967.

Schafer, Roy. *The Analytic Attitude*. New York: Basic Books, 1983.

Schappert, David G. "Selected Bibliography of Primary Materials." In *Psychology and Literature in the Eighteenth Century*. Ed. Fox. 303–45.

Schneider, Herbert W. *Adam Smith's Moral and Political Philosophy*. New York: Hafner, 1948.

Scholtz, Gregory F. "Anglicanism in the Age of Johnson: The Doctrine of Conditional Salvation." *Eighteenth-Century Studies* 22 (1988/89): 182–207.

Schwartz, Richard. *Samuel Johnson and the New Science*. Madison: University of Wisconsin Press, 1971.

———. *Samuel Johnson and the Problem of Evil*. Madison: University of Wisconsin Press, 1975.

Sherburn, George. *The Early Career of Alexander Pope*. Oxford: Oxford University Press, 1934.

Smith, Adam. *The Theory of Moral Sentiments*. Ed. D.D. Raphael and A.L. Macfie. Oxford: Clarendon Press, 1976.

Stone, Lawrence. *The Family, Sex, and Marriage in England, 1500–1800*. New York: Harper and Row, 1977.

Temmer, Mark J. *Samuel Johnson and Three Infidels: Rousseau, Voltaire, Diderot*. Athens: University of Georgia Press, 1988.

Tompkins, J.M.S. "Didacticism and Sensibility." In *The Popular Novel in England, 1770–1800*. 1932. Rpt. Lincoln: University of Nebraska Press, 1961.

Tomarken, Edward. *Johnson, Rasselas, and the Choice of Criticism*. Lexington: University of Kentucky Press, 1989.

Tracy, Clarence. *The Artificial Bastard: A Biography of Richard Savage*. Cambridge, Mass.: Harvard University Press, 1953.

Trotter, Thomas. *An Essay, Medical, Philosophical, and Chemical, on Drunkenness and its Effects on the Human Body*. 1804. Ed. Roy Porter. London: Tavistock Reprint Series on the History of Psychiatry, 1988.

Tuveson, Ernest. *Imagination as a Means of Grace: Locke and the Aesthetics of Romanticism*. Berkeley and Los Angeles: University of California Press, 1960.

Uphaus, Robert W. "The 'Equipoise' of Johnson's *Life of Savage*." In *The Impossible Observer: Reason and the Reader in Eighteenth-Century Prose*. Lexington: University of Kentucky Press, 1979. 89–107.

Vance, John A. *Samuel Johnson and the Sense of History*. Athens: University of Georgia Press, 1984.

Verbeek. E. *The Measure and the Choice: A Pathographic Essay on Samuel Johnson*. Ghent: E. Story Scientia, 1971.

Vesterman, William. "Johnson and the *Life of Savage*." *ELH* 36 (1969): 659–78.

Voitle, Robert. *Samuel Johnson the Moralist*. Cambridge, Mass.: Harvard University Press, 1961.

Wahba, Magdi, ed. *Johnsonian Studies*. Cairo: Privately printed, 1962. Distributed outside U.A.R. by Oxford University Press.

Wain, John. *Johnson on Johnson: A Selection of the Personal and Autobiographical Writings of Samuel Johnson (1709–1784)*. London: J.M. Dent, 1976.

———. *Samuel Johnson*. New York: Viking Press, 1975.

Watkins, W.B.C. *Perilous Balance*. Princeton, N.J.: Princeton University Press, 1939.

Watt, Ian. *The Rise of the Novel*. 1957. Rpt. Berkeley and Los Angeles: University of California Press, 1971.

Weinbrot, Howard. "The Reader, the General and the Particular." *Eighteenth-Century Studies* 5 (1971): 80–96.

Wharton, T.F. *Samuel Johnson and the Theme of Hope*. London: Macmillan, 1984.

Whyte, Launcelot Law. *The Unconscious Before Freud*. London: Tavistock Publications, 1960.

Whytt, Robert. *An Essay on the Vital and other Involuntary Motions of Animals*. 1751. 2nd ed. Edinburgh: Hamilton et al., 1758.

Willey, Basil. *The Seventeenth-Century Background*. Garden City, N.Y.: Doubleday, 1953.

Willis, Thomas. *Two Discourses concerning the soul of brutes*. 1683. Quoted in Zilboorg,
    A History of Medical Psychology. 261.
Wimsatt, W. K., Jr. *Philosophic Words: A Study of Style and Meaning in the "Rambler"
    and "Dictionary" of Samuel Johnson*. New Haven, Conn.: Yale University Press,
    1948.
————. *The Prose Style of Samuel Johnson*. New Haven, Conn.: Yale University Press,
    1941.
Zilboorg, Gregory. *A History of Medical Psychology*. New York: W.W. Norton, 1941.

Index

This book has been set in Linotron Galliard. Galliard was designed for Mergenthaler in 1978 by Matthew Carter. Galliard retains many of the features of a sixteenth century typeface cut by Robert Granjon but has some modifications that give a more contemporary look.

Printed on acid-free paper.